Death In Riyadh
dark secrets in hidden Arabia

Robert Corfe is the author of a number of thought-provoking books in addition to several autobiographical works describing his varied and adventurous life. He is best known for his authoritative 3-volume work, *Social Capitalism in Theory and Practice*, which is not only a critique of an irresponsible and failing economic system, but a detailed study of constructive measures for ensuring a stable, free, and prosperous society. The present book tells the story of his remarkable experiences as a businessman in the Gulf region in the 1980s, and how these anticipate the changing relationships between the Islamic and non-Islamic world and the unexpected rise of terrorism at the present time.

By the same author –

Autobiographical –
My Conflict With A Soviet Spy
the story of the Ron Evans spy case

The Girl From East Berlin
a romantic docu-drama of the East-West divide

This Was My England
the story of a childhood

Sociological –
Land of The Olympians
papers from the enlightened Far North

Deism and Social Ethics
the role of religion in the third millennium

Islam and The New Totalitarianism
fundamentalism's threat to world civilisation

Populism Against Progress
and the collapse of aspirational values

Political –
The Future of Politics
With the demise of the left/right confrontational struggle

Social Capitalism in Theory and Practice
(3 volumes)

Egalitarianism of The Free Society
and the end of class conflict

The Democratic Imperative
the reality of power relationships in the nation state

The Death of Socialism
The irrelevance of the traditional left and the call for a progressive politics of universal humanity

Death In Riyadh

dark secrets in hidden Arabia

Robert Corfe

Arena Books

Second edition 2017*

First published in 2000 by Arena Books under the author's pseudonym
of Geoff Carter.

Arena Books
6 Southgate Green
Bury St. Edmunds
IP33 2BL

www.arenabooks.co.uk

Corfe, Robert- 1935
Death in Riyadh *dark secrets in hidden Arabia*

British Library cataloguing in Publication Data. A Catalogue record
for this book is available from the British Library.

ISBN 978-1909421-95-0

BIC categories:- BGA, BGBA, BGHA, HRHP, BTH, JFCX, HBJF1.

Printed & bound by Lightning Source UK

Cover design
by Jason Anscomb

Typeset in
Times New Roman

FOREWORD

The events recorded in this book took place between 1980 and 1986, that is, some 21 years before the age of Islamic terrorism if the latter is dated from 9th September 2001 with al-Qaeda's destruction of the Twin Towers at the World Trade Centre in New York. Although the 1980s was a decade of relative peace in the Middle East, and certainly a place that felt secure for visitors to the region (if we except the separate nations of Yemen, North and South), there were nonetheless intimations of trouble ahead as often expressed in a cautious undertone by concerned businessmen at the time.

As described in an early chapter in this book, there were already underground shelters in Kuwait and visitors required an Entry Permit (in addition to visas when the latter were needed) and several years' later bombs were to fall on the City State. In a chapter towards the end of the book an English resident expresses his dread at the prospect of Crown Prince Abdullah succeeding to the throne in view of his alleged reactionary temperament. When King Fahd suffered a debilitating stroke in 1995, Abdullah assumed the role of de facto regent, and with the death of the King in 2005, he ascended the throne.

Abdullah's early rule was marked by conflict with King Fahd's full brothers, known a the "Sudairi Seven," and later in 2003 and 2004, by a series of bombings and armed violence in Riyadh, Jeddah, Yanbu and Khobar. Abdullah pursued a policy of minimum reform and clamped down on protests, and although he carried out some reforms for modernisation, the country may be said to have regressed rather the progressed over the following 20-year period. Regression was noticeably marked by the increasing influence of Sharia law and religious authority on many spheres of life including new restrictions on dress codes and the behaviour of foreigners in the Kingdom.

It is difficult to measure the responsibility of the monarch, and for that matter, of previous monarchs, for enforcing an ever-more restrictive religious life, but there is one accusation from which they cannot escape censure. This is in regard to the billions of dollars invested worldwide in the name of Islamic religious education that more correctly should be denominated propaganda on account of its intensity, and sometimes, crude hostility towards other established religions.

The governments, or Emirs (for there is little difference between the two) of the other Gulf States, have also contributed to these investments on a huge scale, and unexpectedly, the repercussions have rebounded with violence on the donors of these generous gratuities. To understand the reason for this, it should be noted that the kind of Islam exported is the purifying and puritanical Wahabism that emerged in Eastern Arabia in Dariya in the 18th century, and spread its message throughout the peninsula in league with the successful military exploits of the Saudi tribal leaders over the following centuries.

Wahabism became diversified or corrupted through the intensity of its proselytising endeavours, and al-Qaeda, the Mujahideen, Isis, Daesh, Boko Haram, and other Jihadist movements are natural offshoots of the original Saudi sect. It should not thereby be suggested that Sunni Islam, of which Wahabism is a part, is solely responsible for the religion's violence, for Shia Islam has hardly been less aggressive throughout history, quite apart from the mutual hatred between the two that has ensured an ongoing conflict throughout the Middle East.

The Islamic terrorism that has spread like a contagious disease amongst its co-religionists since the start of the present century, is shocking and usually incomprehensible, not only to Westerners, but to the peoples of the Far East, the Americas, and elsewhere on our planet. What makes young men and women turn themselves into living bombs, and what attracts them to join the most brutal army of bandits imaginable? What kind of culture thrives on a self-destructive religious fanaticism, and on those who one moment appear peaceful and sane in their home or working environment, and the next are engaged in horrific acts of violence that seems to contradict all normality? To the majority of people throughout the world such perverse behaviour is contrary to human nature.

The present book does not offer a rational explanation for Islamic terrorism, but in describing in detail Arabic customs and attitudes and all that is foreign to them, and in reporting verbatim their opinions on many aspects of life, there is probably conveyed a clearer understanding of Islamic civilisation than could ever be made through a purely intellectual approach. Most foreign visitors to the Gulf region in the 1980s – or at least those with whom I came into contact – were fearful for the future of their peoples. Predictions for the future were nearly always negative because there was so great a chasm between the Islamic and non-Islamic world perspectives. All the hospitality and graciousness of the Arab towards his foreign guests was unable to cancel out the imperative of Islamic priorities transcending all other values.

The Gulf region is populated by many nationalities seeking higher paid employment, the majority being from the Indian sub-continent, followed by Westerners and those from various Far East countries. Money is the sole attraction in a region that offers little freedom and few opportunities for open socialising or public entertainment. Whilst in the smaller Gulf States the conditions of life are accepted in a spirit of fatalism; in Saudi Arabia there is permanent caution and a feeling of dread of inadvertently stepping out of line. It is very rare to encounter anyone who admits to actually "liking" the country, although of course, there are Westerners who have converted to the religion and gone so far as to change their nationality. Such persons may sometimes be found in the media or as TV presenters.

Whilst this book is predominantly descriptive in eschewing comments on what is observed or said by the many personalities who appear on its pages, it becomes already apparent in the first chapter that there is a total incompatibility between the Islamic and non-Islamic views of the world. This in itself is sufficient to indicate the potential for conflict and the impossibility for the hope of cultural integration. It also helps explain the psychological need for Islamic peoples to establish their own systems of Shariah law, and the creation of ruling councils or "parliaments" wherever they decide to settle outside their own societies. The creation of a state within the state spells danger wherever it occurs.

Democracy or freedom, as understood in a modern technological society, is not only incomprehensible to the Arab-Islamic mentality, but is received with aversion and disgust as something leading to anarchy and chaos. The only authority to which the Arab gives credence is the law of God, and Divine law is seen as contradicting the Man-made law of the infidel peoples of the world. The fixity of these attitudes allows little room for discussion. As noted above, this book is not concerned with intellectual arguments, and those wanting the latter should turn to my more recent book, **_Islam and The New Totalitarianism_** _fundamentalism's threat to World Civilisation_.

The present book not only describes the manners and attitudes of Arab peoples from a neutral or disinterested viewpoint but also those of ex-pats with whom the former come into contact. The book could not have been written unless I had been able to draw on the source material of hundreds of long letters I had written describing my experiences on a daily basis. Hence the veracity of the spoken dialogue that appears throughout the book.

I feel that all those with whom I cam into contact are shown in a positive light, and those few that are not were mostly non-Arabs. I was everywhere met with courtesy and friendship, and where misunderstandings occasionally arose this was not the intention of any individual. Arabs have always been known for their generous hospitality, and in the years following the events described in this book, my wife and I sought to reciprocate this friendship when we took in Arab students who visited Britain to improve their English language facility.

But it should be noted that however friendly relationships may be developed on a personal basis between those of differing cultures is no assurance that groups, or nation states, follow in the wake of this in the same spirit. Good manners and the friendliest intentions on a personal level can only go so far. Economic factors giving rise to conflict can arise in a thousand ways, and overnight the closest friendships may be destroyed by war or lesser modes of struggle.

Economic differences, however, are not significant in undermining good relationships between Gulf Arabs and the rest of the world. This is because the former have always been very well rewarded through the sale of their oil reserves, and the world has always been intent on maintaining good relationships so that it might not put at risk the filling of its petrol tanks.

The risk of conflict between the Arab-Islamic and non-Islamic world stems from a quite unusual cause in the history of global conflict. It stems from a purely cultural, or more specifically, a religious cause, bearing in mind that in ages past most religious wars were motivated by underlying or partly hidden economic factors. The oil wealth of the Gulf is being used aggressively to proselytise the Islamic faith as a worldwide religion, through prioritising religion over national boundaries and national loyalties, and by demanding privileges and rights in creating parallel states within the state.

Such an ideology and such a strategy can only lead to increasing conflict with non-Islamic peoples irrespective of the latter's beliefs or non-belief. Islam chooses to see the accelerating struggle as that between Divine authority versus Secularism or Man-made (if not atheistic) law, and such an interpretation of the facts may be accepted with little controversy by both sides in the argument. Up until the present time the non-Islamic world has hardly comprehended the nature of the conflict, and despite the continuing terrorism from the start of the present century, has not been able to form a politically defensive strategy of any kind due to the fear of contravening the principles of political correctness. The uncertainty of the world in responding to this attack is unlikely to be prolonged forever, but the new political groups and voices emerging in all parts of Europe and elsewhere, give no clear indication as to where those counter-measures might be directed.

Although the main theme of the book is centred around a public execution I witnessed in Riyadh, and the mystery as to who was the offender and the nature of the offence, which is not revealed until the final chapters, the discerning reader will also note there is a serious sub-plot to the account that is of historical significance. The author describes his battle to promote the cause of British exports against increasingly difficult odds. It should be remembered that this was during the difficult years of the Thatcherite period.

The author, who at the time, was the Export Field Sales Manager for a major company and a household name, was not only struggling against the rising exchange rate of the pound, and the de-industrialising polices of down-sizing and out-sourcing, leading to the closure of thousands of manufacturing enterprises and the unemployment of millions; but was also confronted by the vicious internal politics of his own company. The author was in alliance with the UK's Company Chairman and sales team and those employed on the factory floor, against the suicidal policies of the marketing men who wanted to close down sections of the manufacturing plant in exchange for placing British labels on Far East products.

The author was dissatisfied with his achievement in increasing sales year by year as his success failed to match the far greater percentage increases of the competition, and when he reported on the true situation, and produced assurances from leading customers in the Middle East for far larger orders if only we would change our tooling and produce the desired products, he found himself in a conflict situation.

When attempts were made to restrict the circulation of his reports to those who might have enabled desirable policies for the company, his days were numbered. Consequently, within several years of his leaving the company, the enterprise was taken over by a Chinese concern, and over 500 British employees lost their jobs. This, of course, was a situation repeated thousands of times over throughout Britain in the 1980s.

For the above reasons, other names have been given to companies named in this book, and despite considerable changes that the surviving enterprises must have undergone over a period of almost 40 years I did not wish to give cause for embarrassment. Likewise, the names of persons have been changed, although they may nonetheless be recognised from the illustrations produced in this book, by those with a sufficiently long memory. These changes have not been made to avoid causing offence, for as noted above, I believe that none has been made, barring perhaps a single exception, and that individual was not a native of the Gulf. A major reason for changing these names was to avoid causing simple embarrassment, bearing in mind an Asian sensitivity not always shared by the Westerner.

This book is dedicated to developing a better understanding between the Arab and non-Arab world, and this may only be achieved through a candid presentation of facts and attitudes so that differences can be discussed in honesty and openness. As noted above, good manners and graciousness alone can achieve little in the longer term in a potentially conflict situation. Misunderstanding between peoples of different cultures can only be successfully resolved through the expansion of knowledge in tandem with the spirit of toleration.

Robert Corfe, January 2017

Contents

***

Illustrations between pages 114 and 115

1. The Great Mosque & Clock Tower in Deira Square, Riyadh, a car park on week days, & a place for public executions on Fridays after *Zohar*, the second daily call to prayer.

2. Mr. Chander (from Bombay) a director of Ramesh & Sons, Dubai.

3. Feasting in Nazeer Badanah's flat, Masharafa, Jeddah. Nabeel carving and serving guests.

4. Said & Nabeel Badanah by the Red Sea in Jeddah.

5. Saad Aakef (from Pakistan) General Manager of Al Qasim & Co. (seated), and Hamad Zohair, a Palestinian salesman, Kuwait.

6. Hamad Zohair with his car and & Tea boy.

7. Darshan Devi (from Poonah) a General Manager in Salalah, Oman.

8. On tour with General Manager, Ali Al Oud, Muscat, Oman.

9. Ali Al Oud at the Beach Club, Muscat.

10. With friends at the Beach Club, Muscat.

11. Fahah Munof & Sulaiman Kamel in Dariyah near Riyadh.

12. Mountain road to the south of San'a, North Yemen.

13. Beach, Hodeidah, North Yemen.

14. Denny Mohen (from Kerala) with his wife & daughter in Bahrain.

15. Denny Mohen with daughter & camels in desert, Bahrain.

16. Larry McEwan & Denny Mohen at Bahrain Fair.

17. Abdulla Assaf (an Egyptian), Departmental Manager of the

Contemporary Department Store, before the Clock Tower & Emiri Palace, Doha, Qatar.

18. Mr. Gamdi (an Egyptian) salesman, Doha, Qatar.

19. Nazeer, Larry McEwan, & Nabeel Badanah at the Jeddah Spring Fair.

20. Evening at Mousa Badanah's house: l. to r. Pierre Legouis, Mousa, John Crawley & Samir Badri.

21. L. to r. Larry McEwan, Nabeel, unknown guest & Pierre Legouis.

22.Swimming in Mousa's pool after the evening meal.

23.L. to r. Pierre Legouis, John Crawley, Rob Haworth, Nabeel & Nazeer.

24. Pakistani guide at the camel market in Al Ain.

*

CHAPTER 1
Gateway to anxiety and fortune

"One day brings the punishment which many days demand."

Publilius Syrus, *Sententiae*, No. 692.

As the booming rhetoric blared from the black speakers aloft the four minarets of the Grand Mosque, as crowds of men from all directions poured into spacious Deira square towards the hour of noon, a sense of tension and foreboding filled the air.

This was heightened by the mounting hysteria of the Friday sermon as the deafening metallic voice resounded off the jungle of modern concrete blocks and construction sites surrounding the open space; and by the quickened pace of groups of excited men - many in colourful attire - as they approached the area between the Grand Mosque and the Palace of the Governor of Riyadh.

The mosque was full, for in the rising heat of the day, a crush of hundreds were assembled on the southern side of the building, many with prayer mats in preparation for *Zohar* - the second daily call to prayer. But the call to prayer was not that which drew the crowds from the surrounding streets - from Al Dhahirah and Al Suwaylim streets to the north, on either side of the cloth market; from Jadeed and Gadeen streets to the west and the direction of the souk for household goods; from Tumari street in the east and the main commercial centre; or from the direction of the Clock Tower to the south, and the several alleyways leading into the vegetable and gold markets.

That which brought the crowds after Friday prayers was anticipated, yet publicly, always unannounced. A large semicircle had already begun to form in front of the Governor's Palace, on the southern side of the square, close by the Clock Tower, kept in order by a dozen or so khaki-clad policemen armed with stenguns and headropes. Several police cars and a hearse-shaped ambulance bearing the Red Crescent were parked nearby - an indication of an imminent occurrence.

There was a magnetism which conspired to arouse the curiosity of all those who set foot in the square; stopping them in their tracks, and drawing them towards the grim walls of the Governor's Palace. It was an irresistible attraction, at once touching a sense of fear and a sense of horror. This was a scene and a situation beyond the ordinary experience of the Westerner. It was something strange, something incomprehensible. It belonged to a different world and a different consciousness, and such contiguity with the finitude of life was a sober reminder of the transience of human existence.

In a God-fearing society where all events were the will of God, there was sometimes to be seen a grandeur in death itself. The desperate anger of the preacher's voice, as the Tannoy reverberated off the buildings all around, seemed to express a damning denunciation of the evils of mankind. Such a religion of conviction with its uncompromising call to avenge the ills of the world had little time for the milder feelings of mercy or doubt in the call to executing the will of the One-God. All were entrapped by fear and excitement that Friday in Deira square - those from both East and West alike, for when the law exhibits its ultimate and most dreadful power, reactions are everywhere the same.

Although the outward manifestation of uneasy expectation might vary between individuals from sickly silence to excited hysteria, all were equally over-awed in their own way, by the prescience and reality of death. A theatrical setting was in preparation in response to crime and the call for punishment, hallowed by Shariah law and ancient custom, so buried in the mists of time that it preceded even the birth and memory of Western man.

As with all in the great throng, pulled by the magnetic force of an inexplicable fascination towards the teeming semicircle of surging and pushing humanity, I made my way towards the walls of the Governor's Palace. The colourful crowd of many nationalities gave way at my approach, but soon closed in to form a phalanx as soon as I had reached the front. I was trapped and then there was no escape. As the crowd thickened, the pushing and shoving became a dangerous crush, as with ceaseless energy it moved forward and backward - forward with the thrusting of those from behind, desperate for a better view; backward in response to the shouting and threatening gestures of the police in keeping an open space.

In apprehension of being pushed over and crushed by a mob becoming evermore uncontrollable by the minute, I got down on my haunches - it would anyway give a better view to those behind - only to be told to stand upright and hold my ground. More police were called into the semicircle to drive back the crowd in enforcing some semblance of order - a task more arduous as the minutes passed.

It was a struggle to remain immobile, pressing back against the sweating bodies of the crowd in the sweltering heat; and here and there, shouting hysterically and struggling for a better place, with clenched fists and flailing arms, a man would fight for a better view. Resentful at such arrogance, cries of anger responded immediately to these sudden outbursts. But hysteria is deaf to other's feelings, and deaf to the bellowing fury of the police, who drew out *aqas* (head ropes) from their pockets, beating the offenders' heads with all their might - as frightened stampeding cattle might be beaten in an enclosure on market day.

As the excited and heaving mob moved to and fro, like the sea in storm, the police alone, it seemed, were able to prevent injury to life or limb. It was the minority only who made disorder, hurting others in their frantic scramble, and it was to the police one shouted in desperation above the din, to beat this person or that, so that others might be saved from knocks and bruises in the terrifying mêlée. Whilst some in front, in fear of assault by the police, cried, "Keep back, keep back,!" others behind, struggling for breath and to twist their bodies in the packed multitude, set up the refrain in their alarm of, "Easy, easy!"

For self-protection in anticipating the next surge of the crowd, I turned towards the mob, watchful for the next wave of movement thrusting with oceanic energy through the throng. Such a sea of faces, nationalities and races - some laughing, some angry, and some fearful for their safety! What had brought them to this place on such a day? What common factor united them in their diversity?

Their clothes alone identified their nationality. The majority hailed from the Indian subcontinent. There were Pakistanis in great number in their white loose cotton trousers and knee length-shirts; tall Afghanistanis with loose wrapped turbans and *shalwar* or puffy leg-wear in brown or grey fastened at the ankles; darker skinned Indians from

Kerala and the southern provinces; Egyptians in khaki military-style attire; slim black Eritreans with their delicate features and curly hair; Sudanese in *dishdash* tunics and skull caps; here and there a few "locals" or Arab residents in red check or white headscarves; and Filipinos and others of indeterminate south and far east nationality, in Western dress and brightly coloured shirts.

Most were expatriates - guest workers - privileged to be living in the petroleum goldmine of the world, yet residing and working on the sufferance of their richer sponsors in the God-centred land of the True Faith. They were men struggling for a better life for themselves and their families, those who had fought for and won visas to work in the cornucopia desert states of the Arabian peninsula. They were officially categorised as "Celibates" living in dormitory accommodation on the periphery of towns and cities, yet most were married and all had families in their home countries to whom they usually remitted the greater part of their earnings.

Home remained the Third World territories from which they came, not Saudi Arabia or the smaller Gulf states, which secretly they loathed as places of never-ending restrictions and the ever-present "No" to inclinations of natural pleasure. Most were construction workers, but many worked in offices or shops, and some were managers of enterprises with total responsibility for developing "profit centres," yet none were owners of the businesses they ran. All were ultimately responsible to an Arab sponsor - all controlling ownership was Arab-based - and sponsors held the passports of their employees or other dependents.

Muslims from the Indian subcontinent and elsewhere were held in condescending benevolence, for finally they were brothers in the True Faith, equal in the mosque, beside whom one stood and knelt in prayer, reciting the same words in the same language the world over, but all others were infidels - albeit in a descending order of merit.

The Christian had a false conception of God, but he shared the same prophets and legends of religious inspiration, and with time and careful cultivation, he might be converted to worshipping the One-God. The Jew was a close relative for the language and peoples had a common origin, but tragic political circumstances of the recent past had driven a stake between their common understanding, creating a hatred between them, and as the Jew was barred entry to the Kingdom - or any part of the Gulf, there was little chance for a common meeting of minds.

As for those beyond the bounds of Semitic religious civilisation, they were the "godless" peoples whose religion was "no religion." Those non-Muslims from the far east, irrespective of their nominal faith, were the most despised of all, being held in contempt out of a mixture of religious and racial discrimination, by a people who were otherwise generous in their racial attitudes.

Worse treated than these, at the very bottom of the social scale, were the unseen hundreds of thousands confined in the flats and compounds of private houses. These were the female domestics from the far east (and sometimes elsewhere), who unable to imagine their eventual fate, became the chattels and sometimes the slaves of masters and mistresses subjecting them to physical and mental abuse. Such women, kept under lock and key, their passports confiscated, sometimes unpaid, were often reduced to the status of mindless cattle.

It was money and the hope for a better life alone which attracted expatriates to work in the cities and refineries of the desert lands. Many must have taken the final plunge with trepidation as wives and loved ones were left behind - maybe for years at a time. The Asian guest worker crossed a daunting barrier on entering the desert Kingdom. The laws of illegal seclusion, rigorously enforced, ensured a segregation that was total between men and women. Those confined to the dormitory camps on the periphery of towns and cities were fated to endure the lives of monkish celibates.

As I stood amongst the heaving throng, my recollection was drawn to the Filipino I had met just two days earlier on the flight to Riyadh, and what I felt was his mounting apprehension as we approached the Royal Capital. On boarding the giant jumbo jet among a surging crowd of hundreds of Asian construction workers at Dhahran airport, I felt a momentary pang of anxiety. During the previous weeks I had flown on smaller less crowded aircraft, in the more placid company of other businessmen, to the less populous cities of the Gulf, but now I was confronted by the crush and turmoil of those with uncertain feelings in facing the new experience of a destination unknown in all but name.

Dhahran airport was the eastern entrance to the Kingdom and the largest arsenal in the Middle East, confronting Iran across the Gulf, and Iraq some 300 miles to the north. It was just eight minutes flight from the island state of Bahrain, and several miles south east of the huge ARAMCO compound - an American city in the desert, defended by armed guards and wire fencing - isolated like a plague bacillus from the Islamic civilisation beyond its gates.

As the plane slowly moved off towards the runway, passed radio masts, barrack blocks, rocket launchers, and lines of camouflaged bombers marked UNITED STATES AIR FORCE, I found myself seated beside a young Filipino in his mid twenties. He was excited by the new experience of entering the Kingdom. He came from Manila and was married with a baby daughter. This was his first time abroad, and already he had been flying many hours since leaving the homeland. He was on a two-year contract with a construction company. As he looked intently out of the window he expressed surprise at the sight of endless monotonous desert.

"I didn't think it would be all sand," he exclaimed. "How can they grow anything to eat?"

"Oil,!" I replied. He looked confused. "Everything has to be imported," I added.

"Is Riyadh a beautiful city,?" he enquired.

"It's a vast construction site like everywhere in the Middle East. A city of over two million people."

"What is there to do?"

"There's the souk and several small museums. As soon as you're outside the centre there are few places to visit. Everywhere there are long straight roads, and compounds enclosed by high walls. There are guarded gateways to different ministries or palaces. There are guest palaces, palaces of the King, and palaces of the many princes."

"The King has a big family then?"

"There are five thousand princes - all descendants of King Abdul Aziz bin Saud the Great. The last four kings have all been half-brothers and sons of the first king who died in 1953."

"And what about the churches?"

"There are no churches. Only one religion is allowed in the

Kingdom."

An expression of dismay flashed across his face, and after a pause, he asked if I was Protestant or Catholic. His thinking had taken another turn. Was he already touched by a feeling of isolation or loneliness? He told me he was Methodist and a practising Christian.

"You have to understand you're entering a world which is very different from your own and different from the West," I began to explain above the engine noise. "The Saudis have every modern gadget and convenience of Western technology, and yet when you come into this country, you're going back two thousand years in history. And as for Riyadh, it's at the same time the most modern and most ancient of any city in the Gulf."

"Why's that,?" asked my travelling companion.

"Thirty years ago it was little more than a township of mud and daub houses surrounding a Turkish built fort. It's an inland city. The people are traditional and conservative. They tend to be introverted and suspicious. There's a large bedouin population - and it's the centre of the puritanical Wahabi sect."

"The people are not friendly then?"

"They're all right when they get to know you. If you want to get a feel for Biblical history - to know what Jerusalem was really like two thousand years ago - you couldn't do much better than spend a few weeks in Riyadh. After all, they have much the same dress, the same customs, the same laws, the same thinking, almost the same language, and even the same bearded grey-visaged pleasure denying Zealots. But in Riyadh they don't call them Zealots, they're known as the *Mutaween* - the Religious police."

"And so it's a New Jerusalem?"

"No, an Old Jerusalem," I corrected. "And perhaps the most significant parallel is that they have the same loathing for Western humanist values. Whilst the Jews in old Jerusalem hated the cultural values of Romano-Hellenic civilisation, so the Wahabi Arabs are similarly opposed to the humanist mind-set of contemporary Westerners. In this country a religious interpretation is given to everything."

"Is that good?"

"You'll have to make your own mind up on that," I answered.

"You know so much. Are you a missionary,?" asked the Filipino.

"I'd hardly be allowed in the country if I was," I laughed. "And what do you hope to do in your free time?"

"I enjoy the cinema."

"Then you won't be doing that here," I responded. "Cinemas were closed in Saudi Arabia several years ago. They were condemned by the Religious police as centres of immorality - even though only men were allowed in. Places of public entertainment hardly exist in Saudi - although they do have sports stadia."

"Then I'll walk in the park," said the Filipino.

He looked contemplative, and minutes later the huge belly of the roaring jet descended low over the outskirts of Riyadh over portacabins strewn untidily around the desert; over quarries gouged out of the rock; over the criss-crossing of six-lane highways in the vicinity of nowhere; over fleets of earthmoving equipment; and over convoys of slow-moving trucks loaded with rubble in the wake of great clouds of dust.

"Goodbye, enjoy your stay,!" I said to the Filipino as we parted, and at once I felt the callousness and crass stupidity of such a parting gesture.

Earlier that day I had observed a more alarming incident. It was shortly after arrival in Dhahran following the eight minute flight from Bahrain. Entering Saudi Arabia is always a daunting experience, and leaving it is usually accompanied by a sigh of relief. Baggage inspections are thorough and sometimes destructive to personal effects. As suitcases and holdalls are unlocked and opened, it is difficult to avoid a twinge of discomfort - and even a spasm of unnecessary guilt.

Always there is the fear that perhaps inadvertently something illicit remains in one's luggage which will be uncovered with devastating results. Clearly the discovery of a girly magazine would amount to a criminal offence, but even a copy of the *Guardian* or the *Daily Telegraph* is liable to be seized as an obscene publication if the naked limbs of a woman are portrayed. Most European dailies are on sale at the bookstalls but only after having passed through the censor. Papers may be bought intact but illustrations of uncovered arms or legs will have already been blacked out with the censor's marking ink.

On this particular day as I waited in a slow patient queue for customs inspection, we were confronted by a sight - some way ahead - of a stocky young man of far eastern appearance who was clearly in trouble. His personal effects were strewn out on a counter. It was apparent he had a fondness for colourful silky clothing, mostly shorts and sleeveless tops. And then he seemed to have innumerable packets of white pills, wrapped in small quantities in little envelopes.

Two grim-visaged customs officers were standing by. One was armed with a knife. He slowly picked out the packets, slit them open, and emptied their contents into an oil drum. Then he picked up each article of clothing in turn, slit it down the middle, and dropped the two pieces into the steel container. All the while the young man stood quietly by with an inscrutable expression.

"What's going on,?" whispered a Brit just in front of me to a colleague.

"His suitcase is full of indecent clothing," replied the colleague. "They wouldn't dare do that to a European. It's appalling the way they treat these Asian manual workers."

"They haven't taken a liking to his tablets either."

"If those are drugs he's carrying, he won't be leaving this country alive - that's for sure!"

But Saudi Arabia was not the only country in the Gulf meting out rough justice to innocents and new arrivals with permits to work in the promised land. I remembered an incident several years before, when a PIA jumbo jet had landed at Dubai with a full consignment of Pakistanis, and how apparently the authorities had been unprepared for such a number. I had myself just arrived on the short flight from Doha, capital of the Emirate of Qatar, that peninsula of desert jutting into the Gulf to the south of Bahrain. It was always a pleasure to be in Dubai after several days in the drab city of Doha with its dry hotels and restaurants. All is relative, but Dubai was lively and prosperous - an ancient and well established trading post serving India, Iran and Arabia, as well as the east coast of Africa further afield - and at least it was possible at the international hotels to obtain a refreshing glass of beer.

Its greatest attraction was the Creek meandering through the city like a river, and then curling for about ten miles into the desert until it became lost in the formation of a small lake. On the east side of the

Creek was Deira, lined with dhows, the quayside usually piled with merchandise for importation or transhipment, and beyond that, the skyscraper blocks of offices and hotels, and main commercial centre. On the west side of the waterway was the older town, with its quaint alleyways and substantial houses from a bygone age, ornamented windtowers rising from their roofs like vast chimneys with a suggestion of 19th century gothic. Meanwhile, from early morning until late at night the Creek was busy with the criss-crossing of chugging *abras*, each jam-packed with twenty or so passengers seated back-to-back, as the small craft plied to and fro between the steps of the noisy and crowded landing stages, situated near the souk areas on either side of the city.

On this particular day on arriving at the modern newly extended airport, we passengers off local flights were diverted to a special customs clearance area, as the hundreds of Pakistanis who had landed from Karachi, were milling around blocking the exits to the arrival hall. They looked confused, lost, anxious and exhausted as they stood around in groups, their possessions tied into huge bundles of cloth. They were a colourful and docile crowd, newly arrived as construction workers, but as their papers needed to be checked and double-checked, their permits and visas endorsed, and their baggage examined for illicit items, they were destined for a wait of several hours. Non-British Europeans had to queue for the endorsement of their 72-hour visas, but Brits were waived this obligation, for Dubai as part of the former Trucial States, and presently one of the United Arab Emirates, had been a protectorate of Britain.

On having reconfirmed my onward flight (everywhere a necessity in the Middle East to ensure a seat) and emerging into the arrival hall, I was surprised to see that dozens of the newly arrived Pakistanis had somehow overflowed, like wandering cattle, into this section of the airport. Moments later a hullabaloo broke out as a contingent of police in khaki uniforms and berets, entered the terminal, shouting at the Asians in a language not their own, driving them back through the doors they had entered, pushing and buffeting the human mass like a herd of cattle.

There were travellers and travellers! I was dismayed - sickened almost by the monstrous disparities of degree which divided the human race. Whilst some were undeservingly treated as cattle - the hard-working and semi-skilled but low in the enjoyment of privilege; others with little right to demand better recognition, were accorded every comfort and obsequious gesture from all with whom they came into contact. I decided that that night I would tell my Indian friend and agent, Mr. Chander, about the congestion and scandalous scenes I had witnessed at the airport earlier in the day.

Mr. Chander was not expecting my arrival in Dubai. I had not wanted him to know of my impending trip. In truth I was unsatisfied with his performance as an agent and currently exploring other possibilities for transferring the company's business. But tact was necessary for changes to be made - not that my company was tied by any meaningful contract in English law - but there always existed the possibility of prosecution in the Dubai courts in selling products to outlets other than the agency officially registered at the Ministry of Trade. Ramesh & Sons had held the agency for more than twenty years, but this did not excuse their failing to stem the relative sales decline of our products in the region, even though they may have increased our actual turnover year by year.

As I crossed the Creek at twilight (for I stayed at one of the newer hotels on the Deira side) a warm yet refreshing breeze wafting off the water in the heat of a November evening, I decided on the conditions to impose if the agency was to remain. Ramesh & Sons was situated in the old town, and I needed to be prepared against any counter-proposals of Mr. Chander, for he was a slippery customer and a great teller of tales.

By the time I jumped off the *abra* and leapt up the steps of the landing stage, it was already dark. I walked through the noisy and crowded souk, cutting through the sandy unpaved alleyways passed the bustle of open-fronted metal working shops and cabinet makers, into the teeming and colourful crowds of Talib road - a major shopping centre. The majority in the streets were from the Indian subcontinent, for they represented almost 80% of the population of the United Arab Emirates. Indeed, most of my business in the smaller Gulf states was conducted with Indian nationals although of course, they were never wholly owners of the managed enterprises.

Talib road comprised small shops of all kinds, the greater number selling textiles or made up saris. Ramesh & Sons was squashed between a laundry and a TV radio shop. As soon as I entered, taken aback by the heavy scent of burning joss sticks but relieved to be away from the din of hooting vehicles, I saw through the dim light at the back of the shop, the fat figure of Mr. Chander lolling back in an armchair in the company of several friends seated on a sofa. He welcomed me with a nonchalance as if he had seen me the previous day. He may have sensed my surprise, for he immediately continued, "I knew you were coming today."

"Did you contact my office,?" I asked in surprise.

"I had no need to. My special sense told me you were coming," replied Chander, and he expatiated at some length, to all three of us present, on his remarkable psychic powers. He could always predict the future! It was lucky I had called this week and not last week as he had just returned from a trip to Bombay.

At that moment, Mr. Sikander, an elder brother, a huge man with an obtuse intellect, whose life was restricted to the retail side of the business emerged from behind a curtain in the storage area. His days were spent sitting behind a small table at the front of the shop. No sooner had greetings been exchanged than a small boy, scarcely six years of age and wearing a *dhoti*, entered the shop with a tray and glasses of tea.

"Bring another glass for my good friend, Mr. Robert," cried Chander as soon as the boy had waited on those present.

There was a relaxed and cosy atmosphere, and for the next few hours we settled down to an evening of seemingly aimless conversation and conviviality. Nearby was a shrine from where the smoke of joss sticks rose slowly to the ceiling, and behind that, fixed to the wall, an ornate picture decorated with gold and silver leaf of the god Krishna cradling the head of the sacred white cow, Dhavali, as he looked lovingly into the eyes of the divine creature.

Time is of little account in the eastern half of the world, for hurry is not merely perceived as unmannerly but as uncivilised. There is a fatalism about business as there is about life itself, and during the final working hours of the day, if business was to be won it was through the chance of passing custom and not through any efforts of the hard-sell or pro-active ingenuity.

Mr. Chander, B.Sc., came from Bombay, being one of eight

brothers, three of whom were partners in the Dubai business. The third brother, Kamlesh, managed a video shop, in an alleyway on the other side of Talib road - just two minutes away. Chander had trained as a biologist but wanted to join the airforce, and it was only on his father's insistence that he came to Dubai to become the salesman for the company. His native language was Sindhi, but he quickly learnt Arabic and Urdu to communicate on easy terms with most commercial prospects.

He wore flared trousers and garish short-sleeved shirts, and when not boasting about his "good friendship" with various local notabilities and the importance this had for trade; or bemoaning the recession and the loss of business, he was either recounting the exotic adventures of various acquaintances, or presenting elaborate accounts in demonstrating the validity of reincarnation. In following his conversation it was difficult sometimes to keep track of reality and fantasy, for the two were often inextricably intermingled.

No customers visited the shop that evening to make an actual purchase, and so Sikander sat behind his little table immobile, expressionless, and silent, but several visitors came to see Chander to ask a favour or re-present bounced cheques for re-endorsement - a common occurrence in the area which hardly raised an eyebrow.

A young Arab in a dirty brown *thobe* (tunic) and a red check headscarf worn in a slovenly fashion, strolled lazily into the shop, scraping the soles of his sandals along the floor. He wanted a private word with Chander. It was unusual in the Middle East to request such confidentiality, for the private office was a thing unknown. Business negotiations and deals were settled amongst constant interruptions, and comings and goings of visitors or other staff, and even in the presence of competitors sitting close by as they sipped their tea or cold drinks. It was not unnatural then, when the Arab left the shop, that curiosity got the better of me and I asked the reason for the visit.

"He wants a job," said Chander.

"Then you've got unemployment here too," I responded.

"He doesn't *need* a job," said Chander laughing. "He's got more money than you and all of us in this room together will ever have. There's no Gulf Arab without wealth. They're all sponsoring some business or other. Sometimes they just get bored with doing nothing - that's all. Many take on any menial job to fill in time."

A little later an unkempt unshaven elderly man in a *dhoti* and soiled cloak entered the shop, and if it was not for his briefcase and papers, he might have been taken for a beggar. Chander, however, received him with respect, and after entering into an arrangement, and the passing over of cheques amounting to several thousand US dollars, I was introduced to the newcomer as Mr. Lamchal.

"He's the richest and most highly respected businessman in the Indian community in Abu Dhabi," confided Chander.

After the visitor had departed it was explained that his unwashed and ascetic appearance was maintained for religious reasons. He owned a large warehouse in Abu Dhabi, just two hours along the highway to the south, and all his time was spent in collecting cheques - always walking on foot - whilst his two sons, who were also in the business, drove around in vans delivering goods to customers.

Mr. Lamchal, with his watery red eyes and sad voice, bemoaned the increasing difficulties of the Indian community in Abu Dhabi. They were being persecuted by the Sheikhs. Anyone found taking a second job was arrested and deported. Many Indians were employed as civil servants by the UAE, but office hours were only between 7.0 am until 1.0 pm. It was unreasonable to expect Indians not to take second jobs or set up businesses of their own. What else could they do in their free time? Indian people were not pleasure seekers - they were only used to work. The Arabs were so lazy! They couldn't appreciate the energy of those with more initiative than themselves. It was all unfair.

"And the recession doesn't help," said one of the other visitors.

"It's a little better in Dubai," said another. "Sheikh Rashid protects free trade."

"That's because it's an ancient international emporium here," said Chander.

"But there's no security of law or tenure for the Indian community anywhere in the UAE," continued Mr. Lamchal. "No one knows what will happen tomorrow. Politically the area is too unstable: with Iran and the Shiites to the north, and Iraq threatening Kuwait and the rest of the Gulf."

It was after a bearded man in a jewelled cap, long shirt, and baggy cotton trousers had visited the shop, whom I correctly surmised was a Pakistani manual worker, that I recollected the episode at the airport that afternoon, and I mentioned this to Chander. He took up the topic with relish. These new arrivals were innocents, having no knowledge of what to expect. They were very tightly controlled, and every item of luggage was thrown about and closely examined at the port of entry.

"What do they expect to find,?" I asked.

"Hashish, and possibly, opium," said Chander. "Hashish is smoked as a matter of course in their own country."

"And if they find it?"

"If they find it - and they always do - and they always arrest one in every two hundred arrivals."

"Then what?"

"The punishment is strict for offenders. Firstly, spikes are forced under their fingernails, and then they're strung up by their arms and given a hundred and fifty lashes with wire whips. It always results in death."

CHAPTER 2
The Tales of Chander

"Injustice, swift, erect, and unconfin'd,
   Sweeps the wide earth, and tramples o'er mankind,
   While prayers, to heal her wrongs, more slow behind."

Iliad, Homer, Bk. ix, 1, 628   (Pope's trans.)

During that first evening in Dubai there was little opportunity to confront Chander with my concern over the indifferent progress of our sales in the area. But the following morning I insisted we visit existing customers, and possibly, other prospects also. Chander had little option but to agree to the programme I suggested.

Chander was on a diet - he had a "heart condition" (or so he claimed) - but despite this and his overweight, he had an uncontrollable liking for snacks. It was difficult for him, during any hour of the day, to pass by a snack bar without surrendering to the temptations of entering and consuming at least one or several dishes. As long as I remained in his company I was inevitably implicated in this gastronomic activity, and on this particular morning with unfortunate results. I was a reluctant epicure, but he was persuasive and insistent.

"I don't believe in eating a lot," he said to assuage my reluctance. "I don't indulge in big feasts."

"I tend to keep to regular meals," I responded lamely.

"This is a very special place," he said stopping before a refreshment bar in the Bastakia area. "The manager's a good friend of mine. They have some exceptional delicacies."

"I only breakfasted two hours ago," I pleaded.

"You can always make room for a snack," he said. "And besides, I've got some business with my friend."

We had already made two calls that day, and it was time for a break. We entered the tiny bar which was spotlessly clean and seemingly hygienic, although the decor of lavatory tiles extending to shoulder height and the dark green ceiling and upper walls tended to be de-appetising. There was only room for four people to be seated at two small tables. By the entrance was a basin for patrons and staff to wash their hands, and below that a bin with used tissues.

After introductions and an effusive welcome by the manager, Chander ordered *puri* (a potato and curry soup), bhaji, and green chillies, and moments later, a number of small plates were set before us. The walls of the kitchen beyond were painted black, and in the half light, I espied a bare-footed Indian naked except for a *dhoti*, crouched on his haunches, frying vegetables in a pan on a small burner.

Chander insisted I eat the chillies together with the soup and bhaji, and reluctantly and in no small discomfort, but determined not to lose face in repudiating his hospitality, I complied. Both he and his friend expressed joyful surprise that an Englishman was capable of relishing such highly spiced delicacies, and even the cook was called out of his cubby hole, and all three were grinning and laughing in appreciative wonder. Later than day I pondered whether this was all part of a clever conspiracy to sabotage the programme I had initiated.

Earlier that morning Chander and I had visited the old souk on the Deira side of the Creek, and everywhere he was greeted by friends and acquaintances at different stalls, until at last we came to a small shop of a "very good friend," Mr. Mohammed Abdulla Raisa. Mr. Mohammed, who sat behind a small table in the cramped space, said he could not place another order for our company's products as they were "far too expensive" by comparison with those of competitors.

Whilst I drank tea with Mr. Mohammed, Chander sat on a bench beside the proprietor's brother, each holding one another's hands, and laughing and joking in each other's company as if it was the most enjoyable pleasure in the world, and from a Western perspective, it almost conveyed the impression of a lovers' tryst.

After an hour or so Mr. Mohammed was brought round to the purpose of our meeting. His confidence had been won over, and his attitude softened, and Chander and I came away with a £4,000 order.

"He's one of the wealthiest Arab traders in the Deira souk," explained Chander. "He has a huge carpet store on the outskirts of the town and an office on the fourth floor of a modern tower block, but he feels more comfortable sitting in the traditional quarters of the souk."

After leaving the snack bar we made our way to visiting Chander's

Arab sponsor. He worked at the Central Post Office as a "director" of the Dubai postal service.

"He's very important to the business," insisted Chander. "Through our friendship I have access to all the ministries. It's invaluable! We overcome so many governmental hindrances.   With the right introductions and minimum baksheesh, we're assured any favour."

Ahmed Salem Ziyad worked in a noisy open-planned office, giant swirling fans suspended from the high ceiling, in the hall-like interior with its grey walls, and frosted tall rectangular windows. Ahmed was a small reticent insignificant looking man in his mid-thirties, with the obligatory moustache worn by most men in the Middle East, but I immediately gained the impression that he was a clerk rather than a director at the Central Post Office.

It was only after Chander began buttering him up as an important personality that he began to emerge from his shell.

"Ahmed's a partner and we couldn't do without him," exclaimed Chander placing his arm around the Arab and squeezing him two or three times as the two sat side by side on a bench.

Ahmed gave an embarrassed laugh.

"I couldn't do without you," he responded. "You manage the business. I'm dependent on your good judgement. I'm just a sleeping partner."

"You're more than that. Who has the connections,?" exclaimed Chander with a laugh. "You're the one who pulls the strings. That's why I wanted our supplier, Mr. Robert, to meet you. My dear friend, don't underestimate your value to the business. And you have invested your own capital."

Ahmed giggled awkwardly, and in his modesty, averted his gaze to the floor.

"Chander's been threatening to leave the country and return to Bombay," burst out Ahmed suddenly, turning to me.

"Don't tell him that," responded Chander with feigned hurt feelings. "You know my dear friend, I'd never leave Dubai - not as long as I have your friendship."

"If you ever attempted to leave Dubai," began Ahmed looking into the eyes of his partner, I'd come to the airport and drag you feet first off the plane."

The three of us laughed at the very idea. Chander seized the hands of his sponsor, squeezing them tightly.

"It'll never come to that," he assured.

It was to be some time before I witnessed the outcome of this assurance.

By now I was already queasy. By the time I returned to the hotel and laid down on the bed, I was dizzy and feverish. Foolishly, I had broken the golden rule of eating outside the international hotels with their assured standards of hygiene. I was little better after four hours of sleep, and by 5.0 pm I had to be back at Ramesh & Sons. Now I was afflicted with diarrhoea, and this was to lead to another embarrassment which was cultural rather than just medical.

That evening we visited Mahabeer & Sons, one of the largest and most reputable Indian trading establishments in Dubai, with numerous shops throughout the UAE. As Chander and I sat in the office with one of their senior executives in the modern headquarters building in the Al Mussalla district, I was forced to excuse myself from their presence. The executive, with a dismissive gesture, told me how to reach the desired place, seemingly peeved that I should make such an extraordinary request. I traced my steps along several corridors, down a small flight of stairs, and through a doorway into what I hoped was the proper destination.

At once I was confronted by two Indian ladies washing their hands over a row of basins. I apologised and made to back out, exclaiming, "I'm only looking for the gents." Momentarily, they looked at one another and then at me in incomprehension, then one of them exclaimed, "You mean the lavatory?"

"Yes, that's what I mean," I responded.

"You can use this," she said.

"But where's the gents,?" I persisted.

"There's nowhere else," said the other lady. "You can use any of these," she added indicating the row of cubicles.

I went into one, and then several, and then all. There were no toilet seats and no sign of paper. There were jars of water standing in each cubicle; there were shoemarks on the porcelain seats; and the walls were stained with faeces. I hurriedly left the filthy and stinking cloakroom, but was obliged to return, moments later, with a wad of paper torn from my notepad. I recollected how on one occasion when visiting the toilets in Jeddah airport, I noticed that affixed to doors within the cubicles were illustrations of correct and incorrect ways of using Western toilet pans, together with texts in several languages.

It was therefore a relief when we returned to Ramesh & Sons, and I was able to relax on a sofa for the remainder of the evening, refreshed by frequent glasses of tea to ease my aching stomach. On our return, Sikander's five year old daughter was playing in the shop. She spent all her time in the shop whilst her mother worked as a clerk in a nearby office. She had no toys, but constantly pulled down products from their shelves, climbed onto the laps of seated visitors, occasionally shouted at her father, and was a constant nuisance. Sikander, with his dull expressionless face, occasionally grunted at his daughter, tried to control her behaviour with awkward gestures, or just ignored her mischief as his huge form sat slumped behind the little table.

I sat beneath a framed portrait of Sheikh Rashid, the Emir of Dubai, for throughout the Gulf, portraits of the local ruler were almost obligatory in shops and offices. We had already succeeded in drumming up more business during that one day than we had received over the past twelve months. Chander did not want to acknowledge this as resulting from my visit to the Emirate, but instead he was out to impress on me the good character and business acumen of his family. None of his family indulged in the vices of "smoking, drinking or dancing" - and neither did they visit clubs or places of pleasure. They were hard-working and money-making. The trouble with the Arabs is that they were too fond of "wine, women and song."

Occasionally men entered the shop with video cassettes, to be redirected to the new premises across Talib road. Chander confided to me that the firm even had access to *The Death of A Princess*, but only on a private basis and not from the shop. It was a dangerous item to have around and the police would be outraged on discovering a copy in private possession.

Occasionally, during a lapse in the conversation, or when Chander directed his attention to a business matter in response to callers, I took up a copy of the *Times of India*, lying on the adjacent coffee table. Established in 1838, it was a newspaper whose format belonged to a past age, with its front page layout of classified advertising, similar to the London *Times* of fifty years ago, and the convoluted 19th century prose of its reports and features. It seemed hardly to have changed since the days of Macaulay, and indeed, the great Whig statesman and historian, had been instrumental in promoting the liberal press in India, and the *Times* had actually been established during his final year in the country before returning to England.

When Chander saw that I was still queasy - and I had never suggested the cause - he insisted on reading my hand, so that I might take appropriate measures to safeguard my health in the future. I was reluctant to play along with his charlatanry, but he had such a seriousness and conviction in his psychic power, that it would have been churlish to have resisted the invitation. That morning he had read the palm of his sponsor, Ahmed, and the latter had told me that Chander's powers were almost "magical." Earlier that day he had predicted that Ahmed would come into a "great fortune" but only if he "prayed for the sincerity of his different friendships to be blessed by God, for ill thoughts destroy good fortune!"

I offered my hand. It was explained that the right hand was for men and the left for women, but that the left hand of men needed to be read with regard to a wife and marriage. He correctly described my family status, adding that I tended to be moved by reason rather than intuition. On confirming his findings, he assured me he was incapable of error in matters of palm reading, and if he was thought to be in error, it was usually due to misunderstanding or a failure in the mental powers of the subject. I had a good character, he said, and as I was destined for a long life, there was little to trouble me with regard to health. Finally, he assured me that belief in God was the supreme protection against dangers offered by the world we lived in.

Having captivated my attention, he then began to instruct me in the beliefs of his Hindu faith. Reincarnation was the most valid doctrine of all. He could not understand why Muslims repudiated this belief, as reincarnation had been demonstrated as "scientific" since time immemorial. It was even brought to the consciousness of many people through the intimations of a previous existence.

He cited the experiences of other Hindus who had recorded their tales, and in particular, that of a four year old Hindu girl who began unaccountably reciting Moslem prayers, and who on one occasion, on dropping a casket of jewels, miraculously exclaimed the word, "Allah!" Her parents took her to certain learned doctors, and she led them to a street where she had lived in a previous life, and she encountered and fell into the arms of a much-loved uncle. It was whilst in this house that she pointed to a slab in the floor, which when removed, revealed a box of long lost treasure!

Respectfully, I indicated surprise at this story, for by now it was impossible to engage in any meaningful discussion. I could only sit as a pensive listener. By now the conversation had entered a domain where communication was impossible between the rational intellectualism of the Westerner and the abstruse and chaotic musings of the Easterner which seemed to founder in the realm of fantasy.

The Westerner might share the sentiments or religiosity of his Eastern brother in so far as specific doctrines were abstract or metaphysical, but as soon as attempts were made to explain their nature, then the Westerner was confronted by the inexplicable which failed to lend itself to the logic of scientific rules of his thinking process. What seemed astonishing in this mental divide between East and West was the eclecticism of the Indian mind, and the outrageous contradictions necessitated in putting together ideas and beliefs from opposing poles of the world. And even more surprising was the fact that these tales were being narrated by a man with a scientific training.

And yet the East did exert a beneficent influence on the Western mind in a convoluted fashion. Reincarnation, despite its initial absurdities, embodied an ethical system of inestimable value to those corrupted by or borne down by the callous pride of the three great Semitic religions which had conquered the Western world. An angry monotheistic god had little interest in the fate of anything subordinate in status to his proudest creation. In a world slowly awakening to the fragility of the terrestrial environment; in a world increasingly conscious of interrelationships and interdependence between fauna and flora, there was a need to respect less sentient creatures or other forms of life.

The modern Occidental found himself overcome with dismay at realising the increasing callousness and cruelty to animal life the closer he approached the geographical source of his religion. Reincarnation demanded respect for all animal life, and in a strange way, its ethical values were more in accord with the facts of contemporary science than the more jealous and abrasive religions which had leapt so destructively from the desert lands. Surely, all shedding of blood was evil. Schopenhauer, that philosopher of Buddhism from a Western perspective, had long ago remarked that cruelty to animals was to be geographically identified with the circumcised peoples of the East.

By contrast, how much more ethical seemed the rules of the Brahmanic faith and how much more apt the fate of law-breakers. Hell with its eternal tortures, of the three great Westward moving faiths, seemed merely the vengeful fantasy of life-hating prophets. Hell, with its glorification of sadism, could only frighten children and simpletons, not grown men and women who understood the psychology of vicious motives.

How ill this contrasted with the greater justice of reincarnation expressed in the rebirth of souls into higher or lower categories of existence! How deserving and comprehensible were the penalties or rewards in ensuring respect for the universe and all creation. Such ethical commonsense, and the practicality of the doctrine, was sufficient to prevent, or at least subdue, the blind fanaticism and warlike cruelty which had characterised the three great Semitic faiths for two millennia.

The topic of reincarnation led Chander to tell me about the Maharishis (the religious sages) of the Hindu faith. Most Indians had a favourite Maharishi, and he reminded me how earlier that day I must have noted the framed portraits of a cherished teacher on the stalls of many Indian traders in the souks. There were many classes of Maharishis and the highest class of all had already lived on earth for aeons of time, usually alone in remote mountain regions, and they were only revealed to chosen individuals. He assured me the truth of these facts by recounting the story of the Englishman, Paul Britton, who sixty years ago had come out to India seeking a particular Maharishi revealed to him in a vision.

After five years his search was rewarded, and he recorded his

experiences in his book, *In Search of Mystic India*. He then related of
how when the British were tunnelling for a railway in a mountainside in
northern India, the coolies had broken through to a cavern in which two
oil lamps were burning, and in their terror, the workers ran back to the
British engineers. Asleep in this cavern lay an ancient Maharishi, and on
being rudely awoken by the engineers, he calmly informed them that if
they moved their tunnel twenty feet to the left, they would meet up
correctly with the excavations on the other side of the mountain, and as
it transpired, his calculation was correct to the final inch.

Just as Chander finished his account of this strange story, a lively
young man of middle height and Western dress, entered the shop, being
welcomed with a mixture of pleasure and awe by those present. His
friendliness extended even to showing an interest in Sikander, whose
quiet presence in the shop was usually ignored by all. The visitor was
introduced as Sandhu Aggarwal, and after half an hour's discussion with
Chander and reaching a business arrangement, he left.

"The adventures that that man's experienced would fill a book,"
confided Chander as soon as Sandhu had closed the door behind him.
"He's only thirty-two, but in his time he's achieved a reputation as one
of the most successful smugglers in the Gulf."

He then related the story of Sandju's eventful career. He had been
brought up in a hilly agricultural area in northern India as the son of a
poor farmer, with whom he quarrelled as to the pattern of his life's
future. So bad was the relationship between father and son that the latter
ran away from home at the age of seventeen with the idea of working for
a distant relative who was a smuggler. Sandhu travelled some four
hundred miles to the known home of this man to discover that he rarely
visited his permanent abode. He was met by the smuggler's wife who
explained that her husband was at home for hardly more than five days
in any year, and that his appearances were always unannounced and of
unpredictable duration. Cash remittances were sent regularly to the
smuggler's wife, but never accompanied by a note or letter. Where then
could the smuggler be found?

The wife directed the young relative of her husband to a coastal
town just to the north of Bombay, but there was no contact address, and
so Sandhu travelled another two hundred miles. On reaching the town,

and searching everywhere for his relative, he was told that such a man was "unknown," but he was struck by the suspicion and strange response of all those he approached. Intuitively, he felt himself the victim of a silent conspiracy. It was clear that the town's inhabitants would reveal nothing to strangers. Unknown to Sandhu, the population of the town derived its income from the smuggling trade, mostly entailing the importation of European luxury goods in dhows sailing from Dubai.

After some days Sandhu found himself sitting on the beach, forlorn and hungry, on a dark night, when he was alerted to the fortunate accident of events which led to his eventual prosperity. The inhabitants of the town slept by day to awake at night, so they might guide in safely the smugglers' vessels, unload cargo, and bury it deep in the dunes in readiness for immediate sale to inland traders. The entire coastline, for many miles north of Bombay, was an area of buried treasure, only known to and guarded by the towns' and village peoples' comprising the secretive smuggling communities.

On this particular night a boat had broken down in the bay, and was drifting dangerously in the vicinity of shifting sands, when Sandhu was suddenly approached by a group of desperate seamen. Did he understand the motor of a sea-going boat? Hungry and keen to ingratiate himself with anyone who might offer food or drink, he answered affirmatively, for although he had never seen a boat engine, he had learnt to maintain and repair the motors of generators and road driven vehicles. Risking the accusation of deceit, he accompanied the seamen back to their vessel, and after applying his intelligence in examining the motor, he at last succeeded in repairing it. This done, he then asked again if any knew the name of the relative he was seeking.

The captain of the dhow, who was standing in front of him, identified himself as the person sought. Sandhu, in his excitement threw his arms around the long sought-for relative, immediately asking to be taken aboard as a fellow crew member; but the four or five others standing by, dampened his enthusiasm, by responding that this was not such a simple request.

Smugglers could only be recruited from amongst those of exceptional competence and character. Courage, invariably, was the most necessary quality, for smugglers' vessels were often chased by the

Indian sea police, and frequently, there was an exchange of gunfire, although it was rare for smugglers to fail in outrunning their pursuers. Over the next few days Sandhu was obliged to undergo a series of tests, all of which he passed with little difficulty, and a week later, he was initiated into the smugglers' fraternity.

In the years which followed, he became a highly intelligent engineer, devising engines which outpaced the fastest boats of the Indian sea police, and eventually, he captained his own dhow, choosing his own merchandise from the Dubai traders in maximising his profits on the Gulf-West Indian coast trade run. This success, however, was only to last for several years. The Indian government, under the leadership of Mrs. Gandhi, frustrated at its attempts to stamp out this illegal trade, at last decided to call in the aid of the armed forces. Whilst the Indian army attacked and destroyed the smuggling settlements north of Bombay, the navy meanwhile, laid in wait for the returning dhows with their loaded treasure, which they attacked and sunk in the bays and hidden coves along the Indian coast.

Deprived of his livelihood, Sandhu turned his talents in another direction. Unable to return to his native India, where a price had been put on his head, he settled in Dubai as a watch repairer, opening a small shop in an alleyway just off Talib road, and it was there where he had first met Chander. He was so successful in this business that he rented out the shop, meanwhile obtaining highly paid work in the harbour as a ship's engineer, and this led in turn to an offer by a European company to work in a managerial position taking him to all the Gulf states. Sandhu, however, turned down the last offer, for as he was still unmarried, he was without the need for such a high salary.

"Shouldn't he think about obtaining a wife," I suggested, "since he seems to have everything else?"

"He has a strong desire for a wife, but it's difficult for him," replied Chander. "Here in Dubai it's difficult for such a man to find a wife suited to his requirements. But the greatest difficulty is his father. A wife has been reserved for him in his native village, but Sandhu refuses to marry a girl who has no skill other than that of a water carrier.

"Father and son still do not see eye to eye. And so whilst Sandhu is made unhappy by his inability to obtain a wife of his choice, as he can neither return to India and nor is he prepared to accede to the wishes of his family; his chosen and rejected fiancée is reduced to sadness and despair. And so, as she ages by the year, her chances of marriage recede to an ever more distant horizon."

Later in the evening we were joined by several business acquaintances, and an Indian souk trader, a customer of Ramesh & Sons, began to deplore the false imitations of quality products regularly and illegally dumped onto the Dubai market - usually originating from Taiwan or Indonesia.

"It's very very bad," persisted the trader, "because British goods are always the best - the very best in the world."

I was suffused with a mixture of feelings at this generalisation: surprise, delight, flattered, and sceptical at the validity of such a contention, but there was no doubt about the sincerity in which it was made.

Chander explained how the substitution of letters in a word was cleverly used in an attempt to evade the law in the illegal importation of products. He cited the example of Sandon socks, for which he held the agency, the products bearing the label, "Made in England," together with a Union Jack, so that there could be no ambiguity over the true origin of the goods. After several months of successful selling, a Taiwanese company began selling "Sendon socks" which bore the label, "Mode in England," but still carrying the Union Jack, and these were retailed in the souks at half the price of the real product.

The Taiwanese manufacturers claimed that the word "Mode" had no connection with the word "Made," and that no deceit had been intended. The word "Mode" was innocently used as a synonym for fashion. Nevertheless, Ramesh & Sons prosecuted the offending firm and won the case, and the merchandise of the offending firm was confiscated and burnt.

I recounted how I had been similarly deceived only the previous evening. I had bought from a chemists a tube of what I understood was Colgate toothpaste, only to discover on disposing the box the following morning that two letters had been cleverly substituted in the brand name. I had bought a tube of "Calgete" toothpaste manufactured in Malaysia, but the design of the wrapping was identical with that of the genuine article. The deceit was in the artwork rather than in the substitution of two letters in the brand name, for the prospective purchaser in a hurry would never have bothered to glance closely at the text.

The visiting Indian trader related a tale of Japanese skulduggery in which he was directly involved. He was the UAE agent for the Japanese made President brand briefcase, but on one occasion he received from them a container load consignment which was half filled with cases bearing the famous "Samsonite" label, being exact imitations of the American original.

As Samsonite were already registered with an agent in Dubai, the customs stopped the consignment pending authorisation. In response to their embarrassment, the President company in Japan requested the Dubai agent to present a letter to the authorities certifying that the container had been shipped via America. This the latter refused to do since it would have compounded the deceit and put him in a compromising situation from three directions at once: viz., the Port of Dubai, the recognised UAE Samsonite importers, and the US manufacturers of the genuine product.

The most uncomfortable situation experienced by the Indian business community in the UAE, however, occurred through the religiously motivated discrimination of the *Shariah* (Islamic) courts in litigation cases. These usually occurred in prosecution for the payment of bills or the collection of other debts. The religious judges, or *Qadis*, felt a sense of outrage that Muslims should be made answerable to non-believers. Consequently, the final adjudication of the courts commonly stated that payment cannot be made as, "this man states he is without the necessary financial resources," even though it may be common knowledge that such a man was a wealthy merchant.

Alternatively, and hardly less vexatious to a plaintiff, it was sometimes declared that a debt should be repaid in such easy stages over so long a period, that the aggrieved party was never fully compensated because of the cost of capital. Chander stated that the situation in this regard was particularly bad in the emirates of Fujairah and Ras al Khaimah, where the local Arabs had gained the dubious reputation as the least honourable of any in the Gulf in settling debts.

By now the discussion was reaching a climax of excitement.

"The trouble is, there's no predictability," exclaimed Chander. "There's no proper rule of law. The Emirs have absolute power of life and death over anyone in their Emirates. That's not justice!"

"And do you know whose fault it is,?" exclaimed the Indian trader fixing me with his glance. "It's the British! For a hundred and thirty years they occupied this place when it was known as the Trucial States. They brought British law. It was firm but just. You knew where you stood. The British government should never have pulled out of this place when they did in 1971. They handed everything over to the Sheikhs. That was wrong! The British protected the Indian community."

"You're so right," responded Chander. "The British have a moral obligation to protect Indian communities wherever they are found."

"But why,?" I asked.

"Because wherever the British have gone, the Indians have always followed in their wake: in the Gulf, South Africa, Kenya, Uganda, Guyana and the Caribbean, Fiji and the Pacific - everywhere. We helped them build the Empire. Isn't it right they should protect us now from the arbitrary authority of the mullahs?"

"But Gulf Arabs are terrified by the imbalance of population," exclaimed the visiting trader. "They're swamped by aliens. Expatriates represent eighty per cent of the population."

"Who invited them here?"

"The Arabs themselves," said the trader. "They had to spend their oil money somehow. They wanted to build cities in the desert and so they brought these problems on themselves."

"There are things which would never happen here if the British were still with us," began Chander, and he told a story of homicide concerning a son of one of the seven rulers of the separate emirates.

No long ago the son of a ruling Sheikh was driving along a motorway in his new sports car accompanied (as customary) by his armed retinue of motorcyclists, when suddenly he was forced to reduce speed due to slow moving traffic ahead. The cause of the delay was a truck with trailer, which could not be easily overtaken, due to the unstable swerving of the trailer as the vehicles annoyingly occupied the middle of the road. It was not the truck, however which was to provoke the incident. Closely behind the truck - nose to tail - drove a taxi. It was this vehicle which aroused the ire of the Emir's son. He hooted violently, indicating that he wished to overtake the taxi, but the hired vehicle stubbornly maintained its position behind the trailer.

At last the prince could bear the frustration no longer. He gestured to his bodyguard and the taxi was forced to stop amidst a blaring of sirens. As the prince emerged from his car, the taxi driver, a Pakistani, was dragged from his vehicle and kicked and beaten with headropes; the Emir's son all the while shouting in rage and urging on his security guard to carry on their punishment. When the beating ceased, the Pakistani, bruised and bloodied, protested his innocence, and when this led to a further altercation, and an exchange of insults, this was more than the prince could endure. He pulled out a revolver and pumped six bullets into the prostrate Pakistani.

This was an incident which could not easily be suppressed. The Emir's son was already notorious as a problem to his family for his fits of paranoia and violence. The case was brought before the Shariah court, and in Islamic law, the penalty should have been death, but such a sentence could not be enforced on a member of the ruling family. Instead, the court turned to the question of compensation (or blood money) and evaluated the life of the taxi driver. The *Qadis* awarded 50,000 dirhams (£6,300) to the relatives of the dead man. This sum was adjudged sufficient in view of the fact that those relatives were poor villagers living in the Sind in a backward area in the Indian subcontinent.

The Pakistani community were outraged at the court's decision. After all, they too were Muslims, and they expected equal treatment as if a local had been murdered in similar circumstances. Within days a demonstration was organised, and thousands rallied around the Emir's palace, demanding vengeance. A petition was launched and the protesters undertook to raise a further 100,000 dirhams as compensation for the dead man's relatives providing that the Emir would authorise the execution of his son. Neither the authorities nor any individual in power offered to increase the original compensation figure laid down by the court. Instead, the Emir ordered his son out of the country, sending him to the safety of London."

"Surely such cases are an exception," I put in, "and surely such stories tend to blacken unduly the calm and peaceful nature of life in the emirates. For example, at least you cannot deny that the streets are safe at night. Women are unmolested everywhere and at all times."

"That, too, is a myth," exclaimed Chander, almost before I had finished the sentence, and he began to elaborate on the recent increase in rape cases in the UAE. "It's not so bad here in Dubai, but in Abu Dhabi, several men have been convicted for rape in recent months. They say it's something to do with the warmer air, and the sand, and the more saline drinking water which acts as an aphrodisiac. Not long ago a serial rapist was caught and executed in Abu Dhabi. He was a young fellow of twenty-five. He had raped fourteen woman over a period of months."

Chander then related the story of a rape case which had aroused considerable concern amongst the Pakistani community a year or so previously. It concerned the wife of a high ranking Pakistani general - a woman allegedly of great beauty. She was due to meet her husband at Karachi airport, and a taxi had supposedly driven her from the house of friends to Abu Dhabi airport, but it never arrived. When the police appeared dilatory in unravelling the crime, the Pakistani general, at last, in exasperation, flew to the UAE and petitioned the Emir of Abu Dhabi for justice. The petition was granted and action initiated, resulting finally in the arrest and conviction of the rapist.

"What's the punishment for rape,?" I asked.

"In that case - for it was murder also - two hundred and fifty lashes followed by stoning," replied Chander.

"And who are the people who carry out the stoning,?" I asked.

"It's always carried out by very religious Muslims - usually prayer leaders," answered Chander. "They try to choose people of unblemished character. First they must undergo ritual ablutions in the Mosque. They alone are fit to carry out an execution by stoning."

CHAPTER 3
In a Saudi home

"There is a mercy which is weakness and even treason against the common good."

George Eliot, *Romola*, Bk. iii, Ch. 59.

Struggling to keep upright, as I pushed my back into the crowd behind, several drops of perspiration fell from my brow onto my cheeks in the sweltering heat, and moments later, my lips were suffused with a salty liquid. What crazy purpose had brought me to join this mob? I recollected the words of a Noel Coward song about "Mad dogs and Englishmen out in the midday sun."

In front of us, the gates in the compound wall surrounding the Governor's Palace were slowly pushed open, and seconds later, three companies each of sixty men, marched out in perfect formation in files of two, raising their arms to shoulder height in correct military precision. Armed with small automatic weapons suspended from their shoulders, and wearing berets and khaki uniforms, they took up positions before the crowd facing inwards towards the empty space.

Behind us, we were surprised by the noise of a vehicle in the square which previously had been cleared of traffic. A huge dirty sandy brown Dodge truck was slowly making its way across Deira square accompanied by a small escort of police. As soon as it reached the outer limits of the crowd pressing towards the Governor of Riyadh's Palace, it went into reverse, and amidst the shouting of the police and the movement of the human mass to create a space, it eased its way into the open crescent formation, shuddering clumsily with every gear change.

At last the giant vehicle came to a halt. Two men jumped down from the cabin and released the tailboard. One man went to the controls behind the cabin and began to operate the lift. A loud crash filled the square as several tons of stones and rubble were emptied onto the roadway, and a brown cloud of stifling dust rose in the airless heat.

"It's to be a stoning," exclaimed someone nearby.

"Then it's got to be an adulteress," retorted an American who had just pushed his way to the front.

That so much technology should be needed to implement so basic a method of execution,! I pondered. After all, even apes can throw stones at an enemy. Surely, this is not how it could have been two thousand years ago! The mixture of old and new in the Saudi culture never failed to astonish. Arriving in the Kingdom is always a culture shock, for the divide between the West and the Arab world is too great ever to be bridged. And the first arrival of all in the desert Kingdom is an experience never to be forgotten.

On arriving in Jeddah, the Red Sea port and commercial capital, on that first occasion, I was supposed to be met at the airport, but nobody was there. It was past 7.0 o'clock and a dark humid evening, and after waiting in vain for three quarters of an hour, I took a taxi to the Al-Attas Hotel in Al Jamjoum street. As the taxi drove down the broad busy boulevards, amongst the constantly hooting vehicles, beneath the giant full colour portraits of the King and two leading ministers who were also half brothers of the monarch, suspended at regular intervals across the breadth of Al Matar road, looking down benignly at those below so that first time visitors would never again forget the faces of the country's rulers, I reflected apprehensively on the reception I might receive.

For two months I had waited for the required invitation from Badanah Brothers, our sponsors and agents in Saudi Arabia. Without such an invitation it would not be possible to apply for a Visitor's visa from the Commercial section of the Saudi embassy in London. As requested, I had sent photocopies of my passport and baptism certificate - the latter document being required proof that I did not belong to the hated "Jewish enemy." I had sent letters and urgent telexes, but all had been unanswered. What were the Badanahs playing at? Why were they so unco-operative? They had successfully represented our company for more than twenty years, but how could trade be effectively maintained if they adopted such unbusiness-like and lackadaisical practices?

Finally, as a short cut, I had persuaded the company to pay the £200 membership fee in joining the British-Arab Chamber of Commerce, for it was then possible to obtain a business Visitor's visa within a week. Had the Badanahs possibly taken offence at this short-cut measure? There was no knowing how they might have reacted. I remembered my predecessor's warning, shortly after I had taken on the job, that the introduction of a "new face" was always a problem in the Middle East.

Arabs don't do business with a "company." They only do business with an individual. They hardly understand what a "company" means, together with all the legal complexities of limited liability. Only relationships between people have meaning in the Arab mind. Relationships between tribes and families and individuals make sense, but relationships with an incorporated body is incomprehensible.

"In any case, they're not going to do business with you until after they've got to know you as a person, and if they don't like you, it's no order in the bag. If you can't socialise with them as an equal, you can't do the job," concluded my predecessor.

Once settled into the hotel room, I phoned the Badanahs' office, asking for Mr. Mousa, the elder brother and my main contact with the firm. I was gruffly told that Mr. Mousa was not there, but "elsewhere," tied up in business with a friend. When would he be available? It was unknown, but not before 10.0 pm. I explained to the office manager, Fallah Abdullah, at the other end of the line, that I was expected. Abdullah said that he couldn't help, but that I would be contacted by a "family member" later in the evening.

A fine start to the visit,! I thought to myself. So much for the reputation of Arab hospitality! Where was this going to lead? My lingering apprehension that something must be wrong took firmer told. Perhaps I had been too pushy in insisting on making the trip - but what other alternative had there been? I was paid to do a job. Then I consoled myself on the abruptness at the other end of the line. Arabs often sounded unfriendly on the phone. This was partly due to the staccato sound of the language with its poverty of vowels, and the awkwardness of Arabs in telephonic communication.

Or perhaps there was a more ominous explanation stemming from underlying problems in promoting business in the area. Momentarily, I fell into the paranoid suspicion shared by Accounts Department colleagues back in the Basildon factory. To them, all foreigners were "bad," and exporting was a headache best left to fools.

Just two weeks earlier, Steve Barnes, a dyspeptic clerk who had been raised to the position of a little dictator as head of Credit Control, had stormed into my office without knocking, railing against the idea of doing business with Saudi Arabs.

"These Badanahs are bloody crooks," he exclaimed, dropping cigarette ash over my desk.

"They're our third biggest export customer," I said defensively.

"They never pay their bills."

"Don't give me that crap because it's not true. They pay at sight by confirmed irrevocable letter of credit. What more do you want?"

"They're supposed to pay at sight, but they still hold onto the money."

"Then it's the bank's fault. They negotiate the bills."

"We don't get this problem with other customers."

"Okay, I'll look into it when I see them in two weeks."

"And we haven't had an order from them for over a year."

"That's because no one's been there for over a year."

"They could have sent something through the post."

"That's not the way they operate in the Middle East. If you don't go in person, you don't get the business. It's as simple as that. Remember, their last order was ten container loads."

"I'll never understand these bloody foreigners - you never know where you are with them. You export bods can deal with them in your own way," he said, and stormed out of the room as hurriedly as he had entered.

Apprehensive at what the next few days might bring, I felt the loneliness of my position. Everywhere there was misunderstanding. I alone was the connecting link between the great cultural chasm which divided our Saudi business partners from what I now perceived as the unsympathetic myopic provincialism of the management at the Basildon factory. I was exhausted after a long day and several connecting flights across the peninsula, and I decided to retire. The room was cold, for the control on the air conditioning unit was defective; there was no spare blanket; and no way of opening the windows to let in the sultry night air. I would visit the Badanahs' office the day after tomorrow, for it was now a Thursday night.

Hardly half an hour had passed when I was startled by the bedside telephone. A Mr. Obeid Badanah was waiting for me at the desk. Surprised, I hurriedly dressed, and some minutes later met a diminutive and reticent young man in his teens who introduced himself as the son of Mr. Mousa. He was wearing a white thobe and *kaffia* (or skull cap), but no *gutra* or headscarf. He explained he had been asked to take me to his father.

We went outside and climbed into a huge black American saloon. Obeid was dwarfed behind the controls of the car, his head hardly reaching the height of the windscreen.

"Where is your father,?" I enquired as we drove off.

"In a big big place," was his only reply.

"Then he's not in his office?"

"No, he's in a big place with many many people."

My curiosity was aroused. I tried to make polite conversation, but Obeid was shy, and we succeeded in little more than the exchange of civilities on passing sights along the road. The journey seemed endless, but after forty-five minutes we arrived at what looked like the approach to a giant supermarket: hundreds of parked cars and thousands of people milling about an expansive low-built structure. After we left the car and began tracing our way through the crowds, it was evident we had reached an exhibition ground, and on the building in front of us, the word INDIA was illuminated and dozens of Indian flags fluttered in the wind on either side of the sign.

Behind the main building huge rectangular marquees had been erected for exhibitors, and it was into one of these we entered in reaching the Badanah Brothers stand. The firm was managed by three brothers, assisted by their numerous sons aged from their late teens to mid twenties. There was much bustle, and several Pakistanis were removing products from display areas and packing them carefully into crates whilst several of the Badanah sons were acting in a supervisory role.

Amidst this confusion, on a dais, the two elder brothers sat side by side behind a table, with the detached authority of Roman Consuls, calmly surveying the scene. They were plump stocky men, and although only in their mid forties could have been taken for sixty. Nazeer, the younger of the two, had a dark grim complexion, fixing prospective customers and business associates alike with a look of constant suspicion. He wore a white headscarf, and I was never to see him with a headrope, and so the *gutra* which draped freely over either side of his visage, not only made his complexion all the darker, but gave him a strangely nunnish appearance. The elder brother, Mousa, had a more good-humoured demeanour. He was benevolent with an impish sense of fun, and a protruding lower lip and hunched shoulders gave him a clownish appearance.

"You're very very welcome to Jeddah," exclaimed Mousa with warmth, clasping my hand in both of his. "We show you all Jeddah, Mr. Robert. We make your stay very good. Your first time in Saudi Arabia? We'll make your trip very special."

He sat me down in a place of honour beside him at the table on the dais, and immediately ordered a glass of tea. Minutes later I was introduced to several other Europeans who had been working on the stand. The Badanahs had been exhibiting the products of a world brand leader with manufacturing plants in Sunderland, the US and France. I met Dick Wadsworth, the American Product Manager, Pierre Legouis, the French representative, John Crawley, the Export Manager from Sunderland, and Rob Haworth, who managed the overall Middle East sales operation from an office in Amman.

Mousa spoke good pidgin English: "I no talk good English but I can say what I want," he apologised. His brother, Nazeer, spoke no English but understood more than he was prepared to admit, and would only enter into business negotiations through an interpreter when he would press for a hard bargain.

"Next year we'll exhibit your products, too, at the exhibition," assured Mousa.

John Crawley gave me an excuse to leave the table and we were soon in conversation.

"This is the end of a ten-day fair," he said. "It's been like this every day - absolute chaos! You wouldn't call this a trade fair in the West."

"Sponsored by the Indian government,?" I suggested.

"That sign outside isn't supposed to be there," he said with irritation. "This is supposed to be the Jeddah Spring Fair, but the Indian

Ministry of Trade bought up so much space they persuaded the Saudi organisers to put up all those flags and call it an Indian trade fair. The public have been conned! It isn't a bloody trade fair at all. It's been a glorified bazaar! The public have been let in from day one, and all we've done is sell our products over the counter as fast as we can unpack the containers, from ten in the morning until ten at night - bar a four hour break until 5.0 pm. The public think they're buying at wholesale prices, and on several occasions, the police have been called in to control the crowds at the entry points. It's been total chaos! We haven't had a chance to meet dealers for serious negotiations. They don't bother to come here. This place is just a joke! Our purpose in exhibiting was to find agents for other Middle East markets. None of us are bloody shop assistants - we're export sales managers!"

By this time Mousa had left the table and was standing in the middle of the display area, holding Rob Haworth by both wrists, talking to him intently. Rob was a convivial overweight man in his early fifties, and he was nodding affirmatively and laughing in some embarrassment at what appeared to be a good-humoured remonstration.

"Mousa's worried about Rob," confided John Crawley. "He's been on at him all the week."

"What about?"

"He's not married," replied John. "Rob's great company - I love him dearly - but Mousa doesn't seem to understand he's not the marrying kind. It's his hormones."

"Couldn't someone drop a hint?"

"Not likely! They don't understand that kind of thing here - not when it's amongst friends."

"But surely -," I began.

"It's a taboo topic," snapped John.

"No man should sleep alone. It's not good," persisted Mousa waving a finger reprehensibly in front of Rob's face. "Sleep alone is bad. You must a wife."

"But I haven't found anyone yet," protested Rob laughing.

"No problem! We make arrangements," said Mousa. "You live in Amman?"

"And how can I find a wife in Amman?"

"Different from your own country, eh? Easier to find a wife in England, yes ?"

"Yes!"

"Then let me help you," said Mousa, and he took Rob by the hand and began walking him backwards and forwards on the stand.

By now the attention of us all was alerted, and the Europeans began laughing openly at Rob's discomfort at the comical appearance of these disparate individuals engaged in such a bizarre interchange.

"You want to get married don't you,?" persisted Mousa, as they walked to and fro.

"Of course," said Rob.

"Good, because only bad men don't want to get married," said Mousa reassured, and patting the back of his friend's hand. "Now we've known each other for five years. You're a good friend. I like you. You're a good man."

"I hope so," said Rob laughing awkwardly.

"I've a proposal. Now listen carefully. You'll stay in Amman?"

"As long as the job lasts."

"You like Amman?"

"Yes."

"Then you'll spend your life in Amman! It doesn't matter about the job. If you lose the job, God will always find you another."

Rob laughed nervously, apprehensive as to what was to follow.

"I've a second cousin here in Jeddah," began Mousa solemnly, fixing Rob in the eye. "She's well-built and beautiful. And she's well-educated. Her English is much better than mine. She'd make a good wife. Good family! She'd make you happy. And you'd never sleep in an empty bed again. My friend, I can arrange everything."

"He would, too," confided John in my ear.

"How old is she,?" asked Rob.

"Sixteen!"

"Far too young," said Rob laughing.

"No, not too young," protested Mousa. "You need a young wife. She'll give you good babies - and a son."

"Too much responsibility," cried Rob.

"She'll be no worry," responded Mousa. "Good Muslim girl! They

make the best wives. And, my friend, we've often spoken about the
Koran. I know you'd make a good Muslim."

"I'd have to think about it," said Rob .

"Come, my friend, let me talk to you in confidence," said Mousa
leading his friend away from the stand. "These are bad men here. Don't
listen to them. They're only mockers," he added turning to the rest of us
with a broad grin, and he led Rob down the aisle between the stands,
towards the far end of the marquee.

"Is he serious,?" I exclaimed incredulously to John Crawley.

"He is," replied John.

It was already 10.30 pm, and the lights began flashing for visitors
and exhibitors to leave the building. Minutes later the Badanah brothers,
joined by their youngest sibling, Kamal, began taking down cartons
filled with cash from a shelf behind them, emptying them onto the table
so that the day's takings could be counted. Wads of cash, tightly secured
with elastic bands, began to pile up on the table.

"Just look at that," exclaimed John in overawed astonishment. "If
this was back home it'd be a robbers paradise! It's been like it every
day."

At last the daily total was announced: 70,000 riyals, or £10,000.

"Now we go to eat," announced Mousa, as the three brothers rose
from the table and stuffed the bundles of money into the deep pockets of
their thobes.

The sons, of which there were nine milling around the stand
engaged in various tasks, had already gone ahead to the fleet of cars, and
we Europeans followed the three brothers as they strolled in the slow
Arab fashion towards the car park.

"You couldn't get away with that down the Old Kent road at half
past ten on a dark night," joked John, nodding towards the walking
mountains of cash.

"What do they do with it when they get home,?" I ventured.

"I guess they put it on the mantelpiece," said Dick Wadsworth, and
we all laughed.

"This must be a security salesman's paradise," I said.

"You're joking,!" said John. "Electrical surveillance for property
protection is practically unknown here."

"Robbery, the way we experience it back home, just doesn't take place in Saudi Arabia," said Rob.

"With the penalties they hand out, you don't exactly get a second chance," laughed Pierrre. "After all, one-handed burglars must be pretty thin on the ground."

"Where are we going now,?" I asked.

"Search me," said Rob.

"They've got houses and flats all over the town," said Pierre.

"We've been eating in a different home almost every night," said John. "The Badanahs never eat in restaurants. It'll be in one of the residences of the brothers."

"The extended family all eat together," said Dick. "I don't think there's ever been fewer than eighteen of us sitting down to dinner."

"The brothers plan everything in advance, but they never let on what the arrangements are," said John.

When we reached the three ceremonial-looking black saloons, the sons were already standing by and the drivers were seated for departure. The brothers were ushered into the front passenger seats first, together with a third person, and then we Europeans were conducted into the more spacious area at the rear of the vehicles, followed by the other sons.

"Where are we going tonight,?" asked Pierre cheekily of the driver, as the car with its quiet motor drove at a leisurely pace down a broad street.

"Masharafah," replied Mohammed, the son who was driving.

"Is that Nazeer's flat over the new household goods shop?"

"Yes."

On arriving at the Badanah Supermarket, we entered a side entrance into flats, and climbed two storeys with beige polished stone steps and walls, until we reached the imposing double-door entrance to Nazeer's flat.

The doors were opened by sons who were already within, and we were welcomed with smiles of pleasure and effusive gestures of hospitality. It was a long entrance hall with a marble floor, washbasins at either end, lit by two crystal chandeliers. Before entering the Majlis, or lounge area, we were invited to wash our hands, and having removed our shoes, we entered a spacious carpeted room with low-seated soft upholstered sofas placed against three sides of the wall area. The fourth wall consisted of a frosted glass partition leading into an adjoining room. There was no article of furniture in the centre of the room, but in the corner in the direction of Mecca stood a small table on which lay a mother of pearl box in which was kept a copy of the *Koran*, also decorated in mother of pearl. This was the prayer corner. On one wall was suspended an elaborately framed text from the *Koran*, the script standing out in white against the traditional Islamic green. In another corner stood a TV set below which was a library of video tapes.

We were bidden to be seated, and we found that our backsides were scarcely above floor level as we sunk into cushions which seemed to embrace our bodies. Two younger sons, both grinning in delight, and possibly, in some embarrassment, and hardly ten years of age, stood before us. One carried a brass tray bearing porcelain cups, but of a size and shape more resembling egg cups than the receptacles usual in the West. The second boy held an ornate brass pot with a long spout. We each took a cup, and green tea was served.

The three partners entered the room bare-footed, less *gutras* which gave them quite a different appearance, since their hair and the shape of their heads was now visible for the first time.

"Now is the peaceful time," pondered Mousa contentedly, and the three took their seats on the soft furnishings, not cross-legged, but kneeling sideways or pulling their feet beneath their haunches.

Then an elderly man entered, supported by a staff, and introduced as a distant relative, and he was given an honoured place beside the brothers, and then a number of sons noisily entered, taking up places at the opposite end of the room to their fathers. Finally, a short dark-skinned man in a red turban and Yemeni skirt, danced comically into the room carrying an enormous *Kolyan* (water-pipe) or hubble-bubble, to shrieks of laughter from the children. The latest arrival was introduced as Samir Badri, a friend who lived on the floor below.

There was an exchange of banter between Mousa and Samir, followed by a peal of laughter, and even Nazeer's grim visage broke into a smile, and he offered a witticism of his own to the amusement of the company.

The hubble-bubble was four feet high, a superb and beautiful smoking requisite and article of furniture, with its silver, mother of pearl, and gold inlay on the shapely brass pipe and water vessel. The supple snake-like six foot tube leading from the water vessel to the mouthpiece was draped in red cotton and tassels. As Samir prepared the water pipe for use, placing red hot charcoal in the earthenware receptacle, and *gurac* (a black sticky paste of decomposed fruit and vegetable matter with spices added) above that, and sucked at the end of the long tube until smoke from the *gurac* had passed through the water container, John Crawley identified discreetly for me several of the elder Badanah sons involved in the business.

"That's Nabeel," said John, pointing to a plump young man whose countenance was more serious than the others. "He's one of the eldest and a son of Nazeer. He's very reliable and spends a lot of time in the firm although he's studying business administration at the University here. The one behind him is Said, a son of Mousa. He's very presentable and perhaps the most intelligent of the clan. He only works for the family when the pressure's on, so we don't see much of him. He's studying medicine in Riyadh. I can relate to him more easily than the others. He does have some understanding of the West.

"That one in the middle laughing and pushing the younger ones around is Ismail. He's just happy-go-lucky. He's another son of Mousa. He's been a terrible headache to his father. About a year ago he spent six months in London. He got into bad company, and got mixed up with alcohol and women. He had a flat in Bayswater and ended up visiting knocking shops in Soho seven nights a week. He cost his father a packet! As soon as he got back his father arranged for him to be married almost at once."

After ten minutes the hubble-bubble was ready for smoking and now the mouthpiece could be handed round to each in turn.

"Give it first to our honoured guest, Mr. Robert," said Mousa.

Samir handed me the mouthpiece, and the younger boys in the room crowded round the sofa, laughing in anticipation that someone was going to be embarrassed.

"You don't have to smoke it," whispered John.

"It's not a cigarette. Go on, breathe deeply," cried Pierre. "Fill your lungs. You mustn't stop until you hear the water bubbling."

As soon as the water bubbled, the smaller boys clapped their hands, jumping up and down on the floor.

"You like it, Mr. Robert,?" asked Mousa.

"It's like nothing I've experienced before," I responded. "So smooth and refreshing. You can't compare it with tobacco."

"You'll make a good Arab yet," laughed Mousa.

"Come on, pass it over," said Dick who was two places to my left.

"Not yet, I haven't had my fill," I said blowing out clouds of smoke.

"Look at him, lying there like a real Arab," cried Ismail in excitement. "He can't even take it from his mouth. And he hasn't even choked yet. Everyone chokes the first time. He's a marvel!"

The elder men laughed appreciatively, and I handed along the mouthpiece to John.

"Not me - I've given up smoking," he responded.

"I'm a non-smoker, too, but this is different," I said as the mouthpiece was passed to Dick. "What a beautiful ornament," I added, passing my fingers down the brass pipe.

"You like it,?" said Samir.

"Of course," I responded.

"You shouldn't have said that," whispered John nudging me in the side.

"What do you mean,?" I said startled.

"Never tell an Arab you like something which belongs to him."

"Why not?"

"Because he'll give it to you. It's their style of generosity. The greatest pleasure of the Arab is giving."

Some days later I was to discover the truth of this.

At last, the glass partition to the adjoining room was opened from within, and Nabeel emerged, inviting us to take our places for dinner; and I was asked to enter the dining area first, followed by the brothers, and then the other guests, and last of all, the numerous sons.

Two giant stainless steel platters, three feet in diameter, loaded with rice and roasted chickens, lay on the white table cloth spread out on the floor. On each place setting was a bowl of vegetable and a bowl of sauce, and although no knives or forks were in evidence, spoons had thoughtfully been placed where the Europeans were to sit. We sat on large colourful cushions, and I abstained from using the spoon, determined to comply with the table etiquette of my hosts. I made sure that only my right hand should be used for passing food to the mouth, but the left hand was allowed for tearing apart the flesh and bones of the roasted meat which had been thrown onto our plates; and I burnt my fingers on the hot rice as I squashed it into a ball for ready eating, cooling them in the sauce bowl. The two eldest sons, Nabeel and Said, acted as hosts, ensuring that the best pieces were given to the Europeans and that their plates were kept full.

The elder Arabs ate with great relish and rapidity as if they had not eaten for a week, sucking the bones dry before throwing them back onto their plates, and after the first course was finished, the smaller boys passed round bowls of warm lemon water and towels to wash our hands. Swiss ice cream was served for the main dessert, for which we were all given spoons, and finally, we were offered a selection of fresh fruit: oranges, apples and bananas.

On returning to the lounge area we were again served green tea, as being good for the digestion, and amidst a highly convivial atmosphere and much jollity, the TV was switched on and videos shown on the screen, but no tape was allowed to run for more than five to ten minutes. There was a pot-pourri of entertainment, purely visual and aural, with the minimum of dialogue: a King Fu film with the Chinese villain made easily identifiable with his anomalous Hitler moustache and forelock; a violent all-in wrestling match, and finally, what seemed to me, an indifferent black and white Hollywood film of the 1950s.

In the enjoyment of this escapist entertainment, it surprised me that this latter piece aroused more amusement from the company present, young and old alike, than anything else which had preceded it. There was little that was amusing that I could see in the film. It comprised only of sequences of stereotypical scenes of American domestic life constructed around the story of a detective thriller.

"Western life-styles have about as much bearing on reality to the Arab mind as a Tom and Jerry cartoon to us," explained John in response to a comment I had made. "The fact that a man and woman should sit together at a table in a public place is so absurd and unreal that it's impossibly bizarre. Hence the laughter. They never follow the plot of a Western made film - they can't understand the dialogue anyway. When it comes to serious cinema they rely on Egyptian films - and that's a vast industry."

The last video was removed and a regular TV programme appeared on the screen, being a channel from Kuwait. It was a musical programme narrating an epic love story. As a blind elderly musician chanted the words, accompanying himself on a *saz*, a kind of three-stringed guitar, he was surrounded by a rectangle of some fifty seated men in their thobes and *gutras*, clapping in unison, and occasionally, singing in chorus, and at different intervals, between two and six of their number would jump into the rectangle and perform the *Ardha*, a traditional but unstructured form of dancing. It was such a scene as might have been witnessed in primeval Greece or in the baronial halls of early medieval Europe in the age of travelling minstrels.

As the evening mellowed and we were served black tea, and as Nazeer reclined at full length on one of the sofas, blowing out clouds of smoke from the hubble-bubble, he issued an instruction to the older sons across the room, and they immediately left. By now, the two other brothers, Mousa and Kamal, had left their sofas and were seated on cushions on the floor where they seemed more at ease. Moments later, the four or five sons re-entered the room, carrying babies and small children, none more than three years of age. At first they were handed to their grandfathers who kissed and fondled them, and a sweet little girl in a blue dress and brown locks ran happily round the room, and then the children were passed from one person to another to be admired by the rest of the company.

"Ismail's son is only four weeks old," explained John, "and the little girl is Said's daughter."

After ten minutes the children were taken out again, and by now the younger sons were fatigued by the late hour. Mousa was stroking the head of his youngest son, Faisal, as he dozed dreamily against his father's breast, whilst Nazeer affectionately pressed the hand of a younger son as he leant against his father. It was a scene of such domestic bliss and contentment with the "best of all possible worlds," as would rarely be met with in a Western household. It was already past 2.0 am, and Dick Wadsworth rose from his seat, saying that all good parties must come to an end, and that later that morning he had a flight back to Chicago.

The rest of us took the cue and rose from our seats. Pierre Legouis embraced each of the three senior brothers in turn, and then the other elder Arab guests, kissing them on each cheek. We Anglo-Saxons could not bring ourselves to make the last gesture, but we embraced our hosts and the elder men, just touching cheeks. Samir, the hubble-bubble man, gave me an especially warm embrace. Nabeel was to drive us back to our hotels.

"God be with you," exclaimed the brothers as we left the apartment.

Pierre was the first to be dropped.

"See you tomorrow," he said to Nabeel as he left the car.

"Inshallah," qualified Nabeel grimly, as if to remind the Frenchman of his mortality.

"Of course, inshallah (by the will of God)," responded the Frenchman. "Everything's 'inshallah'! Nothing can be said without 'inshallah.'"

Over the following days I was to learn the importance of this phrase. At first the Westerner tended to interpret this term, when he heard it from the lips of an Arab, in the sense of the Spanish *mañana*, i.e. as an excuse that anything may be left undone out of carelessness or idle choice. But "inshallah" had quite a different meaning.

Initially, it always gives rise to misunderstood feelings, since just as the Arab cannot understand the Westerner's secularism and self-confidence in his power as a free-willing independent agent; so the latter cannot give credibility to the Arab's total belief in the omnipotent power of God. Hence, at first, the term "inshallah" is either perceived as an expression of hypocrisy, or else as a light-headed excuse that an anticipated event may never occur. It is only after the Arab constantly corrects his Western partner in insisting that the latter always uses the phrase whenever he expresses an intended action, that he learns to comprehend the true meaning of the term.

CHAPTER 4
A family in Jeddah

"Exact justice is commonly more merciful in the long
run than pity, for it tends to foster in men those stronger
qualities which make them good citizens."

J.R. Lowell, *Among My Books: Dante*

Concern at the possibility of failing to achieve sufficient business
during my first trip to the Kingdom, continued to haunt me over
the next few days. This was not because of lack of attention on
the part of my sponsors, for their hospitality could not be faulted, but
because of their apparent reluctance to touch on the topic of company
business.

I would bustle around making my own researches on price
comparisons and product design and quality in their various shops and
wholesale display stores, but they took little interest in my note taking or
in any comments I offered. Their only interest in my existence seemed
to be a relaxed socialising and tea drinking, from early in the morning
until the close of business at 10 o'clock at night - and even after that
hour, there was feasting and more socialising.

There was a timelessness to their lives. Business was something
that you sat and waited for. Trust and optimism in success was always
there, for it was a gift of the deity. As someone experienced in the
sophisticated north European markets with their emphasis on efficiency;
 the importance of maintaining time slots for given tasks throughout the
day; and the obsession with modern methods to increase the speed of
business completion, the ways of the Middle East were a disturbing
contrast. To the Westerner, with his Protestant work ethic, unproductive
time was felt instinctively as immoral. And yet Arab ways seemed to
serve their own purpose! Was there not something more to life than just
closing the deal?

Those who demonstrated super-efficiency - or more correctly,
those intent on maintaining its appearance - were disdained in Arab

business circles. Germans, especially, with their subjectivity, were often knocked off balance by the cultural shock of a first visit to the Kingdom, and it was not until they subdued their dynamism, falling in with Arab ways, that they realised success.

I was later to meet a young German banker, who on a flying visit, had not merely been so foolish as to visit in July but also during the period of Ramadan. As he struggled in the unbearable heat, covered in perspiration and desperate for shade, denied sustenance from dawn to sunset, as he made his way from one office to another, walking at the pace he was accustomed to in Frankfurt, he collapsed in the street and needed to be hospitalised for de-hydration. Not only had he not achieved any business, but his air fare and hotel costs had been a wasted expense. Perhaps the age-old Arab ways, with their more leisurely pace, contained a wisdom from which the West could benefit.

The following day, a Friday, and so a holiday, I was fetched from the hotel by Nabeel, Ismail, and Ali (a son of Nazeer), to be shown the sights of Jeddah. The attention of three guides assured lively company for the day. They were most intent on showing me the newer sights of the town as these reflected on the modernisation of the country, and this struck me as an irony in view of entrenched traditional modes of thought. I was shown the Hajj City, comprising thousands of self-catering accommodation units for pilgrims from the four quarters of the globe, for Jeddah was the gateway to Mecca, a mere 45 miles to the East; and the third airport of the city, a brand new complex which was yet to open its passenger terminals.

"Mrs. Thatcher and King Khalid will jointly open the airport in two weeks time," explained Nabeel.

As we drove passed a garage near a roundabout by the city centre, Ali pointed out that Eve was buried under the concrete forecourt.

"Who's Eve,?" I asked naively.

"The first woman," replied Nabeel curtly, as if shocked by my ignorance. "The garden of Eden was situated around Jeddah," he added in all seriousness.

"Really," I only replied in stupefaction.

As we drove down a motorway, and through a monumental entrance about three times the size of Marble Arch, I enquired after the significance of the building.

"It's a private entrance to the grounds of one of King Saud's palaces," explained Nabeel. "He was a great spender! The palace was confiscated from him by his brothers, shortly before he was deposed in 1964. This motorway runs for several miles through part of the garden. Another corner of the garden has been given over to building an entire suburb. Most of the remaining land has been given over to the people as a public park."

We drove through a suburb of superbly designed ten-storey flats - or so they seemed - but I noted that the streets were deserted and the buildings empty.

"The project's a white elephant," explained Nabeel. "No one lives there. It was built for bedouins coming in from the desert. Several years ago they had goats living on sixth floor balconies, and camels were getting stuck on staircases half way up the building. Then floors began to crack and collapse onto the storeys below, after fires had been lit for traditional cooking. Windows were broken to let out smoke, and electrical fittings and bathrooms were smashed. The flats were fitted with all mod cons, but the bedouins didn't know how to use them."

During the afternoon, as we drove through the streets, we passed by several accidents, which was unsurprising in view of the reckless driving habits of many, although the driving of the Badanah sons could not be faulted for its care. We drove passed the new University with its ultra-modern apartment blocks, passed endless palaces and construction sites, and down through the diplomatic quarter to the corniche.

"The embassies and ministries are gradually being transferred to Riyadh," said Nabeel, as we strolled along the coastline.

We passed families playing on the beach, and watched men, children and fully clothed women bathing in the sea.

"This area is for families only," said Nabeel. "Single men go to the Celibates' beach in the next bay. They're nearly all foreigners here: Egyptians, Sudanese, Syrians, Palestinians, Eritreans and others. Saudis don't like to expose themselves on the beach," he added superciliously.

"It's like Brighton on a Bank holiday," said Ismail joyfully.

Later in the afternoon we went to an Arab snack bar in a major shopping centre, enjoying a delicious slice of *Shawarma*, a sliver of roasted lamb carved from a spit and served in Arabic bread.

"What do you like doing in the evening - going to the cinema,?" I asked.

"Cinemas are bad places," said Ali.

"They were closed down by the government three or four years ago," said Nabeel.

"Why are they bad places,?" I asked.

"They're dark! People get involved in fights," said Ali.

"Decent people never went there - only foreigners," added Nabeel.

As we walked over the Zebra (or more correctly) the Suicide crossing, for Saudi traffic accelerates rather than slows in the face of pedestrian impediments, to rejoin the car, I reflected that the Badanah boys had little wish to show me the historical sights of their ancient trading city. I was soon to learn that not only did the Arab have little knowledge or interest in history, but little aesthetic sense for architectural form or visual representation. Their princely palaces were hideous monstrosities with corrugated roofs, or else lame imitations of Western structures. Their artistic sense and ability was reserved for calligraphy or abstract design.

Although the Badanahs had no objection to my using a camera on their tour, and indeed, seemed flattered when I photographed them in close up against a chosen background, I soon encountered a problem when alone. The old and many-storeyed Turkish buildings, with their latticed windows, were aesthetically the most appealing structures in the older quarter of the town, but in response to the interest I expressed, the Badanahs were dismissive, saying that such houses were "dirty and decrepit," soon to be pulled down in place of gleaming new tower blocks.

When during the long siesta of the following day, I ventured out to photograph these buildings, I was abused and shouted at for daring to use a camera in a public place. Thenceforward in Saudi Arabia, when not in the company of friends, I was only to venture forth with a camera concealed in a plastic bag and to use it only with the greatest circumspection.

It was early evening when we returned to the hotel, and I invited the Badanahs to my room for soft drinks, and no sooner were we seated than Ismail turned on the TV, which we ignored as we engaged in intensive conversation.

"Arabs get a bad reputation for the way they treat women, as soon as they leave the country," said Nabeel.

"That's because when they're abroad they treat women like donkeys," said Ismail. "Arabs don't get the opportunity to meet women in their own country."

"But if they treat women badly, it's their own fault," said Ali. "They're not modest! What can a woman expect if she wears a short dress? A man has only so much self-control. It's human nature."

"But in Saudi Arabia women are always treated well," assured Nabeel. "We respect them. Islam protects women."

"And everyone knows that," said Ali. "That's why Arab men keep their distance from women. For example, if someone was to touch my sister, I'ld kill both her and the man together - and so would anyone else in similar circumstances."

"But what about if your sister had been seduced or forced, and it was not her fault,?" I queried.

"I'd still kill her," replied Ali.

"But why?"

"Because she'd have been besmirched," said Ali. "She'd have lost her value. If she was allowed to live the family would never regain its honour."

"But you'd be in trouble with the law."

"The Shariah courts would be sympathetic. They can't go against the moral law of God."

"And so women can walk anywhere, day or night," said Nabeel. "They'll never be touched."

"Is that because they can never be seen,?" I suggested.

"We have many beautiful women in Arabia," retorted Nabeel, offended by what he misinterpreted as an implication that I thought Arabian women unattractive.

"I believe that," I replied.

"In the West there are so many troubles between the sexes," said Ali. "We don't get those problems in Saudi."

"So many young people in England are unmarried," said Ismail.

"That's why there's so much trouble between men and women. Everywhere there are prostitutes. There are no prostitutes in Saudi. In England the temptations are so great. All men are promiscuous. You don't get that here."

"It's very difficult being in London," began Nabeel. "Last Summer my father and I were there for three weeks on business. We stayed at the Mount Royal Hotel. Resisting temptation is very difficult. My father and I had a great struggle to keep ourselves clean. Everywhere in the streets are semi-naked women, and with all those men and women in the hotel, your imagination goes wild with what must happen in the bedrooms. You don't get hotels like that in Saudi. My father and I had to use all our willpower to resist temptation."

"We don't have to suffer such agonies in Saudi because we marry earlier," said Ali.

"Are you all married,?" I asked.

"Of course we are," they replied in unison.

"Families in Saudi ensure their sons are married as soon as they're out of puberty," said Nabeel. "It's very bad when a father doesn't arrange an early marriage for his son. It leads to trouble. You see it all the time with youths on street corners. They get into bad company - and eventually crime."

When they learnt that I had not married until the age of thirty-four they expressed horrified surprise.

"That's far too old," said Ali.

"You need to marry young so children can grow up quickly to help in the business," said Ismail.

"For example, a man should never need to drive a car after the age of forty," explained Nabeel. "My father never drives a car - or hardly ever. Why should he? He has sons to do it for him."

On the TV the half hour English language news bulletin was drawing to a close. The final item concluded with the announcement that two men had been beheaded in Jeddah that afternoon for sodomy.

* * *

Early the following morning I went to the British Embassy. I needed to check out Badanah Brothers, not only for my own information but to satisfy the Accounts Department in Basildon. Sitting in the office of the Commercial Secretary, I wanted first to check out certain aspects of marketing and sales strategy, including clearance for our printed brochures, before dipping into the confidential file of the Badanahs.

"This publicity literature is totally offensive to Arabs," began the Secretary who was a woman, as she passed the expensive and recently produced glossy brochures in Arabic text through her hands. "You can't possibly display women in sleeveless tops and knee-length skirts. And as for these children's items with 'Miss Piggy,' they'd be seized and destroyed at the port of entry. The pig is a taboo animal in the Arab world."

"We wouldn't ship those in any event," I replied.

Once again, I realised that the Marketing Department had made yet another blunder, but I said nothing. The academic marketing boys with their qualifications in pure as opposed to applied studies, as so often in British companies, had once again formulated their own decisions behind closed doors without liaising with Sales. Their desk-bound ignorance and ivory tower approach to business was only matched by a supercilious arrogance. They felt their jobs were dependent on picking ideas out of the sky and running rings of confusion around the board, for they were either afraid of commercial realities or effected to despise them.

The over-refinement of their upbringing had so narrowed their vision of the wider world, that anything beyond the suburb in which they lived or the local golf club meant little to them. This was just the last in a long catalogue of disasters. I had always believed that in the cause of practicality Marketing should be kept firmly under the thumb of Sales, and not vice versa. Several thousands of pounds of publicity material would now have to be binned. Was it any wonder that British manufacturing was in decline!

The Commercial Secretary opened the Badanah Brothers file. The company had been established in 1925 by the grandfather of the present brothers. Commercial morality: "Of the highest repute." The firm had a substantial paid up shareholding of several millions, and had never reneged on its debts.

"I'll get you a photocopy to take away," said the Secretary.

I explained the problem with regard to the negotiation of at Sight documents and the tardiness of receiving payment.

"I'm afraid it's a special problem here in Saudi Arabia between the banks and their customers," replied the Secretary. "I'll send someone along to the Badanahs to have a discreet word. That's the only way we can handle it. You may find more sophisticated partners in Saudi Arabia, but you'll be hard put to find anyone with better integrity. In general, the Arabs have a high degree of commercial morality - far higher than to be found in Third World countries. When they make an agreement, they usually stick to it. It's only their determination to drive a hard bargain which gives them a devious image."

The topic of conversation then turned to the status of women, and since the Secretary was herself a woman working in a particularly male-dominated society, her comments would be of especial interest.

"Non-Muslim women aren't really seen as 'real' women," she began. "Although it may be safe for veiled Muslim women to walk the streets anywhere in the Kingdom, because of the horrendous penalties carried out on those who commit physical attacks of any kind, it's extremely dangerous for a European woman to be out alone at night, and virtually impossible for her to use a taxi. There have been many attacks on European woman, here in Jeddah, over the past few months, and several cases of rape.

"The problem is that the Shariah courts usually take the side of the man: firstly, because she was provocatively dressed - and any Western dress is judged provocative; and secondly, because as an infidel, the court cannot accept her evidence in good faith. However, these problems should be alleviated somewhat by a new law coming into force within the next few months. This will make it obligatory for non-Muslim women - as well as Muslims - to wear the *chador* or *Abaaya* (the traditional black garb) over her other clothing whenever in public."

Early that evening I was fetched by Kamal, the youngest of the three partners, to be shown the different shops and factory of the Badanah business. Kamal was an especially ugly little man with a protruding jaw and a sloping forehead, but as with the rest of the family, he was intent on conveying the best possible impression. Between our scheduled visits, he stopped at several grocery stores, made purchases, and loaded cartons into the back of the estate car. My curiosity was aroused and I passed a comment.

"In our family, the men do the shopping," he explained as we drove along. "We like to help our wives. We share the tasks. I buy the meat and my brothers buy the rice, vegetables and other items."

"That's very good," I answered.

"It shouldn't be necessary for women to leave the home," he continued.

"Why not?"

"Because modern life is too stressful. The city is too big for women to get about. They're forbidden to drive, taxis are unreliable, and buses infrequent. See what I mean," he added pointing to the kerb as we stopped at a junction.

Four or five veiled women, standing by the back entrance to a single decker bus, were engaged in fisticuffs, as they quarrelled as to who should enter. The back of the bus was already packed with women.

"But the bus is empty," I cried in astonishment. "There are only three or four people in the front section. Why don't they move down the platform."

"That's the men's section," corrected Kamal.

I then noticed that a partition near the back of the bus constituted a squashed standing-space only compartment for women.

"It's terrible when women start fighting amongst themselves," said Kamal nodding his head in disapproval. "That's another reason they should stay at home. What are their husbands going to say when they see their bruised faces?"

"Do your wives *ever* leave home,?" I ventured.

"Of course - on special occasions. We sometimes drive to the desert for picnics. It's a special treat for the women. It's wonderful! Just the sand and the sky. In such solitude one communes best with God. There are no worldly distractions."

On the outskirts of the city, near the company's main warehouse, I was shown the Badanah factory, which consisted of two blow moulding machines producing watering cans for the local market: one manned by a team of Pakistanis and the other by a team of Turks, and neither was able to communicate with the other. It was explained that the government gave an on-going subsidy to maintain the factory, and as it was only necessary for one person to operate each machine, as several of the workers were stretched out smoking or playing cards, and as the unit costs of production must have exceeded that of equivalent imported merchandise, it struck me that the entire project was a total waste of money.

Finally, Kamal took me to the radio and TV shop, in the old souk in the town centre, situated between Abd Al Aziz road and King Faisal street. This was manned by Mousa, sitting behind a large desk set on a high platform at the back of a long narrow shop which offered him a perfect overview of the crowd of customers. Ismail was moving boxes behind his father, and several other assistants were busily working on the floor of the shop. I sat beside Mousa for the next hour or so, and glasses of tea were constantly set before us, and I was astonished by the fast turnover of products which moved with the rapidity of items in a grocer's store.

"They go on holiday to their own countries," explained Mousa. "They take radio cassettes and TVs back to India where they sell them for four times the price. Electrical appliances are the best currency!"

Before leaving the shop that night, Mousa took down three cartons stuffed with banknotes, already in elastic bundles, from a shelf behind him, and he and Ismail began to count the bundles. Meanwhile, loose notes were already dropping to the floor at our feet, every time Mousa opened the drawer of the desk. When the money had been counted, it was replaced in the cardboard boxes, which were sellotaped over with the amounts endorsed in felt tip, and put back on the shelf, where the totals of packaged cash could easily have been read by anyone entering the shop.

When Mousa and I left the shop, we made the four minute walk to the Badanah offices round the corner in noisy Hifny street opposite the Rehab Hotel. We climbed the stone steps to the second floor of the grubby building, and in the inside office I was introduced to Fallah Abdullah, a Sudanese, a genial giant dressed in a *kaffia* and thobe, who was seven feet less several inches tall.

This was the Office manager and the man responsible for communicating with the outside world. He sat behind a spacious desk, nearby a telex machine and typewriter, and if any written communications were to be made by the company, he alone would execute the task. All orders to suppliers issued from this desk alone, and as he sat back like a king in his revolving armchair, he dwarfed Nazeer and Mousa who sat hunched up on folding chairs in front of him. This was the office where the three partners usually spent the last working hours of the evening, where they reviewed the day's business and planned for the future. Beyond the office was the wholesale display area for visiting retailers.

Fallah was a man with whom I felt entirely comfortable discussing business, and indeed he immediately raised the question of a problem on one of our products, and this led to a lively discussion, as an elderly bearded Yemeni (who was employed for no other purpose) prepared and served glasses of tea. Just as I was trying to clarify a point, Nazeer - rudely (to my mind at the time) - interrupted the discussion by rising from his seat, with the words, "We must go to pray."

All the men rose from their places.

"We must go to the Mosque," explained Mousa. "We'll be back in twenty minutes."

Outside the office was a tap and a footbath, and before leaving the building, the men performed *wudu* or ritual ablutions, washing their faces, arms and feet. I was left alone, in silence, in the building, and it was the first of many occasions throughout the Middle East, when business discussions were peremptorily interrupted by the call to prayer.

The broken discussion was not to be renewed that night, for the Badanah brothers were in a more relaxed socialising mood, and soon they were joined by several sons. Mousa joked about Fallah's height, saying he was still gaining an inch every month, and when the topic turned to children, I was asked about my own family.

"You must have a son," urged Mousa, when I revealed I had three daughters.

"It would be expensive to have more children," I responded.

"Why worry about money? God will give you money," insisted Mousa.

I smiled with incredulity. Mousa was irritated that I failed to take him seriously.

"God gives you everything - everything,!" he insisted. "Pray for what you want, and God will give it. You need a son for companionship in old age. Someone to talk with! You can't talk with daughters."

"Daughters don't count," laughed Ismail.

"Don't say that when he's got daughters," reprimanded his father.

On leaving and locking up the office at 10 o'clock, Mousa said he would drive me back to the hotel, but before fetching the car, I was amused by an anomalous episode which might have embarrassed many men in the West if they had found themselves placed in a similar situation. I went with Mousa to a chemists shop where he bought a giant supply of sanitary towels in their own carrier bag, which he then carried through the crowded souk without any suggestion of awkwardness, as if the event was an everyday occurrence. Perhaps there were areas of life to be uncovered where the Westerner actually felt a greater coyness than the Arab.

On driving off, Mousa switched on the radio to the channel to which he said he was always tuned. It broadcast a magnificent chanting in all the poetic beauty of the Arab tongue, and even if one could not discern the meaning of the words, the musicality of their cadences alone was sufficient to uplift the spirit.

"It's the *Koran*," explained Mousa. "It's broadcast throughout every hour of the day and night. No one, at any time, in joy or sorrow, need ever be deprived of the words of the Prophet."

* * *

As I wished to carry out marketing research on the retail presentation and customer response to our products in a variety of major stores in Jeddah, independent of the Badanahs, I was obliged to use the city's taxis, and soon discovered what an unreliable mode of transport they were in moving quickly from one place to another.

I encountered the worst example of this the following morning, when travelling from the hotel to the Al Sawami Supermarket (one of the most famous and largest in Jeddah) situated in Sharafiyyah. As the hotel porter had clearly instructed the driver, I did not anticipate a problem, but after driving what seemed an endless distance, and also in circles, and after sensing that the driver had lost his way but was afraid to admit it, he suddenly stopped by the kerb, declaring in Arabic, "This is Sharafiyyah."

"It's the Al Sawami Supermarket I want," I insisted impatiently.

Nervously, he re-started the engine and drove off, but it was evident he had lost all sense of direction but was afraid to admit his predicament. It was not the cost which concerned me for taxi fares were negotiated in advance (by anyone in their right mind) but the loss of time. I ordered him to stop in a crowded street, and having found a passer-bye who knew the whereabouts of the store, I asked him to kindly direct the driver.

After the driver had left the vehicle and listened to instructions for five minutes, he threw up his hands in despair, indicating that he still had not understood. Our guide, who had a car parked further up the street, offered to lead us most of the way, which he did; but it was not until after we had lost our way down several cul-de-sacs, stopped at several stores which the driver supposed to be our destination, but which the signs indicated otherwise, and followed the instructions of another guide, that we eventually reached our journey's end.

During the long lunch break I rested by the hotel swimming pool, which was not well frequented for a reason I was soon to discover, for I suddenly realised that my book cover, and everything around, was covered by a grey film of dirt; and that the entire area was polluted with cement dust from a vast factory belching out clouds of chemical minerals twenty-four hours a day. Such are the tribulations of a city in the throes of never-ending construction!

On mentioning the taxi problems I had encountered that morning to Kamal, when he fetched me in the late afternoon in taking me to his brothers, he was full of consolation.

"It's a lucky man who gets anywhere in a hurry in a Jeddah taxi," he said. "Only the worst educated Saudis become taxi drivers. None can read or write. They're bedouin from the desert, and as soon as they get into the city, they lose all sense of direction. In the desert they can travel thousands of miles and never lose their way, but in the town, all is confusion. If you take a taxi in Jeddah, you must carry a map and direct the driver every part of the way."

As we approached the centre, and the muezzins' call began to resound off the rooftops against the reddening sky of approaching dusk, I reflected on the melodic beauty of the cadences, for irrespective of faith or non-faith, the calls to prayer were always refreshing and always uplifting in the urgent grandeur to obey the Prophet's command. Kamal's thoughts, too, were turned to religion, during this reflective hour of the day.

"In Islam, we too believe in Mary and Geesa (Jesus)," he began solemnly. "We believe in the same prophets that you believe in: in Abraham, Moses, Isaiah, and all the others. It's a bad Muslim who does not love Geesa. But we believe in one God. God has no colleagues - no helper! God is the highest. He sent Geesa to mankind as amongst the greatest of prophets - but he's not a God. God sent Mohammed as the last of the prophets to teach the True Faith. And Mary is the greatest of women because she was untouched by man. Her purity is an example to all women. That's what we believe in Islam!"

Serious business discussions were packed into the last two hours of my final evening in the city. Together with the three brothers, I was seated in front of Fallah's desk in the office in Hifny street. Fallah was taking the initiative in discussing the prospects for the company's products in Saudi Arabia. I was shown three articles originating from Taiwan and Japan. They were innovative products, with an attractive and distinctive Arabic design. They stood on Fallah's desk, and each of us in turn took them up and examined them with interest.

"They're not yet on sale in any of the shops," said Mousa.

"They're still under wraps," said Fallah.

"A business friend of Nazeer got them from the competition," said Mousa.

"Can you produce them,?" asked Fallah.

"The company will try its best," I responded thoughtfully, handling one of the articles.

"If you can deliver, we'll place an order for two million pounds - cash on sight of documents," thundered Nazeer bringing his fist down on the desk.

"In six months they'll be all over the Middle East - that's for sure," said Fallah. "These Far East manufacturers don't wait around."

"But if we could have these from a British factory - and especially from your factory - then when it comes to sales, the sky's the limit," said Mousa.

"You have to understand that British products still have a great mystique in this market," continued Fallah, "especially amongst Indian, Egyptian, and African peoples, who came under British influence."

"Give us these products, and in twelve months, we'll quadruple your sales in Saudi Arabia. That's a promise," said Nazeer.

"I'll do my best," I said, and I did.

On returning eventually to the UK, I was optimistic on the prospects of the company manufacturing these articles asked for by the Badanahs, for not only was the factory equipped with the world's most up-dated machinery for producing these technologically specialised items, but it was machinery which had never been used for more than fifty percent of its capacity. Surely, here was a marketing opportunity which needed to be seized, but speed would need to be the essence, if we were to develop and fill this market gap.

Over the next few weeks, after my return to England, I produced detailed reports and forecasts in trying to fulfil the wishes of one of our best export customers. As we were the world brand leader for this range of articles - and moreover, they were products with a brand name which at the same time had become a generic term - I felt that the company had everything to gain by exploiting this exceptional situation. But my task was difficult.

"No bloody chance - not over my dead body," moaned Steve Barnes, the Credit Controller. "If you think I'm going to pass through a two million pound order to Planning, from those bastards, you've got another thing coming. I don't care a shit what the terms are!"

"You can have our products in any colour you want, or any design you want," said the Product Controller grinning with greasy condescension. "But you can't have anything needing new tooling - and changing the shape of the product means a major investment."

"But the Far East boys are creating new tooling all the time," I answered.

"But we've got our investors to think of. They wouldn't wear it. Investors' profits must come first," explained the Controller. "In the Far East it's different. They're not dependent on equity funding. Whenever they need to invest, all they do is go to their banks and borrow long term at low cost. In this country we don't have such lending institutions. Your request is a non-starter and impossible!"

And so the required products were never made. And Fallah's prediction was proved correct. When I revisited the Kingdom six months later, the market was flooded with these innovative Taiwanese and Japanese products - and they were selling like hot cakes! A golden opportunity for Britain had been lost forever.

On that last evening in the Badanahs' office, we turned away from the new products to consider the requirements for our existing lines. As always in negotiating an order with Arabs, there was a protracted argument over prices. A generous discount would always be insisted upon, and of course, we had taken the precaution of going in with substantially uplifted prices, and these had been printed in giving them credibility. At last a price was agreed upon, which was still fractionally above our standard FOB rates.

Nazeer made a grudging gesture as if he had been hard done by. He took an envelope out of the wastepaper basket, and maintaining a disagreeable expression, began writing out his requirements. I sat by silent and tense, daring not to open my mouth. As far as I was concerned, there was nothing more to be said. After ten minutes, he passed me the envelope with a dismissive gesture. There was an order for a quarter of a million pounds - twenty container loads - more than double the value of business for the previous two years! I kept my dignity, and thanked him with the casualness as if he had just passed me a cigarette.

"But ship it quickly," said Mousa. "We'll soon be out of stock."

There was a noise outside. Samir Badri, walked into the office carrying a huge elongated parcel tied up with strong.

"Mr. Robert,!" he cried in his comical fashion.

"I think this is for you," said Fallah rising from behind his desk.

"What is it,?" I exclaimed in astonishment.

"You'll never guess," said Mousa with a broad grin.

The bearded Yemeni entered with a tray bearing glasses of tea, and amidst greetings and laughter, we began to relax for the evening ahead.

CHAPTER 5
To be rid of a wife

"Justice is one; it binds all human society, and is based
on one law, which is right reason applied to command
and prohibition."

Cicero, *De Legibus*, Bk. 1, Ch. 15, Sec. 42.

Suddenly, the sermon ended, and the stones of the buildings
surrounding spacious Deira square, seemed to fall silent, as they
ceased to throw back the words of the preacher in the heat of the
day to the thousands below. But moments later, another voice was to be
heard from the Tannoy transmission aloft the minarets of the Grand
Mosque: more personal, less rhetorical than the sermon; the urgent
intensity and deep base recitation of prayer.

There was a rumbling murmur, and the sound of mats being laid on
the hard surface, and moments later, thousands fell to their knees in
praying to the One-God, and the suppressed whisperings of the many
filled the square with an awed sound, as the worshippers lowered their
foreheads to the ground.

The slow measured words of the prayer leader, with their
commanding authority and depth of tone, seemed to calm the spirits of
the unruly multitude which had assembled before the Governor of
Riyadh's Palace. There was a numbness throughout the crowd. Now
was a time for waiting - a time for reflection. The police stood relaxed
and motionless - no need now to beat the heads of the hysterical. There
was a silent tension in waiting for the anticipated - an imminent event to
occur soon enough. All eyes and ears were alert for the unusual.

The doors of the Mosque were opened. Five men emerged from
within, tall and proud, dressed in red headscarves, one in a brown thobe,
the others which in the midday sunlight were blinding white. Escorted
by police on either side, they strolled with slow but certain steps towards
the open space before the Governor's Palace.

"Who are they,?" asked someone.

"Must be criminals," answered another.

"They're too confident for that," said a third.

Seconds later, more men in clean white thobes, and cool expressionless faces, emerged from within the dark interior of the Mosque to be escorted through the thick crowd to the open crescent-shaped space before the Palace. At last a dozen were standing huddled together, occasionally exchanging a word with one another, as the skirts of their thobes were gently blown in the warm breeze.

The praying ceased. A silence fell over the square. The air was thick with the tension of the unexpected.

"They must be bringing on an adulteress," said the American.

"But there's no one there," responded another in a tone of exasperation, jumping up for a better view.

Was it really to be an adulteress,? I pondered. Marriage in Saudi and the peripheral Gulf states seemed tranquil enough - at least as narrowly revealed to the visiting Westerner - and Arabs themselves were always careful to draw an idyllic picture of their family lives and social arrangements, comparing them favourably with the dreaded conditions of the West. And yet, where did the truth lie? I recollected several episodes in the Gulf I had personally witnessed, which conveyed a contrary impression.

There was the story of Hamad Zohair. Hamad was an excitable Palestinian, unpredictable in his behaviour, and liable to fall into fits of political moodiness, and once aroused, he would indulge in the luxury of a rhetorical tirade which quickly became incomprehensible to his supposed listeners. European business associates became invariably the unwitting victims of his spleen, but as soon as he recollected the rudeness of his anger, and that he alone was both speaker and listener, he would throw a friendly arm around the shoulder of his hapless victim, followed by effusive gestures of amity and exclamatory assurances of, "my dear friend," accompanying every statement which followed.

Palestinians held a particular status in the Gulf: firstly, they were Arabs - although very different from Gulf Arabs; and secondly, because of their tragic political circumstances and expulsion from the lands of their forefathers, they retained the sympathy of both the rulers and peoples amongst whom they now lived and worked. The Palestinian in the Gulf took on the appearance of a Westernised Arab on several counts: his dress, his racial origins, for he was often fair and blue eyed - and his proportion of Crusader blood may have taken his forebears from anywhere in the northern hemisphere; his thrusting ambition and attitude to Western education; and lastly, his more relaxed attitude to religion and relationships between the sexes. The understandably resentful and possession-less but hard-working Palestinian was to be found in middle management and the professions throughout the Gulf, and in this status he constituted the most successful and fortunate of his kind in a world which had made him an outcast.

Hamad was in his late twenties, a thin angular man with a prominent nose and a Saddam-like moustache. He was an energetic salesman working for an old-established trading house in Kuwait, and I first met him on my first visit to the emirate when he fetched me from the airport for the half hour drive to my hotel in the city centre. As we drove along in his dark maroon petrol-guzzling Pontiac - his proudest possession - prayer beads dangling from the driving mirror, plastic flowers and ornaments obscuring the windscreen, I was exposed to a lecture on the latest development in the Arab-Israeli conflict.

By the time we reached the Bristol Hotel in Fahd Al Salem street, I had not heard a word on our sales situation in the area, and I was feeling impatient. My irritation increased as soon as I had registered in the hotel. It was the foulest hotel I was ever to visit during my years in the Gulf. It had originally been picked from a list of names.

It would have been a change from the multinational American-inspired hostelries where I usually stayed, and anywhere in Europe, the name Hotel Bristol was almost invariably an assurance of five-Star quality, since they derived their name from the patronage of the well-travelled 4th Marquis who bore the title of the great English port. It transpired that this Hotel Bristol was a parody of its reputation - a misnomer designed to entrap the unwary traveller - an angler's deceit in casting his fatal fly - a travesty of all that was true.

Although it was unnecessary for a British subject to obtain a visa, as Kuwait was situated on the periphery of a war zone, it was necessary to be in possession of an Entry Permit, and this needed to be checked, and I had to surrender my passport as the Security police needed to monitor the presence of all who entered the country. There was already the sickly smell of broken drains in the crowded lobby of the hotel, and on completing the necessary forms and taking my key, I was surprised and took it as an intrusion on my privacy when Hamad insisted on accompanying me to my room. What did he want,? I wondered. Why could he not have waited in the lobby until I was ready, as I had suggested?

The accommodation quarters of the hotel had a curious arrangement. Two or three bedrooms led into a shared lounge area with a coffee table, sofa and armchair. The bedroom was cramped, with a dilapidated wardrobe, a forty watt reading bulb over the bed, and no washing facilities. As the window overlooked the busy main street and the Municipal Park, the room was noisy and hot, and as the air conditioning unit was of the ubiquitous Friedrich box variety, as soon as this was switched on the noise became intolerable.

"I'm thirsty. Can I have some of your water,?" said Hamad touching his throat and indicating the Thermos jug by my bedside.

"Of course," I could only answer, and he began to make himself at home.

I went into the bathroom which was reached through the lounge. There was a smell of stale urine which came from a puddle by the leaking toilet. There was a bidet, a mosquito guard which darkened the room and partly concealed the view of a concrete wall which led down to the well of the basement and the disharmony of kitchen noises. Paint and plaster were peeling off the walls, but most disturbing were the cigarette ends strewn about the floor.

On rushing back to my room, I seized the phone and lodged a complaint with Housekeeping. Hamad, meanwhile, seemed to enjoy my discomfort.

"This is a very old hotel," he said. "It was built nearly twenty years ago. Europeans never stay here any more."

"You never told me that when I wrote to you," I said.

"It wasn't my business to interfere with your travel arrangements," he said shrugging his shoulders.

Perhaps I had not expressed sufficient sympathy for his people. He showed no condolence for my situation, and neither did he suggest how things might be put to right.

"I feel tired," he exclaimed, and threw himself onto my bed, lying outstretched. "Do you mind if I sleep for an hour,?" he added.

"I most certainly object," I replied with quiet firmness. "If you want to sleep, you can go to your own bed."

"But I live more than an hour away," he said rising from the bed, hurt and humiliated.

"I'm sorry, but I want a rest before work begins again at four o'clock," I responded. "I've had a long journey."

"There's room for two of us," he persisted.

"Such an arrangement is not acceptable," I said finally.

I declined Hamad's offer to fetch me from the hotel in an hour's time. I would make my own way to the office that was only a ten-minute walk from the hotel. He left my room awkwardly with gestures of apology. I was not tired and did not take a rest that afternoon. Instead I walked towards the coastline, passed the Sieff Palace, and explored the immediate vicinity of the Central Commercial area. I was struck by the frequent signs pointing to the direction of Public Shelters, an indication of the fear of imminent involvement in the Iran-Iraqi conflict.

At four o'clock I was seated in the office of Saad Aakef, the tall fair-haired Pakistani who was the General Manager or Al Qasim & Co. He was a well-informed and intelligent man, sensitive to the political vulnerability of the area.

"There'll be serious troubles in the region once the oil begins to run out and the wealthier foreigners move back to their own countries," he began. "At present everything's rosy, because everyone's well off, but it's not going to last. This was the first of the Arabian Gulf states to be exploited for its oil, and it'll be the first to be exhausted of its resources. The sheikhs are trying to build up local manufacturing but it can't work. Prices are too high for home-originated exports - apart from oil. I'm telling you in confidence: it's a precarious situation in this country."

His predictions were timely, for in several years Iraqi bombs were to fall on Kuwait.

All the while, as Saad was speaking, Hamad was standing behind the desk at his right side, sometimes laying his arm across the shoulder of his boss, determined to convey the impression that he was a trusted confidant and the second in command. Hamad was clearly jealous of anyone who might come between him and his manager, and fearful of any business associate from another company who might see him in a position of diminished responsibility. Therefore, in maintaining an appearance of heightened status, Hamad had developed a lap-dog relationship with Saad Aakef, in manipulating the latter to pepper his conversation with compliments on the qualities of his subordinate.

Shortly after nine o'clock that night I was seated in the restaurant of the Bristol Hotel, watching scraggy cats chase and hiss at one another as they passed between the legs of patrons from one table to another, competing for food, and occasionally, they jumped onto the waiters' table at the far end of the room to retrieve some tit-bit left by guests on the piled up plates. I was off my food, sickened by the smell of broken drains, and pushed away my plate after two or three mouthfuls.

The sloppy unshaven Greek waiter with his baggy trousers and stained white jacket asked if I had finished. I remarked on the cats and questioned the desirability of their presence.

"We must have them," drawled the waiter in a sad matter-of-fact tone. "The lower floors are infested with rats."

"Not much of a recommendation for a leading hotel," I remarked as I sipped my lemonade from a wine glass.

"Today it's an eighth class hotel," confided the waiter. "One of the oldest in Kuwait! You should have known it in its heyday, twenty years back. Then it was patronised by the richest sheikhs in the Gulf."

The following day I lunched with Saad and Hamad in the great height of the Kuwait Towers restaurant, situated on the northernmost coastal point of the city, with magnificent aerial views over the emirate. On mentioning the unusualness of Saad's hair colour he proudly declared the belief that he was descended from one - if not several - of Alexander the Great's soldiers, for his army had occupied the northern Indus valley (Saad's home territory) in 324 BC.

Whilst Hamad was out of earshot, as we drank our coffee, Saad apologised for his "friend's" strange behaviour.

"He's depressed just now," said Saad.

"Over the Arab-Israeli conflict,?" I suggested.

"No, over his wife," answered Saad, but nothing more could be said on the matter as Hamad returned to the table.

Hamad's alleged depression had not been made evident to me. On fetching me from the hotel that morning, he had been particularly effusive in his friendliness, assuring me every few minutes that I was his "dear friend." He was clearly intent on wiping out the bad impression of the previous day. But Saad had aroused my curiosity. When we descended to ground level again and strolled along the seashore, and I was some feet ahead of the others, I turned round to see that Saad and Hamad were walking hand in hand, and that the former was consoling his subordinate.

Hamad's problem was not to be revealed until the following day. It was not until driving from one store to another in meeting the retailers of our products, that Hamad was able to relax sufficiently in unburdening his mind. He needed twelve hours of sleep every day, and he could not afford to forego his need for two hours sleep during the long lunch break. That's why he had been forced to test my patience two days earlier.

Now he was making an explicit apology. Did I understand him? Yes! Could I forgive the way he had imposed himself on my privacy? Of course I could! A smile of contentment spread over his face. Now all was forgiven and I could be treated as a trusted friend. He stretched his arm over the car seat onto my shoulder, squeezing me several times.

He explained that he had a serious problem with his wife. She was causing him a lot of anxiety. She had had four miscarriages and produced no other children. It was all becoming quite an expense - and he was desperate for a son. Never mind, next month he was taking his wife to a gynaecological specialist in Egypt. Perhaps - "Inshallah" - everything would work out all right. Did I have children? Then I could understand his predicament. He could always rely on my support for any decision he took.

When I returned to Kuwait six months later and Hamad met me at the airport, he had a streaming cold, and the floor of his car was strewn with Kleenex tissues. Although his wife had been nursing him back to health over the previous four days from his sick bed, Saad had nevertheless insisted that he get dressed and drive down to the airport to meet me.

"Saad shouldn't have done that," I responded. "I could easily have made my own way to the hotel."

"Saad doesn't always understand me," said Hamad with self-pity.

"How is your wife now? Was the specialist in Egypt able to correct the problem?"

"A lot has happened, my friend, since we last met. The specialist could do nothing. It's finished!"

"What's finished?"

"My friend, I know you can understand me. I'm getting a new wife," he said in the tone of someone about to replace his car. "I've given her every chance. I've spent a fortune! She can't produce children. Now I'm getting a new wife."

"Will that be difficult,?" I questioned.

"No, no problem at all," he answered.

"Then you'll have two wives," I concluded.

"No, not two wives, that's only asking for trouble," laughed Hamad. "One wife's enough. You can't have two wives under one roof. They fight like cats and quarrel about who is to sit in the front seat of the car. Two wives are only for rich people. Besides, modern girls don't like polygamy."

"Then you'll get a divorce," I said.

"That's right, my friend," said Hamad smiling, nodding in satisfaction.

"Is that difficult?"

"No problem. Just a question of the compensation price to be paid to her father," said Hamad. "I have to save up for that. It'll be another six months before I have enough money. That's why I have to sell plenty of your products, my dear friend. In several days I'll give you a big export order. Then I'll sell to the shops. Then I'll have enough money to buy a new wife."

"But what does your present wife think about all this,?" I asked. "Does she agree?"

"Of course she doesn't," responded Hamad.

"Then how can you divorce if she disagrees?"

"You don't understand, my friend," began Hamad. "The court will grant me a divorce because she can't have children. She has no choice in the matter."

"But what's her state of mind about the situation,?" I asked

"She's screaming! She's hysterical! Every day she's screaming," said Hamad. "She doesn't want a divorce. She'll never get a man again. When she's returned to her father she'll be like a widow. She'll be a spent coin. But she'll have her compensation money. She'll be reimbursed."

"How can you live in such an environment?"

"I know how to handle women," said Hamad with a reassuring tap on the back of my wrist. "I tell her not to worry. The day may never come! I tell her it's my family to blame - they demand a son. I know how to be nice to women. One day I tell her I have stomach pain, another day I have headache, another day I am depressed. I show her I need her. I tell her to forget about divorce. She doesn't know when I get the money anyway. As far as she's concerned, it could be five years, it could be seven years. Anything can happen in the meantime. Don't worry, I say."

"But doesn't your wife feel you have some other kind of obligation to her,?" I suggested.

"My friend, I think I know what you're trying to say," said Hamad with intensity. "But these concern things which are not in our hands. If my wife cannot produce children then it's the will of God. I can understand that, and my wife can understand that. The fault lies with my wife and no one else. She must carry the penalty of God's will. Who else is there to blame? That's the way it is. And that's the way the court will see it."

"How long will the court proceedings take,?" I asked.

"When the money's up front, the decision's immediate," replied Hamad as if I had asked the most stupid question. "Everything's decided in advance according to the terms of the original marriage contract. Of course the dowry must be repaid in full. There's nothing more to it than that."

"And how will you get your new wife?"

"No problem," replied Hamad. "I'll just approach a neighbour with a daughter in my home town in Lebanon, and work out an agreement with him."

"Will you be able to see your new wife in advance?"

"Of course! I wouldn't buy a pig in a poke, as you say in your country. I'm not old-fashioned. I believe in modern ideas. I'll be able to meet her four or five times in the presence of her family. We'll both have an opportunity to decide if we like one another. Then we'll marry according to the financial arrangement made with her father. Nothing could be simpler."

Eighteen months later I was to meet quite a different Hamad Zohair - a calmer, quieter, happier man. He had acquired his new wife and even a desired son. On our second evening together he took me to an open air restaurant within an enclosed courtyard, together with his wife and child. He dutifully pushed the buggy, adjusted the baby's bottle, and picked up and cuddled the infant when it began to cry. Meanwhile, I spoke with his wife, a good looking and intelligent girl who had qualified as a teacher, and had had a Western education. Hamad was now a real family man, and I sensed that his wife was gaining the upper hand in their relationship.

A year previously, when Hamad had just sent back his first wife to her father and he had married his second, Saad and I had sat in the rooftop restaurant of the Hotel Meridien, and joked about his changed situation. Hamad was elated. Everything was to change in his life. He had a new car and a new flat, and before eight months were out, he would have a child as well.

"Now you'll have to double your sales turnover," said Saad.

"If Al Qasim & Co. are to keep the agency, that's about the increase we'll need in export orders to Kuwait," I added.

Hamad was not to realise at the time the significance and outcome of this prediction as it was to effect him personally.

CHAPTER 6
Justice in a man's world

"All punishment is mischief. All punishment in itself is
evil. Upon the principle of utility, if it ought at all to be
admitted, it ought only to be admitted in as far as it
promises to exclude some greater evil."

Jeremy Bentham, *Principles of Morals & Legislation*, Ch. 13, Sec. II.

As I stood on the deserted palm-lined shore of Salalah, an hour
before sunset, looking towards the flat expanse of the calm sea,
I reflected how the peace of the ocean was belied by the
deafening crash of the huge rollers which broke onto the white sand.

Night and day the roar of the breaking waves could be heard from
the rooms of the Holiday Inn, set a hundred yards back from the
shoreline on the low-lying land; yet the expanse of the still ocean never
betrayed so much as a ripple as one looked out towards the distant
horizon where sky and water met in the misty distance. There was
deceit in the Indian Ocean!

Over the years, several unwary hotel guests had been claimed by
the merciless waves, and days later, some miles down the coastline, the
sea would throw back their bodies contemptuously, for recovery and
tragic burial. Since my last visit to the province of Dhofar, in this
remotest part of the Arabian peninsula, the authorities had everywhere
erected warning signs along the beach against the dangers of sea bathing.

Meanwhile, the porters in the lobby of the Holiday Inn always
advised guests, "Just keep to the hotel pool!" But the sea was inviting
and seductive with its warmth, its deceptive calm, and the foam that
splashed playfully towards those who approached the water. There was
an apparent innocence that contradicted the fatal power of the Ocean.

"Don't go near the sea," urged an Indian porter expressing his
horror. "If you so much as place your foot in the water, the undercurrent
of the waves will suck you under. Even the strongest man will be
drowned in the Ocean. It's not a place for swimmers."

In this part of the world there was much which was slow, and
tranquil, and seemingly eternal, concealing unsuspected horrors in the

natural world no less than that in the sphere of social relationships. There was not a breath of wind, and I looked along the coastline towards the South West, where the distant mountains met the sea, in the direction of that Russian satellite, the Yemen People's Democratic Republic, some seventy miles along the shore. But the East-West situation had eased since my last visit to Dhofar, for it had not now been necessary to obtain a letter from the Divan to enter the region.

Salalah was several hundred miles south of Muscat, the capital of Oman. Here everything was different. Salalah was situated in that corner of the peninsula that was subject to the monsoon. In Muscat there was the burning dry heat typical of the Gulf. Here in Salalah there was 90% humidity, and so when one stepped from the air-conditioned hotel into the open, one's spectacles steamed over in the heat; and as one drove into the town the windscreen wipers were needed to clear away the condensation which settled on the car. In the countryside there was the rich greenery of banana and coconut plantations, and fields of green, red and yellow peppers and tomato plants.

As I strode across the sand dunes towards the direction of the town (hundreds of giant red hairy land crabs burying themselves at my approach) I reflected on the disaster that had struck Salahah only three weeks before. It had been towards the end of the monsoon season, when after several days of torrential rain, the mountains which descended onto the flat plain some ten to fifteen miles distant, surrounding the town on three sides, unleashed a deluge on the helpless community. It was 2.0 am in the morning when a thunderous roar issued from the distant hills, and the stormy flood water could not be contained by the many wadis which led their course to the ancient town.

By 3.30 am Salalah was under three feet of water: many were electrocuted through short circuits in their homes; houses and other buildings were flattened within minutes; crops were ruined; and an unknown number of people, goats and other domestic animals, were swept out to sea to be drowned in the depths of the Indian Ocean. For three days the flood water remained in the town, for the ground was hard and dry and resistant to natural drainage.

As I walked along the shoreline, I crossed several channels where the flood water had broken through the subsoil in making its escape to the sea; and everywhere there was broken timber, sheets of corrugated metal, uprooted palm trees and wreckage, which was thrown to the sea and back again onto the land - neither willing to accept the rubbish of the storm.

And yet within three weeks the disaster was already becoming a distant memory. The Eastern mind had little inclination to mull over the trials and tribulations of life, or to ask the why or wherefore of an inexplicable event. Such thought patterns were only a luxury reserved for the Western mind. The Arab with his total trust in the One-God was endued with the strength of a fatalism and acceptance of all natural events and most other happenings that influenced his life. As all events were ordained by God alone, it would have been an impertinence to question the why or wherefore of a thing.

In the town of Salalah there was little to indicate the events of three weeks before. Debris had been cleared from the streets, surfaces were hot and dry, and life progressed in the sleepy town of ten thousand much as it had been before. Clouds of dust were still thrown up behind passing vehicles on the dirt track roads; goats and sheep still obstructed traffic in the town centre; and camels (kept for their milk and transport) were still chewing the cud in the back yards of private houses. Even in the Holiday Inn I slept in a ground floor room that three weeks earlier had been under several feet of water. Only the damp musty smell of rotting plaster, pervading the building, was a sign that something untoward had earlier occurred.

But then the inhabitants of Salalah had reason to occupy their minds with other dangers that loomed ahead. Over the past few months many had been fixing bars over the windows of their homes, or erecting steel shutters in front of shops and businesses. This had not been done as a precaution against the threat of floods! Some years earlier the Omani authorities had armed many of the tribesmen in the border area as a protection against the incursion of bandits from the Yemen, but recently the government of the Yemen PDR had sufficiently secured their frontier against the possibility of such attacks.

The Omani tribesmen became demoralised through the disuse of their weapons, and so they turned their attention to the regional capital, leading raiding parties into Salalah: robbing anyone they encountered in the streets; breaking into houses and shops; slaughtering those who resisted; and sometimes carrying off hostages into the hills.

A number of Omani regiments, often under the command of British officers, were stationed in the vicinity of Salalah, but as the camps were situated some miles from the town, and as the tribesmen were so quick and skilled in the use of their horses, and the tactics of unexpected attack, they easily outwitted the slow lumbering movements of the Sultan's conventional forces which were unsuited to the guerilla operation of a pursuit in the hills. The only consolation of the Sultan's men was the constant tribal warfare being fought out in the hills, for this allowed a respite from the untamed tribesmen in their violence on the settled people of the plain.

None of these fearful occurrences would have been evident to the occasional visitor to Salalah, for the slow relaxed pace of life seemed to continue undiminished in what appeared superficially to be the most peaceful of communities. When Mr. Darshan Devi fetched me from the hotel for the leisurely drive to the office, we stopped half way at the fruit market for refreshments. We were served by women in brightly coloured dresses and turbans, and skin as black as ebony.

This was more like Africa than Arabia, for these people were descended from the slaves of Zanzibar and captives from the East coast of the Dark Continent. The tops of coconuts were sliced off with deftness with a machete, and we were given the remaining cups to drink the milky liquid in the sticky heat. The leftover nut was of no interest, and so when we finished the drink, we threw the empty shells onto a pile of rubbish beside the stallholder's stand.

Darshan was a small squat man from Poonah, with a quiet personality, who managed the Salalah office of our Omani agents. He was a married man with two children, but his family remained in India, and he only saw them once a year during his one months annual leave.

"Is that a satisfactory arrangement,?" I had once asked.

"It's the only possibility," he had replied philosophically with that strange shake of the head unique to Indians. "The money's good here, and we have to plan for the future. My wife thinks it's the best arrangement. One day, when I've saved up, we'll be able to live together, and we'll enjoy a comfortable old age in each other's company.

In this life you can't have everything you want. We're working for the
next generation. It's the children who are important."

I felt like remarking on the prospects of children deprived of
fatherhood, but I held my tongue. It struck me that Darshan must be the
loneliest of men living in this quiet backwater in a foreign land, but he
never betrayed the slightest discontent, and it was impossible not to
admire the confidence of his self-surrender for a better future.

Life in Salalah was little less restrictive than in Saudi. The Ibadi
rites of Islam, which were followed in Oman, were closer to the Sunni
sect throughout most of the peninsula, than that of the Shiites on the
northern side of the Gulf. Darshan had warned me of the threat of arrest
facing a man or woman caught walking hand-in-hand in a public place,
and if it was a married couple caught in such a compromising situation,
then the police officer would turn angrily to the woman saying, "Then go
to your home at once, and confine your feelings to a private place!"

For two days only I was to be in Salalah before returning to
Muscat. As I drank the milky liquid, I thought of the tragic
circumstances which were unfolding around Salem Tabili back in the
Capital area, and I was eager to return to Muscat to learn about the latest
episode of the drama.

The following morning I drove with Darshan to the port of Raysut,
some ten miles to the West towards the Yemeni frontier, to see the new
container terminal still under construction. During the journey we were
stopped at several military posts and asked for identity papers, by the
Sultan's bearded men in their great turbans, their curved daggers (or
khunja) sheathed in ornate silver scabbards, part of the obligatory dress
of all Omanis, their bandoliers loaded with cartridges, and their
antiquated rifles.

"It's good the company pay us danger money here," said Darshan
as we drove away from one of the posts. "It's safe if you keep to the
main roads - providing it's daylight. After dark no one wanders away
from the safety of the town. - Did you have any trouble with spies when
you flew into the region on this occasion,?" he added.

"No," I answered.

Darshan was referring to a friendly Omani whom I had met at Seeb airport (in Muscat), who after questioning me on my life story had accompanied me to Salalah and then to the Holiday Inn.

"This place is full of spies," said Darshan. "They do nothing but drink in the bars all day, and then report back to the Divan at night. They'll have you on their files in some government office. It's the Russians they're after. This country's very vulnerable to war. In the north there's the Strait of Hormuz that Iran threatens to block, and in the south there's a Russian satellite at the entrance to the Red Sea. British armed personnel and weaponry are everywhere in this country."

After exploring the port of Raysut, we met a couple of Englishmen who had just returned from the Yemeni border where they had plucked a sprig of frankincense from a bush. We looked towards the dark and threatening mountains in the distant West.

"When Shakespeare wrote about 'all the perfumes of Arabia,' that's where it came from," said one of the Englishmen nodding towards the south west corner of the peninsula.

"And to think that three thousand years ago, in the time of the Queen of Sheba, it was the richest and one of the greatest countries of the world," said the other.

"Such is the fate of rising and falling civilisations," remarked Darshan. "Every country in turn enjoys its high period, and when it's gone, it never again recovers its lost predominance."

* * *

Salem Tabili had had more than his fair share of life's misfortunes over the past two years. He was a short heavily built man, dressed in a dishdasha (the long white cotton garment known as a thobe in most of the Gulf) and a white turban, or *masar*, for the headscarf and headrope were not worn by the Arabs of Oman. He was the leading salesman in the consumer goods section of our Omani agents, and when I returned from Salalah, he met me at Seeb airport for the run to my hotel in the Capital area.

I was keen to learn what had happened in the intervening period of the past two days in the drama affecting his family, but I would leave it to him to broach the sensitive topic, and so I remained silent. As we sped along the modern highway in the direction of Muscat, I reflected on the previous drama in which he had been tragically involved. One dark night as he drove through an unlit street in the new town of Ruwi, in the Capital area, two elderly women dressed in black, one totally deaf leading another who was blind, stepped off the kerb into the roadway, and were instantly killed by Salem's vehicle.

Salem was immediately arrested and thrown into prison. Although insured with a company vehicle, as everywhere in the Middle East, insurance was no protection in the event of injury or death. Salem was tried by the Shariah court and condemned to three years imprisonment. It was his personal financial circumstances that dictated the length of the term for blood money had to be paid for two lives that had been lost. Fortunately, he was only twelve months in gaol, for his company approached the court, defended the character of the accused, paid the blood money, and secured his release. But the stress that now confronted his family was, in a way, closer, more protracted, and more painful.

The Oman was a country of unusual contrasts. It was at once the oldest and most modern of the Arabian states. Until 1970 the country had only three schools, one hospital, seven miles of asphalted road and no street lights; its people living in medieval isolation and poverty under the absolute rule of the ageing Sultan Said bin Taimur. In 1970, the British and Sandhurst educated son of the ruler deposed his father in a bloodless coup, seizing the reins of power as Sultan Qaboos bin Said, and immediately embarked on a modernisation programme under the inspiration of British influence.

As Kuwait in the far north was the first of the Arabian states to be exploited for its world sought-after mineral resources, so the Oman in the south was the last to be developed from the wealth lying deep beneath its sands. Consequently, whilst Oman remained in a state of underdevelopment with more plans and construction sites than completed projects, there were also aspects of its trade and infrastructure which were more modern than those to be found throughout Saudi and the smaller Gulf states to the north.

The Capital area consisted of three major towns, together with other sprawling areas to the West, and ribbon development along the twenty mile highway leading to Seeb International Airport, the total population amounting to 80,000 with eventual plans to accommodate a city of half a million. There was Muscat, the nominal capital, a harbour town at the foot of mountains which descended almost to the sea, its bay defended at either end by the ancient Portuguese forts of Jalali and Mirari, atop precipitous cliffs; then there was Mutrah, two miles to the north west, an ancient port and trading centre, reached from the capital through a tunnel in the hills; and inland, hidden behind coastal mountains, was the huge construction site of Ruwi, which eventually would swallow up the entire area in a jungle of concrete and industrial development, so that Muscat and Mutrah would be reduced to the status of quaint village communities.

Our Omani agents were situated in Ruwi, and Ali Al Oud, the General Manager with whom I finally negotiated business deals for the area, was the most Westernised and liberal-minded Gulf Arab I was ever to meet. He was an amiable, generous, warm-hearted man, intent on emphasising his love for progress and modernisation, walking with an American swagger, and peppering his conversation with idiomatic slang and expletives, as if to suggest that he was no less relaxed in his social attitudes than any European. He had Caucasian features but a black skin, and he wore the Omani cap with gold braid, which he constantly readjusted, usually in a rakish fashion, and sometimes when in a thoughtful mood, he would remove it from his head and turn it over in his hands.

On the occasion when we first met, he took me to the hotel bar for a drink. Although officially the consumption of alcohol is illegal in Oman, it is available in the international hotels, and nowhere else in the Gulf did I see Arabs openly and unashamedly relaxing together in conversation over a glass of beer. When we were served, Ali insisted on pouring his own bottle into the glass.

"These Indians don't really know how to pour a beer without spoiling it," he confided.

We began to discuss the business situation in the area. Ali was no time-waster and wanted to get down to practicalities.

"It's quite different here from Dubai or anywhere else you've been so far," he explained. "Because of the greater size of retail businesses, and the number of supermarkets, selling methods are different. Here in Oman we have a sophisticated marketing situation; whilst in Dubai it remains a purely trading situation."

Ali explained that most of the employees of the company for which he worked (for he, too, was an employee) were Indians on low rates of pay, but as they were given free accommodation and food by the company, in addition to health insurance and return air fares to Bombay for a month's annual leave, the turnover of staff was very low. Occasionally, Ali flew to Bombay to recruit personally for the company.

The following morning, a Friday, Ali showed me around the old towns of Muscat and Mutrah. I remarked on the innumerable "wild" goats, of all sizes and colours, which seemed to wander down from the denuded hillsides, stroll intrusively around the town, pilfering any object they could find for consumption, and generally getting in the way of pedestrians and vehicles alike.

"None of them are wild," laughed Ali. "They all belong to someone. They're kept by ordinary households for their milk. At night they return to their owners' yards for a pail of water which is all they're given, but at daybreak they're let out into the streets again to feed and fend for themselves."

I soon found that the heat in the Oman was a few degrees greater than anywhere else in Arabia. This was because the air was trapped at the foot of mountain ranges, which contrasted with the flat plains to the north west allowing for the free movement of wind.

In Muscat we strolled through the gates of the old walled city, explored the dark unpaved alleyways in the souk area, and emerged into the light near the seafront before the Sultan's magnificent new palace, with its spacious green lawn, kept moist night and day by constant jets of water.

But it was in Mutrah where Ali was enlivened by the sights he wished to show me. This was his home town, and he reminisced on a distant past. He was now forty-one years of age, but as a child the town was still contained within its city walls, and entry and exit could only be made through one of the gates that were under constant guard, and sometimes there were hours of curfew. He had lived in one of the houses in the bay by the corniche, but at that time there was no corniche, and so the shoreline extended to the house fronts.

As a small boy he had spent idyllic days playing on the beach, and when it came to education, he was sent for instruction in a crowded room where a dozen boys of all ages sat on the floor, and where the elder pupils taught the younger. The teacher was unqualified, of course, and worked according to the different fees he could squeeze from parents, and so the children of poorer families were pushed into the background in favour of those who offered a higher remuneration. Text or exercise books were unknown in such an institution, and so all writing had to be done with chalk and slates.

As soon as Ali reached adulthood, he had no other wish (as with many others) than to leave Oman, which in his eyes was a dreary and backward place, with no future for anyone with initiative or talent. At first he went to Tanzania, the coastal region of which until 1856, and for two hundred years previously, had formed part of the Omani empire; and subsequently, he went to Pakistan, gaining for himself a sound Western education, as well as fluency in English and Urdu. By the time he returned to his home country in 1976, Sultan Qaboos had already seized power from his father and embarked on a programme of modernisation.

"Sultan Qaboos is the greatest man in our history - nothing less," concluded Ali. "He's given an opportunity to us all. Where would this country be without him? Still in the dark ages!"

At midday we drove to the exclusive Beach Club, some seven miles south of Muscat, hidden in a remote sandy cove surrounded by brown mountainous cliffs descending to the shoreline. This was an association with all the ambience, exclusivity, and finicky control of a traditional British club. There was a club house - very much like a cricket pavilion - straw canopies giving shade to small round tables, yachts, several motor boats, and families bathing, playing ball, or lying in the sun. Well over three quarters of those enjoying the facilities of the club were Europeans, the others being Omanis in management posts or senior government positions.

Ali found himself completely at home immediately we arrived, greeting old friends, introducing me to acquaintances and buying drinks all round. I was soon talking with an Englishman who was complaining about an airline tardy in carrying his son, on holiday from boarding school, from Heathrow to Muscat, because they thought his NOC (Non-Objection Certificate) had not been properly issued.

"We even telexed his NOC number to the airline as confirmed in Oman," he exclaimed. "And if that wasn't bad enough, as soon as he arrived at Seeb airport the customs seized his toy gun. And as soon as he went back to school again, we had to get the authorities to airmail it back to England. It cost me a fortune! I've heard they've got an entire warehouse at the airport filled with toy guns. It's all so stupid! I'm going to complain to the airport Director. He's a member of this club."

There was a Dublin woman with three daughters, married to a senior government official. She had lived in Muscat for seven years, and during the earlier period, conditions had been intolerable. During the Summer months, the night temperature retained the heat of the day, and when there were power cuts, which were frequent, and the air conditioning broke down, it was impossible to sleep. Her husband would then take the bed sheets, soak them in the bath, and cover his wife with the cold wet linen.

She would sleep for an hour, by which time the sheets would have dried out again, and then the process would be repeated. In Summer when laundry was hung out, the first items were dry before the last had been pegged onto the line. Nowadays there were no power cuts, and they lived in a house with modern air conditioning and all conveniences.

When her husband overheard that I had three daughters, he intervened by saying that that was "very good luck," and that the first daughter especially would bring "good fortune." This was because Mohammed had had three daughters by his first wife, his only children surviving to adulthood, and that the eldest, Fatima, had married Ali, whose reputation gave rise to the foundation of the Shiite sect.

As I was seated amongst a circle of Omanis and foreigners, eating a plate of succulent lean spit-roasted lamb wrapped in Arabic bread with humous, sliced tomatoes and French bean salad, which Ali had ordered, I noted he became involved in an altercation with several of his countrymen.

"It's important our basic lives remain unchanged," said one. "We must preserve our cultural values."

"But we've got to have change," insisted Ali. "Maybe you and I don't like it, but think of our children. It's going to be better for them."

When Ali went off to fetch a round of drinks, one of his

countrymen, with a nod of disapproval towards the bar, asked me, "Is he a local?"

"Born and bred here," I replied in a tone of surprise.

Mumbles of disapproval in Arabic were exchanged between the Omanis at our table. It was then that I noticed two other factors. Ali was dressed in a tea shirt and trousers whilst the other Omanis at the club wore dishdasha and either a *kaffia* or the Omani cap. The other factor was that Ali alone was drinking beer, whilst his compatriots kept to soft drinks.

Meanwhile, the Dubliner and an Englishwoman were engaged in another conversation.

"These Filipina girls are dreadful," exclaimed the Dubliner. "All they think about is meeting boy friends. I sacked mine this morning. Her boy friend brought her back at one o'clock in the morning. You don't know what they get up to! It gives the neighbourhood a bad reputation. She'll be sent back to Manila. She'll never get another job in Oman. My husband works in the Ministry. He'll ensure she'll never get another visa."

"My dear, they can't be worse than the Bangladeshis," responded the Englishwoman. "Mine didn't even know how to use the microwave. She was unteachable! I said to her, 'What do you cook with at home?' She couldn't even answer that. She just stood there stupidly. You're lucky! At least you've got rid of yours. I'm still stuck with mine," she concluded with a laugh.

* * *

When Salem Tabili fetched me the following morning for a tour of the retail outlets, he was clearly in a distraught condition, nervously hesitant with sad watery eyes. I sensed it would be unnecessary for me to enquire after the latest situation in the family crisis.

"Do you mind if we go to the Court,?" he asked as soon as we were seated in the car.

"Of course not," I responded.

"They deferred the hearing until today," he explained. "I'm sorry about this - it's wasting your time."

"You don't need to apologise - I understand," I assured.

I had already spent an entire morning sitting in the entrance hall of

the Shariah Court before the two-day trip to Salalah. Soon we were
there again. There was much hustle and bustle as we entered the
building, and almost at once, Salem was surrounded by three or four
excited women draped in black, and before they had entered the
courtroom, one of the women collapsed onto Salem's shoulder with loud
sobs, as the others crowded around with gestures of consolation.

Salem introduced me to his wife and sister-in-law, both of whom
spoke fluent English, and to several other female relatives, and to other
family members and friends. None of these, however, was at the centre
of the case. There was a sense of urgency and anticipation as a clerk
called out various listed cases to be heard before the *Qadis*. It seemed as
if most of Salem's friends and acquaintances had come to the Court to
give him moral support. It was not long before the case was called.

I sat alone on a hard wooden bench - not being allowed to enter the
courtroom - but minutes later, I heard the loud angry shouts of women,
followed by the deep authoritative voice of a court official, and then
moaning and weeping, and once again, the furious cries of women,
followed by the loud riposte of a disgruntled man.

The case concerned Salem's sister, Aysha, who had now been
under arrest for five days - having been thrown into an airless and filthy
prison cell, which she shared with six other women. Aysha had been
married for nine years, but after five years of marriage, her callous ne'er-
do-well husband left home without warning or explanation as if never to
return. He never wrote or communicated with his wife, or remitted
means to sustain his family, and she had no knowledge of his
whereabouts. Aysha had two children to bring up, and these were now
seven and eight years old. Her husband had meanwhile gone to the
coastal region of Kenya (formerly part of the Omani empire which had
been seized from the Portuguese in the 17th century) where he had
enjoyed the free-living life of Africa, away from the restrictions of
Islamic society, with alcohol and the generous friendship of women.

After four years he returned unexpectedly to Muscat and to the
homely comforts of family life, but in the intervening period Aysha had
changed the locks on the front door, and she refused him entry. Instead,
she called for an immediate divorce and demanded that he no more show
his face at "her door."

With wounded pride and rising anger, astonished at such a rebuff and stubborn "insolence" from a woman, he went instantly to the law, demanding back both his home and full conjugal rights.   Aysha's counter-claim was laughed off and dismissed by the Shariah judges, for in Islamic as in Jewish law, a woman cannot divorce her husband, although in special circumstances she may take certain steps towards the dissolution of a marriage entailing the surrender of property rights.

When the story of the husband's life over the previous four years was gradually, yet inevitably, revealed to the light of day through the spontaneous spread of rumour and the revelation of facts, Aysha used the counter-claim of "alcohol" and adultery as sufficient evidence in demonstrating the impossibility of the marriage, pleading that these should be grounds for dissolution initiated through the Authority of Justice.

Again, the Shariah judges threw out the counter-claim despite its soundness in Islamic law.   There was a lack of evidence and no demonstrable proof. The husband had claimed he was only on business in Kenya. He had never consumed alcohol and never been with other women. A woman's baseless accusations could not be taken on trust.

The judges were intent on upholding the sanctity of the marriage contract. The woman must take back her husband. If she refused the law would show its severity. Aysha had responded by screaming at the judges: "I'll never take him back in a thousand years!"

"Then the case is adjourned for five days," responded the senior judge. "You'll be held in prison until then. If you repent, you'll be released in the meantime."

Five days had passed and Aysha had not repented. And now the Court was sitting again. After half an hour's waiting Salem re-emerged from the courtroom with his relatives and party of supporters. His wife and sister-in-law were weeping, and even Salem could hardly hold back his tears.

"What happened,?" I asked.

"She still refuses to take back her husband - and why should she,?" Salem answered.

"And so what's to happen now?"

"The judge says she's to stay in prison until she agrees to take back her husband," said Salem.

"She says she'ld prefer to stay in prison for ten years than take him back," exclaimed Salem's wife with a mixture of grief and anger.

"It's terrible, terrible! I don't know what'll happen," mused Salem pulling his chin.

"The case has been deferred for another seven days," explained the sister-in-law.

* * *

Half an hour later Salem and I were speeding along the highway of the fertile Batinah coast in a northerly direction towards the ancient capital, Sohar, and the Emirate of Fujairah. There were many villages and small towns along this route which was a well-established agricultural area, situated at the foot of the Jabal Akhdar mountains and the Western Hajar. We stopped at shops and supermarkets in the townships of Seeb, Birka, Al Musana'a, As Suwayq and Al Khabura.

The manageress of a superstore in Al Khabura who was a Greek served us with a bowl of the local sweet speciality, *Hawali*. She had spent the greater part of her life in Uganda, and soon the three of us were in lively conversation. Salem, it transpired, had been educated in Dar es Salaam - it had once been a paradise.

"Africa was a wonderful place to live, and Uganda was the very best place of all," exclaimed the manageress. "It had everything! But now it's been barbarised. Everywhere in Africa, conditions are worsening by the day. Everyone says so. Nowhere's safe any more. You British should never have left. You were bringing law and prosperity to all. But I wouldn't like to live in Europe either. Business life is too hectic there. The Oman suits me. It has a future."

As we drove back towards Muscat early that evening, Salem looked sad and contemplative.

"It's not justice," he exclaimed sorrowfully to himself. "It's not justice! But there's nothing I can do about it."

CHAPTER 7
The grim capital

"It is advantageous that the gods should be believed to attend to the affairs of man; and the punishment for evil deeds, though sometimes late, is never fruitless."

Pliny the Elder, *Historia Naturalis*, Bk. II, Ch. 5, Sec. 10.

The multitude in Deira square was startled by the sound of a police siren, and moments later, over the heads of the crowd, a windowless black vehicle could be seen easing its way through the throng.

The black maria stopped before a row of iron bollards on the pavement in front of the Governor's Palace. Two khaki clad men jumped down from the cabin of the vehicle, and opened the twin doors at the rear. As a black figure was dragged from the dark interior, a loud female wail from within the vehicle momentarily filled the square. All eyes were strained for a better look at the centre of attention, but the distance was too great to distinguish as to whether the figure was that of a man or woman.

The black figure, dressed only in a coarse dark sackcloth skirt, was placed between two bollards, the wrists secured with rope to the iron posts on either side. The gates of the Governor's Palace were opened once again, and twenty uniformed men marched out into the square - but their hands were free for they had no weapons. They were halted and brought to attention in their double file formation before the pile of stones.

The man in the brown thobe, who apparently was someone in authority, addressed the other men in their flowing white robes who minutes earlier had emerged from the interior of the Grand Mosque. Following their leader and walking in a line, with slow casual steps, they approached the sprawling yellow heap, and one by one, each took up a stone.

Moments later missiles were flying through the air. There was a breathless silence from the watching multitude, as they stood paralysed, their feet fixed to the hard concrete surface. The only sounds to be heard in the vast area, were the clang of stones resounding against the iron bollards, the heavy thud of rocks against the pavement or the walls of the Governor's Palace, or the soft thump striking human bone and flesh.

The man in the brown thobe nodded to the non-commissioned officer leading the men who were standing to attention by the pile of rubble. The soldiers, in their turn, each took up a rock and assisted in the work of the public execution. As backs bent forward, and muscles flexed, and a forest of arms thrust violently in aiming towards a single target, the air was penetrated by a shower of deadly objects. The stoning was in progress! How long could it last?

Amongst foreigners this area was known as "Execution square." That I knew. It had been pointed out to me long before, on previous visits to Riyadh, but it was not quite possible to imagine the actual occurrence of a public execution. Riyadh was not merely the capital of the world's richest oil producer. It was also the pivotal centre of Semitic civilisation in all its ancient tradition. As a desert city hundreds of miles from the sea, it was not exposed to the corruption and sins of the outside world.

It was protected by the isolation of the desert, and one could travel from horizon to horizon and still there was only sand which met the sky in the infinity of distance. The desert was a place for contemplation - for despising the things of this world. It always had been. It was a place for hermits and prophets; for recognising the sins of the flesh, and repudiating the temptations of materialism. It was a place for scourging the body - that accursed receptacle of flesh and blood, which placed a barrier between man and God, in his painful struggle to commune with the true deity.

It was also the Old Biblical Jerusalem restored for the modern age, but just as Old Jerusalem need not be identified with what was most progressive in Jewish culture, so likewise, in a future and changing world, modern Riyadh need not be identified as embodying the essence or best in Arab culture. As the greatest achievements of modern Jewry have been achieved through the humanist values derived from a symbiotic relationship with the West; so the higher consciousness of ancient Jewry two millennia ago, was achieved through a symbiotic relationship with Romano-Hellenic values, as witnessed through the Jewish intelligentsia of Alexandria, Pergamum and Rome, and the high esteem and positions achieved by Jews within the ruling establishment.

Might not Arab culture, too, some daybreak through the restraining limits of its mould by engaging the positive aspects of a foreign mind-set? Old Jerusalem and modern Riyadh respectively were and are intolerant, cruel, self-righteous, and introverted cities of religious reaction against those humanist values essential for the development of a multi-cultural world. The life-denying puritanism of both is typified by the swish of the policeman's cane, the fall of the executioner's sword, and the hurling stones of the indignant.

Riyadh was also the home of the puritanical Wahabi movement, or *Ikhwan* (brothers), who under their 18th century founder, Mohammed bin Abdul Wahab, led a *Jihad* or Holy War against the infidels and backsliding Arab peoples who failed to follow in detail the original practices of the Prophet. The fanatical preacher was soon to come under the protection of Mohammed bin Saud, Sheikh of fortified Dariyah, and under the influence of prince and teacher, and the armed horsemen of the Nejd, the new Islamic sect was to embark on glorious conquest.

For twenty years Riyadh - that stubborn city - was to resist, before succumbing to the steady pressure of the new movement - never again to renege on its allegiance to the purified practices of the True Faith. By 1765 all of central and eastern Arabia had been seized and consolidated by the tribesmen of the Saudi princes, for a leading article of the movement called for unity amongst warring factions in condemning the blood feud and tribal raids. During the 19th century the Wahabis encountered serious setbacks and many defeats at the hands of their nominal masters, the Turks of the Ottoman Empire, usually under the command of Egyptian expeditionary forces.

It was only from the start of the 20th century, driven forward by the military victories and political acumen of Abdul-Aziz II bin Saud the Great, that the Wahabi movement, experienced an all-powerful renaissance. With the demise of Turkish power after the First World War and the defeat of leading princes in Hejaz and northern Arabia, by the 1920s the victorious Sheikh from the Nejd was proclaimed King of

several provinces. Finally, in completing a thread of events that had
begun in the first half of the 18th century, a new nation state was
proclaimed in 1932, uniquely under the designation of a family name, as
Saudi Arabia.

But what was the meaning of progress in this nation of the One-
God? Earlier in the century it had meant a greater toleration in allowing
non-Muslims to besmirch Arabian soil with their infidel footprints, and a
more latitudinarian attitude in accepting those abominations of
technology from the West, such as the car, the aeroplane, the telephone
and radiotelegraphy. The ruling sheikhs had had to use care and tact in
recognising the legality of these things in facing the frowning
disapproval of their puritanical mullahs. But now the pendulum had
swung in an opposite direction. Progress had a different meaning. The
Arabs were a mighty force, and Arab power was synonymous with the
True Faith.

There was no longer the need to defer to the infidels of the West.
There was everywhere a new confidence, and now was the time for
rolling back the corrupting evils of an alien civilisation with its
sodomites and adulterers; its apostates and idolaters; its blasphemers and
nihilists. These were the ungodly people who not merely threatened but
even acted out the destruction of family and social life. Was this not
evident even in the published research and media reports of the infidels
themselves? But hope was on the horizon! Fundamentalism in its
different forms, and the revolt against the values of the West, was
everywhere strengthening apace.

Even the two thousand years of tradition underpinning the
development of rational law was eyed for destruction. The iniquities of
man-made law must now give way to God-made law. The foundations
of British and French authority, grounded in the humanism of ancient
Rome, which they developed and adapted for a later millennium, were
now to be replaced by a greater and better power. In Pakistan, in
Algeria, in eastern and even western Africa, in Indonesia, and certain
provinces of Malaysia, and in other Islamic states throughout the world,
Shariah law was to replace the legal codes based on the cold
disinterested systems of the West.

And social custom, too, would be made to adapt, in adhering to the will of the One-God. Ever more restrictions were introduced into the composite body of Saudi law: cinemas were to be closed; women to wear the *chador* - the black drape over their European dress in public places; no woman to sit in the front passenger seat of a car unless it be the wife of the driver; and the sale of Christmas cards to be prohibited throughout the Kingdom.

These were aspects of progress incomprehensible to Western thought. God alone was relevant to the peoples of the True Faith, and so progress entailed those measures helping humankind towards a closer proximity with the Almighty Being. The suppression of material desire - especially of the flesh, and the promotion of spiritual fulfilment - that was progress! What other concept of progress could a theocratic state be properly expected to achieve?

A first visit to Riyadh must always be a memorable experience. The huge arrival terminal at the airport seemed crowded, noisy, and chaotic. I was apprehensive - nervous even - at the size and alien atmosphere of the place. There was an abrasive environment in the air. All were in a hurry, and all were stern, tense, and self-absorbed. There was an immediate impression that this was a different place from the cities stretched out along the Gulf, and so too was it different from Jeddah on the Red Sea.

As soon as I had reconfirmed my onward flight, I struggled with my luggage to the broad flight of steps outside the terminal building. At once I was confronted by a dozen unkempt figures in dirty thobes and grubby headscarves, with raised hands and aggressive voices shouting, "Taxi, taxi!"

"Sir, I'm a poor student, can you give me money? Just ten riyals! Please Sir, thank you Sir!"

A young man in Western dress was holding out his palm in front of me.

"I've no small change," I responded sharply. "I'm looking for a taxi."

"I've got a taxi," cried one.

"No, use mine - I've a licence," cried another.

I must have looked an innocent in attracting the attention of so many amongst the throng.

In an inadvertent moment I put my suitcase on the step. It was snatched up by a short thick set man who began running towards a taxi rank and car park. I had no option but to follow him, and overwhelmed with luggage I struggled to keep up. I was surprised when he ran through the taxi rank and into the car park. At last he threw my suitcase into the back of a mini-truck. This was not on! Never mind - perhaps it was a *fait accompli*.

"How much,?" I asked.

"Two hundred riyals," he replied.

Without further ado, or any verbal exchange, I snatched back my suitcase, just as another taxi driver in a yellow cab drew alongside and beckoned to me. I opened the back door of his car and threw my luggage onto the back seat, before placing myself in the front passenger seat. But that was not the end of the incident. A fist was thrust through the driver's window, and moments later, the two men were wrestling in the street. The driver of the mini-truck was thrown off, cursing and swearing, and my driver jumped back into his seat and accelerated at speed. I realised - too late - that nothing had been negotiated with regard to the fare. I had placed myself in a risky situation. But what else could I have done in these exceptional circumstances?

"Where go you,?" asked the driver.

"Inercontinental," I replied.

"How much,?" I cried at last, as soon as we had left the vicinity of the airport.

"Hundred riyals," he replied.

I remained tight-lipped. I was certainly unprepared to pay him that amount, but an argument would be best left for later. My silent reaction must have aroused his suspicion, for he slowed down, exclaiming gruffly, "You have money?"

"Of course I have money," I responded curtly, and he accelerated again at speed, driving in his reckless manner, hooting aggressively at all vehicles we approached and overtook.

After fifteen minutes he stopped at the side of the main road at the entrance to a long drive. We were in the middle of nowhere. We had driven down the endless length of long straight roads, and passed buildings hidden anonymously behind compound walls. There was the smell of cement dust and dirty sand in the air.

"Intercontinental," exclaimed the driver.

"I can't see any hotel," I replied, and I was determined not to pay him until I had ascertained a reasonable fare with the concierge.

"At the end of the drive," came the response.

"I can't carry my luggage that distance. Take me to the entrance," I commanded.

"Not allowed! No taxies allowed to the hotel. All taxis stop here," explained the driver.

"That's crazy," I responded.

"I stop here. No further," he repeated.

Reluctantly, I left the car and safely retrieved my luggage from the back seat.

"A hundred riyals," demanded the driver standing in front of me.

"No chance," I replied. "I'll give you fifty."

Grudgingly, he accepted the fare, before returning to his vehicle and driving off, and I began the long trek up the path, palm trees and greenery on either side.

By the time I reached half way, a porter immaculately dressed in uniform and gold braid, hurriedly approached to meet me. He was of Indian origin and asked what had happened.

"These people are the scum of the earth," he said after my explanation. "They're illiterate bedouin, just in from the desert."

He took my luggage and we continued towards the hotel entrance.

"How much did you pay?"

"Fifty riyals."

"Far too much! He shouldn't have charged you more than twenty-five riyals (£7.00) for that distance. That's why we only authorise our own licensed taxis. We have our own drivers working on an agency basis, taking residents to or from the airport, or into the town. They're Eritreans - refugees from the war in Africa. But they're dependable and polite."

Minutes later I was ensconced in a spacious and luxurious room with elegant furnishings, three or four 18th century style armchairs, a *chaise longue*, a verandah complete with sundeck furniture, a freezer cabinet stuffed with quality chocolates, nuts, other delicatessen items and a variety of soft drinks, in addition to a radio, and TV with the availability of video films.

Now began the difficult task of contacting Mr. Fahah Munof, the Badanahs' representative in Riyadh, for the shop was not listed in the telephone directory, and with the help of the hotel porters, and after an hour of phoning, and awaiting return calls, an arrangement was made. It was agreed that Fahad Munof together with his friend Sulaiman Kamel, would call on me in my room two hours hence. I laid out drinks and refreshments in preparation for their visit in the early evening.

Fahad Munof was a reticent slightly built man, dressed in a grey thobe and red check headscarf, but he was always to view me with an expression of dark suspicion as if I could not be trusted to refrain from doing him an injury. He would use his headscarf to hide half his face, so that his penetrating eyes could look out defensively whilst concealing his visage. He spoke no English - not even basic salutations - and so I addressed him in my limited Arabic. I quickly formed the opinion that I was the first European he had met - or at least, had had to "deal with" - and so I was a dangerous and frightening infidel.

My predecessor had refused to visit Riyadh or the Eastern province, maintaining that all business could be conducted solely through contact with our agents at the Red Sea port. That was his excuse for entering and leaving the Kingdom in the quickest possible time. Although it was difficult not to feel the intensity of Fahad's dislike of my presence, he was always scrupulously correct, and as will be seen, even hospitable.

His friend, Sulaiman Kamel, was a very different person, being as extroverted as Fahad was introverted. He was above ordinary height, with a chubby jovial face and prominent pouch, and although he had conventional views on life and morality, he was also sensuous and outspoken, and not afraid of expressing his erotic fantasies. Whilst Fahad had scarcely dared to go beyond the confines of Riyadh, Sulaiman was internationally travelled and had enjoyed himself without inhibitions in the "wicked" world beyond the Arabian peninsula. He was an employee of the Saudi American Bank, and was now accompanying his friend as an interpreter.

As soon as I had seated the visitors and served them refreshments,

Sulaiman was relaxed and at home, but Fahad seemed overcome by the luxury of the unaccustomed surroundings. I tried to steer the conversation in the direction of business but whilst Fahad seemed unable or unwilling to express an opinion on any matter I raised, Sulaiman was simply uninterested in the topic. Sulaiman wanted to use his opportunity as an interpreter for enjoyment and leisure. What did I want to do in Riyadh?

If they were so kind as to show me the city, I said, I should be most grateful if they could take me to the Qasr al-Masmak, the fort where the first great Saudi King as a young prince, had scaled the city walls with a select body of only fifteen warriors in January 1902, before defeating the Rashidi governor and liberating the oppressed population. I should then like to visit Dariyah and see the ruins of the fort where the great religious leader, Mohammed Wahab had lived after fleeing from Othman bin Muammar, the ruler of Al Uyaynah.

As I began to enthuse over these awesome historical events, the two Arabs viewed me with an expression of increasing surprise that was unmarked with approval. Had I been seated before two foreigners who were Europeans, and similarly revealing some knowledge of their heritage, it would most probably have aroused in them feelings of being complimented. But not so in this situation!

"Where did you find out about all this,?" said Sulaiman at last, but he seemed to be adding, "How can you fill your head with such useless rubbish?"

"From books," I answered.

The Arabs glanced at one another as if to say, "How can such irrelevant nonsense be published in books?"

I had yet to learn that the Gulf Arab had no historical sense. His mentally static existence, and the many and omnipotent religious controls directing his daily life and thought in unchanging perpetuity as one generation followed another, had denied him the possibility for historical understanding. The Arab lived for the present and the immediate future. The past was dead and buried! Even his nearest and dearest were consigned to the anonymity of sandy unmarked graves, for the Sunni branch of the Islamic faith condemned memorials to the dead as objects of idolatry.

The Westerner, by contrast, could not live without a historical sense, for in a fast moving world, changing decade by decade, it gave meaning to all his beliefs in facilitating a psychological adaptation to change. The explicable past had to justify the present, and if the speed of progress ran too fast for its acceptance, then sentimentality and cherished false illusions about former epochs were used as a prop to rest the shattered soul.

Such thought patterns had influenced Western humanity for more than two thousand years, and although we no longer looked back, as with the Greeks, to a Golden Age, and although we had progressed from a circular to a linear conception of time and progress, we were nonetheless inspired by the truths and myths of history no less than our predecessors in the ancient world. History had become the displaced religion, or secular belief system, of the modern Westerner, in the way it had once been with our Greek or Roman forebears, and if this suggested the return to a modernised form of paganism in a pluralistic society, then so be it!

How greatly this contrasted with the consciousness of the Semitic or Arab mind! All the technological changes and Western conveniences of the 20th century, howsoever they benefited the peoples of the Kingdom, had not yet begun to influence their underlying thought process. Theirs was still a theocratic mind, and so the imposed advantages of an alien civilisation were accepted passively with gratitude as the gift of the One-God.

Real knowledge was neither History nor Science. The jealous exclusivity of the Islamic faith, and its totalitarianism in defining the parameters of belief, life, habit, and morality, had thereby constructed a barrier against the possibility for evolutionary development as a mental process. It was this barrier that made history a sterile study, for it allowed no moral or other inspiration to be derived from the events or heroes of the past. And as for Science: its end results were accepted at their face value with no understanding or sympathy for the mighty conflicts and intellectual battles which had brought them into fruition.

True knowledge was the knowledge of God alone, as set out in the sacred texts of the *Koran* and the *Hadith*. Of course the Arab had an awareness of the past, but only the religious past was relevant. But that relevant past was not history: it was religion - something timeless and eternal. Its understanding was only comprehensible in terms of faith and ethics. To subject it to the rigours of critical thought was sacrilege - the work of the infidel.

Such thought patterns might be compared to Christian theological thought before the Enlightenment, but in pursuing such a comparison, it would be necessary to imagine a Europe deprived of all secular knowledge which had not already been subordinated totally to Church authority. Of course the Kingdom had its universities and their new and impressive buildings were evident in all the different provinces, and such institutions would have taught the memorisation of facts in facilitating a credible examination system. Nonetheless, it has to remain an open question as to whether such educational bodies progressed sufficiently to influence the thinking mind.

That is a description of the modern Arab consciousness. But such a consciousness is a far cry from the reality of Arab history. It has to be noted that Arab history as with Arab culture, as topics for objective study, have almost become the exclusive preserve of the Westerner - at least, in the modern era.

The awe and enthusiasm for Arab life and the magnificence of the open desert, has hardly touched the pen of the contemporary Arab writer, but it has inspired many an Englishman and woman to great descriptive prose, as evident in the work of Sir Richard Burton, W.G. Palgrave, Charles Doughty, Lady Blunt, Gertrude Bell, and T.E. Lawrence - in addition to the more recent and well known books of Bertram Thomas, H. St. J.B. Philby, Freya Stark, and Sir Wilfred Thesiger. Even leading lives of the Prophet have remained the almost exclusive preserve of European scholars - German and French as well as British and American - as well as an inspiration for some of the literary giants of the 19th century, as Washington Irving and Thomas Carlyle - the latter in his book, *On Heroes, Hero-Worship & The Heroic In History.*

Even a superficial knowledge of Arab history is a reminder that there was once an age when they led the world in science, in medicine, in mathematics, in philosophy and the arts - even in the writing of history in recollecting the names of Al-Tabari, bin Khaldun, Hajji Khalifa, and a host of others in the early Islamic era. What became of the period of the Abbasid Caliphs whilst Europe lingered in the ignorance of the dark ages?   Such a civilisation could not have flourished without the humanism and freethinking values of a generous people.   And yet today, such a glorious age is no longer even a faded memory in the Arabian peninsula.

Can the fanaticism of religion be so destructive and so reactionary in wiping away centuries of civilisation from the slate of progress? Yes, because it was so in the West after the fall of the Roman Empire, and it was not for twelve hundred years that the mist of superstition and bigotry with all its cruelty was to lift with the emergence of the Renaissance and humanist thought. That is why the West must initiate a friendly dialogue with our Arab brothers and sisters in promoting a greater understanding on both sides of the cultural divide.

Those were my reflections, sometime later, which arose originally from that evening with Sulaiman and Fahad, as we sat in the peaceful environment of the Intercontinental.

* * *

Sulaiman and Fahad fetched me at 9.0 am the following morning for a sightseeing tour, and we drove through the seemingly endless expanse of the city in the Mercedes of the former. I had never before driven in a city with streets so long and straight and broad, with changeless views from one mile to the next. Even the buildings seemed ashamed to expose their face to the world, as they hid their form behind dreary walls. Every street was the same as another, and once away from the centre, no pedestrian was to be seen, and this gave a strangely empty atmosphere to the urban environment. A ghostly impression pervaded a seemingly motionless and depopulated city, only belied by the senseless rush of traffic - mostly American saloons - moving from nowhere to nowhere.

Wherever there was vegetation, it was coated in cement dust, and wherever there was a break in the non-ending continuum of defensive walls, there was a gateway, often with khaki clad police strolling outside, or lounging against the brickwork, machine guns suspended from their shoulders. I was curious as to the identity of such places.

Most were the palaces of princes, assured Sulaiman, but some were identified as government departments, often with such strange sounding names as: Public Morality Committees General Presidency; Ministry of Pilgrimage and Endowments; General Presidency of Female Education; Committee for The Protection of Virtue & The Prevention of Vice; Disciplinary and Investigations Board; Department of Public Security; Ministry of Justice; Ministry of the Interior; Saline Water Conversion Corporation, etc.

We passed the palace where the King held his regular Monday morning Majlis, where any subject was free to present personally a petition to his Majesty, much in the same way as petitioners were free to present their complaints to feudal barons in Medieval Europe. And as it was then a Monday morning, we saw numbers of petitioners hastening to the palace, each being allowed a minute to present his case to the King. Could I take a photograph? No, said Sulaiman. The photographing of ministerial or historical buildings was forbidden. We then drove the ten miles to Dariyah and saw the ruins of the old city that the Turks had destroyed in 1818. There was a herd of goats atop a hill overlooking the town, and they offered a good photo opportunity. Would it be allowed? Sulaiman conferred with his friend.

"Fahad says it wouldn't be possible," said Sulaiman at last. "The people are very strange here. They'ld take offence. The creating of life-like images is against the teaching of the *Koran*. And if they saw a foreigner photographing their goats, they'd be afraid that an evil spell had been cast on their animals."

On returning to Riyadh we went to Fahad's household goods shop situated in Sibalah Street in the New Market of the Deira souk. Glasses of tea were served, and as Fahah and Sulaiman sat and talked together at a little table, I wandered around the shop making price comparisons and noting other factors for research. I had been assured that none of the marked prices were "real" prices, for they had been raised by 10% - 12% to allow for a negotiating margin. No prospective customer (other than a European) could be expected to accept a marked price as fixed or final.

There were three other assistants in the shop, all men in their early twenties, to whom I had not been introduced. Since they kept their distance from me, and since they were occupied for much of the time with the coming and going of customers in a busy retail district, I did not attempt to introduce myself.

It soon became apparent, however, from their looks and body language that they not only regarded me with indifference or suspicion but the prejudice of deep-seated dislike. The precepts of religion had so made their mark that it was painful for them to endure an infidel in their midst. In these circumstances I felt it wiser to adopt a self-effacing attitude, and so I returned to my chair by Sulaiman and Fahad, and sat quietly observing the business of the shop.

After several days the three assistants became more relaxed in their attitude, seeming to lose their suspicion and bias against the unknown. All three had a working knowledge of English. When we were obliged to drink tea together their mood changed to one of curiosity, and then to friendliness, and even to the communication of intimate truths. Fahad had a seven year old son who in the evening used to run around and shout in an unruly fashion outside the shop.

"He's completely neurotic and out of control," said one of the assistants as we stood in the doorway of the shop. "His father's had a terrible problem with him. He's even taken him to the doctor."

At that point I realised I was no longer regarded as a demon. I might still be an infidel, but I was an infidel who could be trusted and did not grow horns.

Most visitors to the shop were Arab women, rarely alone, usually two or three together. All were heavily hooded and veiled, their silhouettes conveying the impression of black ghosts. I was struck by the mode of communication between customers and assistants that was so impersonal and abrupt, in the eyes of a Westerner, as to be actually rude. Eye contact was avoided, and in negotiations entailing the sale of any item, both parties kept a discreet distance from the other, curtly exchanging their bargaining positions without a suggestion of humour or human feeling. This was in the spirit of the custom and law of illegal seclusion, as well as in view of the prohibition against men and women working in a common place of employment.

But as I sat in the shop, viewing the hustle and bustle of trade, it soon became evident that the heavy black garments worn from head to foot, could not entirely conceal the nature of the beings draped within. None of the ordinances of religion or the ingenuity of disguise could transform flesh and blood into something it was not.

Femininity showed through and so the tempting of the imagination could never entirely be suppressed. Abolishing the thought of sin and the evils of the flesh was not quite such an easy task. Despite all the determination and good intent, and all the decrees of the theocratic state, the religious masters had finally failed in transferring man's consciousness from the contemplation of matter to that of ethereal spirit.

There was an elegance in these women as they walked, or as they stood by the shelves, changing the weight of one foot to another, the drapes of their skirts moving against shapely limbs. And when they reached out for an item, a slim hand would be bared and a well-formed wrist and forearm would be exposed with a smooth and olive skin, inviting to a lover's kiss.

And as the sunbeams shone into the shop, they would wickedly penetrate the concealing drapes, and momentarily, a beauteous form and delicate features were revealed, sufficient to awaken desire in the hardest heart. These girls of Riyadh were shapely and beautiful beings, of pure Arab stock, taller and slimmer and with a lighter complexion than those of the Gulf or the Red Sea coast. Such were my personal and secretive impressions - and purely subjective feelings!

Were these beauteous objects in Riyadh any less of a temptation than their counterparts in a London street? Can the accustomed dress of any society really decrease or increase the awakening of sin or sexual desire? Is nakedness more obscene than the erotic art of clothing the human form? Is not the culture of dress a relative matter that in specific instances cannot be lent to the assumption of a higher objective morality?

And most significantly, is it in the interests of society that this natural form of desire should so become the obsession of religious authority that decrees are made for the control of dress? Attempts at suppression too often find a more unnatural outlet than the cause for their first existence, and in this way greater evils are created out of lesser. It is dangerous to press down the lid on a boiling pot, for it will scald the hand of the cook.

Later in the morning I went with Sulaiman to the Qasr al-Masmak, a few minutes walk from Fahad's shop, and as we returned shortly before noon, numbers of elderly men with henna-dyed beards in brown thobes and red check headscarves, armed with camel sticks, began descending on the streets in the central area. Some were good-humoured but most had the scowling countenance and humourless severity of Old Testament prophets, as they cried, "Assalah! Assalah,!" (to prayer, to prayer), knocking the knobs of their camel sticks on the open shutters of premises, and calling angrily to proprietors and customers to vacate the shops. These were the *Mutaween* or Religious Police, responsible for public morality and to ensure that the muezzin's call was answered by the populace.

Nervous shopkeepers shooed their customers to the exits, and the clanging sound of metal shutters being pulled down to the pavements, resounded everywhere. The Religious Police were responsible for the propriety of dress, and any woman whose arms were uncovered would incur their ire, whilst any man so foolish as to be dressed in shorts would risk arrest. Every shop and business needed to be vacated and locked up by the stipulated time for prayer as published in the daily press, for prayer times altered day by day according to the exact position of the sun as dictated by sunrise and sunset. Only the market women, sitting cross-legged on the ground like black pyramids before blankets with their wares, were left undisturbed allowed to continue their business during the prayer period.

"We must hurry back to Fahad," said Sulaiman, "and then we'll fetch my son from school."

Walking through the central commercial area, it soon became clear that here was a different pattern to business compared with that in the Gulf or even on the Red Sea. A far higher percentage of retail business was managed and staffed by Arab locals, and only one in three shop fronts bore descriptive names in Roman as well as Arabic script. This is not to suggest that many thousands of Indian (and other) personnel were not engaged in other employment, entailing anything from manual work to senior executive posts, but their presence was less evident in the souks.

On meeting Fahad we walked back to the car situated on the huge parking plot known as Deira square. Sulaiman explained that every Friday this was transformed into the execution area, as it was nearby the New Justice building, and if there was no one to be beheaded or stoned for any of the eight capital offences of: Murder; Rape; Sodomy; Armed Robbery; Sabotage; Drug Trafficking; Adultery, or Apostasy, then lesser criminals had their limbs amputated for larceny, and if there were no thieves to be punished, then minor offenders would be flogged for riotous behaviour, causing an affray, or drinking alcohol.

"Have you ever seen a public execution,?" I asked.

"No, only foreigners come here," he replied. "It's too much of an ordinary event to be of interest to locals."

After a twenty-minute drive we reached the school - or rather the compound wall which hid the school building within. Outside the closed gates of the school stood a man with a microphone. The car stopped by the kerb and we waited.

"Aren't you going in,?" I asked.

"It's not allowed," said Sulaiman. "It's a primary school. All the teachers are women. The janitor standing outside knows all the children and the car numbers of their guardians."

Moments later a six-year old boy ran out of the school gates which were momentarily held ajar from within, and jumped happily into the car.

"Do you have parents' evenings,?" I asked as we drove along.

"Yes, but only my wife's allowed to go," explained Sulaiman. "Talking to women in an enclosed place is forbidden by law."

I said nothing but when he spoke again I guessed he had been reading my thoughts.

"In Saudi Arabia we're very lucky," he began. "The law helps and protects us all. Shariah law is God's law and so we can all understand it. If you read the *Koran* you know what's right and wrong, and if you know what's right and wrong you know the law. It's not like that in the West. In the West the law's changing all the time. A man doesn't know whether he's coming or going, or doing good or bad. That's because he has man-made law. That's not justice!

"In Saudi we have very little crime. We watch one another. We have strong family ties. In Saudi we have a life-long responsibility for our children. It's not like that in Europe. In Europe, when a child's eighteen it goes off and does what it likes, and the parents don't care. That's bad! In Europe, parents don't bother to marry off their children, and so soon they get into all kinds of trouble. It's only natural! In Saudi it would be a bad father who didn't find a wife for his son as soon as he reaches maturity."

"Is there enough for young people to do here,?" I asked.

"Of course," replied Sulaiman. "Everything's arranged within the family. That keeps young people happy. It's good we have no cinemas, or clubs, or other public meeting places, because they make people discontented - and you get fights and bad company there. Look at Europe! In Europe people only go to clubs for heroin or promiscuous sex. That's bad! We don't have that in Saudi. In Saudi drugs are illegal."

CHAPTER 8
Values in conflict

"The world does not grow better by force or by the policeman's club."

William J. Gaynor, *Letters & Speeches*, p. 314.

S ince I was unsatisfied with our market share in the Kingdom, which had been declining for a decade, despite our company's substantial increases in annual product turnover during the past five years, I was determined to carry out my own field research in Riyadh and the Eastern Province.

I was not impressed by what I had already seen of the Badanahs operation in Riyadh. It was managed by a shopkeeper who may have had a natural business acumen and a low cunning, but he was uneducated, and not best fitted for the sophisticated and fast changing conditions of the market place.

It would not be difficult to excuse myself from the company of Fahad Munof for an occasional half day during my days in Riyadh, and indeed, he must have been relieved by my absence, and his friend could return to his work at the Saudi American bank. I explained I had some business at the Consulate. It was at the time when the embassies were being moved from the old commercial capital of Jeddah to the nominal and growing political or Royal Capital of Riyadh, where the British government had already established a commercial post.

Besides, in London I had already made contact with a young well-educated Saudi businessman from a noble (or *Assil*) family. He was tall and handsome, with suave aristocratic manners, conveying the impression that he could move comfortably in an international milieu, and I felt we could develop a good relationship. His presentation contrasted sharply with that of the Badanahs. I made an arrangement to meet him early that evening in my hotel for an initial discussion before being fetched by Sulaiman and Fahad for dinner.

The afternoon was spent in field research in the commercial centre and in leading stores in outlying areas. I had occasion to cross Al Foutah Park, one of the few attractive green open spaces in Riyadh, with shaded benches, date palm trees, exotic flowers, and spacious lawns, and in attempting to make a short cut, I came to grief as soon as I stepped from the pavement to the grass. It was a reminder, once again, that only in England is it possible to walk on neatly mowed lawns in public parks, for whilst in Europe such areas are protected by notices announcing, "Verboten,!" here in Riyadh, my foot simply sunk into mud up to the ankle. I should have realised that any lawn in the heat of the desert is only maintained by sprinklers soaking the ground over a twenty-four hour period.

Later in the afternoon I encountered, what seemed, a curious sight. There were dozens of noisy girls rushing out of their secondary school at the end of the day, and whilst they were laughing and swinging satchels at one another, as high-spirited children might naturally behave in any part of the world, all, large and small alike, were heavily hooded and veiled, looking very much like a sisterhood of Ku Klux Klan members in grey attire. Their veils and long skirts were clearly no obstruction to their rough and tumble.

That same afternoon I was also alarmed by an occurrence demonstrating that the inhibitions of young Arab women were not always as strong as might have been supposed. Although it is difficult to imagine a more modest attire than that adopted by the women of the Gulf, I was to learn that that in itself is no assurance of modest behaviour.

Whilst cutting through a narrow unpaved street in an old central residential area, I was startled by the shouting and laughing of three or four veiled girls (whom I assumed could only be teenagers) standing behind partly opened lattice screens on a first floor balcony. My quickened step was not to relieve my feeling of awkwardness, for they shouted all the louder until I was out of view. When I repeated, what I thought were their words to Sulaiman, he assured me, with some embarrassment, they were obscenities that were surprising coming from the lips of women.

Sulaiman was in good form when he and Fahad fetched me that evening. He was also elated - as both men had reason to be. They had just come from the football stadium where they had seen Saudi Arabia defeat Kuwait 1-nil, and this had put the Kingdom into the World Cup. All Riyadh was celebrating! By the time we reached the centre, there was congested traffic moving at a snail's pace.

"It's good women aren't allowed to drive," exclaimed Sulaiman. "Can you imagine the number of cars there'd be on the road then? It would be impossible to move."

By the time we reached Yamamah street, driving in the direction of the stadium, hundreds of cars were parked diagonally on both sides of the street, men squatting on the roofs and bonnets, waving the green Saudi flag and shouting with joy, the horns of their vehicles blaring in an infernal din.

"Just look at that," cried Sulaiman. "I've seen nothing like it before! The city's never seen such sights before. They're all men from good families. They're all sheikhs and princes."

"If that's the case, then there must be more princes than ordinary people," I answered.

"They have to be princes, as otherwise the police wouldn't allow them to behave like that," persisted Sulaiman. "If they were ordinary people, they'd be arrested and put into prison for making a noise and disrupting the traffic. See, the police are doing nothing - just standing there, and letting them shout. It's a great day for Saudi Arabia!"

We drove to a main thoroughfare in the centre, well lit with neon signs, open shops, restaurants and bars, and all the while, cars with hooting horns and flag waving passengers were speeding by in both directions.

"See, you can always feel at home in Riyadh, we have everything here," cried Sulaiman. "Look, there's a Wimpey bar and there a Kentucky Fried Chicken - all the best from the West! We have MacDonalds too. It's just like in Europe."

At last we arrived at our destination, the Al Ahlia Restaurant Co., designated a Steak House.

"You'll like this place," assured Sulaiman as we entered. "It's just been opened. It's designed for European tastes."

As the restaurant was full, we had to wait twenty minutes, sitting on sofas at low tables in the bar area, where we were served exotic drinks described as a "fruit punch." Fahad seemed overwhelmed by the Western ambience, and clearly this was a new experience for him. It began to turn his imagination.

"Just supposing," he said with a smile (as Sulaiman explained afterwards), "that this was alcoholic. What do you think would happen then?"

"It would kill you," answered Sulaiman.

"Have either of you ever tasted alcohol,?" I asked.

Sulaiman replied that neither of them had.

"You see, it's impossible to drink alcohol in this climate," began Sulaiman authoritatively. "It goes to the heart. That's why the government's made it illegal. I once knew someone who had a friend who tried Whiskey. It killed him. He only drank it once, and not much - just half a bottle. Alcohol is very dangerous in the heat!"

At last we were shown to our table in the dining room. This was a restaurant where Arab sponsors brought their Western business associates. The waiters spoke English only and were Italian or Spanish, and whilst the civility of the service could not be faulted, it soon became apparent that the food was appalling: tinned or pre-cooked and pre-frozen meat and vegetables gave a blandness to everything laid out on the hot and cold buffet, although the camel meat did have an unusual tang.

Both Sulaiman and Fahad enjoyed the plush Western environment, and were not too put off by the poor food, of which they left much on their plates at the end of the meal, explaining that they liked their cuisine more highly spiced. Fahad was particularly awkward in handling his knife and fork - implements which he had probably never before used.

"You know, Fahad, you should go on holiday sometime to England, Germany, or France," said Sulaiman good-humouredly, and from his friend's reaction I guessed it was never intended as a serious suggestion.

Fahad shrugged his shoulders awkwardly, smiling coyly as if a wicked suggestion had been made - as if it was perhaps hinted that he should visit a strip joint or brothel. Sulaiman laughed at him.

"You should see something of the world," he said. "You know what's wrong with Fahad,?" he added turning to me. "He's afraid of doing wrong. He doesn't want to trust himself. But one day I'll take him on holiday with me - won't I Fahad,?" he said slapping his hand on his friend's shoulder.

At that moment a young married European couple were shown into the restaurant.

"A beautiful lady,!" Sulaiman confided to me with a wink.

Moments later the couple were seated at a table around which screens were placed in concealing them from the view of other patrons, in accordance with custom and law.

"What do you think they're doing behind that screen,?" said Sulaiman lasciviously, some minutes later.

"Eating," I replied.

"But they could be doing anything," said Sulaiman. "Nobody knows! The waiters would never tell. Perhaps he's taking off her clothes."

"It's unlikely," I replied.

"Perhaps you're right," relented Sulaiman. "European women aren't as we believe. They can be difficult. I found that in London. All they want to do is sit and talk. A man on holiday wants more than that. I don't go to Europe any more - it's expensive and overrated. I go to the Far East. I go twice a year with friends. You should go there. The women are fantastic! You can do anything with them - anything! And they cost almost nothing. And you can have girls of any age. You can have a grown woman and a naked twelve year old - both together. You should try that. In two weeks I'm going again. I asked Fahad to come too, but he says his holiday's a different time. I don't believe him - the liar,!" he added punching his friend playfully on the chest.

It was past midnight when we left the restaurant and began the drive back to the hotel. I was surprised to see numbers of vehicles stopped and asked to pull into the kerb by the police, all along the roadway in the city centre. It could not have been for a breathalyser test!

"Nobody's supposed to be out in the streets after midnight without good reason," explained Sulaiman. "The police are just ensuring good order, so that the rest of us can sleep in peace. They're asking, 'What are you doing out at this late hour?' If the drivers or their passengers are cheeky, they'll be arrested, but usually the police just say, 'Go home and go to bed for there's nothing more for you to do in the town. And if you can't sleep, read a book.' In that way people are kept out of trouble. It's good to have the police around. They take good care of us."

* * *

It had not been possible to reach a business arrangement with Yousef Al Swayyed, the Arab of noble family whom I had met in London, for whilst on the one hand, he had been dismissive of the Badanahs as being originally of Yemeni stock (they had only been settled in Jeddah for a hundred years); on the other, he was not prepared to risk upsetting a family of such well-established traders.

It was suggested I might find small traders to whom I could sell direct without embarrassing any third party. But the Al Swayyeds would only be interested in business with our company on an exclusive agency basis, and this was clearly not possible in the conceivable future. All business in the Kingdom had to be transacted with regard to the sensitivity of family and tribal relationships.

Nevertheless, Yousef wanted to maintain a friendly relationship, for the future could never be anticipated, and he invited me to a dinner the following evening held in celebration for an uncle. He did not explain at the time the reason for the celebration. As other European guests would be present, I would find myself at ease in the invited company.

The party was held in a palatial house in the Umm Al Hamam district on the outskirts of the city. I had been brought by a younger brother of Yousef, and as soon as I arrived at the entrance of the house, I realised that this was a function of some grandeur, as a number of men were mounting the steps, all dressed in their imposing yellow *gambaz* (or cloaks) with gold braid trimming, worn over their white thobes. Yousef's father, an elderly man leaning on a stick, was receiving guests at the entrance.

"Assalamu aleikum" (Peace be on you), I exclaimed taking the hand of my host.

"Wa'aleikum ussalam" (And on you be peace), came the reply.

I passed into a large entrance hall, reminiscent of the foyer of a 1930s cinema, where I was met by Yousef who introduced me to several American guests and a Swiss, and together we removed our shoes, before entering a long room where we took our place on cushions against the wall. Eventually a hundred of us were seated and served coffee in vessels smaller than an eggcup from a *dallah*, or traditional brass coffee pot, kept hot on the burning embers of a *gursi* or brazier in the centre of the room.

Last of all, the host led in an even more elderly man bowed down by age and supported by a staff. He was bespectacled and bearded, but wore a contented benevolent smile as if the world had granted him all its favours. At once, a dozen or so men amongst the guests, rose to their feet, went over to the guest of honour, and kisses were exchanged on either cheek. The rest of us rose to our feet as the guest was escorted to a place of honour, and then we returned to our cushions amongst a hubbub of conversation.

"Who is that guy,?" exclaimed one of the Americans in a frustrated tone.

"It's Hassan Al Swayyed," replied one of the Arabs in a reverential voice.

"Isn't he marvellous! He's eighty-three years old," exclaimed another.

"Marvellous for what? What's the celebration in aid of,?" persisted the American.

"Didn't you know? He's recently got married," said the first Arab.

"Hasn't he left that a bit late in life,?" suggested the Swiss.

"He's been married before," rejoined the Arab. "He already has eighteen sons and five daughters. Some of his sons are here tonight."

"Who's he married - is it a society wedding,?" asked one of the Americans naively.

"A girl from Sri Lanka, Sixteen and beautiful, they say," said the Arab with enthusiasm.

"But that's appalling," blurted out the first American tactlessly. "Now her life is ruined."

"Not at all," responded the Arab, his complexion reddening. "She could never have had a better opportunity. She comes from an impoverished farming family. Her husband bought her without the need for a dowry. Her father could never have afforded to marry her in her own society. Now she's saved! After all, she is a proper wife - not a mere concubine. When her husband dies she'll come into a property of her own. Then, one day, she can return to Sri Lanka as a prosperous lady and help her family. They'll always be indebted to Hassan Al Swayyed."

"But the age difference," persisted the Swiss.

"The world you live in is too comfortable," said the Arab with a smile. "You, in the West, have known prosperity for too long. You don't understand any more that money makes for happiness. Even we in Arabia - at least, those of the older generation - know the meaning of poverty. We were always a poor country. We don't forget that. When you're poor, the gift of riches is everything. Only in the West, with your generations of affluence, do you have such silly notions about love and happiness springing out of sex and mutual feeling alone. You can rest assured, my friends, that that girl will grow to love her husband deeply, and age will count for nothing.

"Maybe the sustaining cause of her love will be his wealth, but her love will be as true as any love between man and woman. Hassan is a good man because he has helped a poor family, and the children of his new wife will know a better future than if she had found a husband in her own country. And her father in Sri Lanka will be a happy man when blessed by Saudi grandchildren. And Hassan will be blessed by God for entering into this marriage."

"I suppose that could be a valid attitude from a Third World aspect," mused the Swiss.

"It's more than that: it's downright commonsense," said the Arab. "In this world, it's only the fool who fails to seize the opportunity granted by God."

Minutes later, the heavily carved double doors at the far end of the room were opened, and we were ushered into the sumptuous dining area, lit by an array of crystal chandeliers over a white dining cloth of monstrous measurements, on which lay giant platters of roasted mutton and mountains of rice. Yousef, who had been paying his respects to his uncle, returned to his European guests, and after we were seated on cushions, he began carving one of the roasted carcasses, serving choice cuts to the Western visitors.

We sat silently awhile, tearing the meat apart with our fingers and stuffing it into our mouths, sometimes with balls of hot rice, or

The Great Mosque & Clock Tower in Deira Square, Riyadh, a car park on week days, & a place for public executions on Fridays after *Zohar*, the second daily call to prayer

Mr. Chander (from Bombay) a director of Ramesh & Sons, Dubai

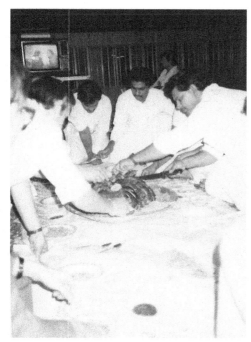

Feasting in Nazeer Badanah's flat, Masharafa, Jeddah. Nabeel carving & serving guests

Said & Nabeel Badanah by the Red Sea in Jeddah

Saad Aakef (from Pakistan)
General Manager of
Al Qasim & Co., (seated)
& Hamad Zohair, a
Palestinian salesman, Kuwait

Hamad Zohair with his car
and Tea boy

Darshan Devi (from Poonah)
a General Manager in Salalah,
Oman

On tour with General Manager, Ali Al Oud, Muscat, Oman

Ali Al Oud at the Beach Club, Muscat

With friends at the Beach Club, Muscat

Fahah Munof & Sulaiman
Kamel in Dariyah near Riyadh

Mountain road to the south of Sana'a, North Yemen

Beach, Hodeidah, North Yemen

Denny Mohen (from
Kerala) with his wife and
daughter in Bahrain

Denny Mohen with daughter & camels in desert, Bahrain

Larry McEwan & Denny
Mohen at Bahrain Fair

Abdulla Assaf (an Egyptian),
Departmental Manager of the
Contemporary Department Store,
Before the Clock Tower & Emiri
Palace, Doha, Qatar

Mr. Gamdi (an Egyptian) salesman,
Doha, Qatar

Nazeer, Larry McEwan, and Nabeel Badanah
At the Jeddah Spring Fair

Evening at Mousa Badanah's house: 1. to r. Pierre Legouis,
Mousa, John Crawley & Samir Badri

l. to r. Larry McEwan, Nabeel, unknown guest & Pierre Legouis

Swimming in Mousa's pool after the evening meal

l. to r. Pierre Legouis, John Crawley, Rob Haworth, Nabeel & Nazeer

Pakistani guide at the camel market in Al Ain

vegetables from our side salad bowls. We were thoughtful as questions rushed through our minds, but our silence could not be contained for long. Soon the conversation we had had in the majlis was resumed again.

"I don't want to sound rude, but I have to tell you, there's a lot I can't understand about you Arabs and your society," said one of the Americans tentatively.

"And there's even more we don't understand about yours," replied one of the Arabs with a smile, "and the reason is that your society is far more complex than ours. Ours is a simple society - by comparison. In many ways we're more fortunate. We have certainties that you no longer have. We're not torn by internal conflict which brings so many evils and so much unhappiness."

"That's the inevitable penalty of progress, I suppose," said the American.

"But what do you mean by progress,?" said one of the other Arabs. "I understand progress as that which makes for a better society. But in the West progress is seen as nothing more than the increasing complexity of technology. The blind assumption is made that that equates with a better society. But we in the East have sufficient sense to know that that's not necessarily true. In Islam we turn to the core values of life, insisting that progress is to be found in them alone."

"But that doesn't mean to say we're opposed to the development of technology," interposed one of the other Arabs. "We only insist that the two should go in harness."

"The problem of the West is that it no longer has a guiding ethical system," continued his companion. "Religion has been corrupted by loss of faith and relativism, and so today it no longer has any practical value. But Islam is as strong and vibrant as it ever was. It guides us during every waking hour of the day. We still have certainties. We know the meaning of good and evil."

"But are those certainties necessarily correct,?" ventured the Swiss.

"Who dares question them,?" responded the Arab. "What other authority is there? How do you justify a system of ethics? Intellectual efforts have always fallen by the wayside in the attempt. That's why we turn to Islam and put all our trust in God and tradition."

"But tradition and God are not the same," said the Swiss. "If relativism is the Achilles heel of the West, then it could be argued that tradition is the vulnerable mark of the East."

"Let me say something concrete on that," began one of the Americans in a tone that was at once intense and tentative. "Let me give an example. Last Friday I did something that I hope I'll never do in my life again. Here in Riyadh, I saw a man beheaded in Deira Square. It was horrific! Now that was tradition."

"So, it was horrific,!" replied one of the Arabs. "It was meant to be horrific. It would only *not* be horrific to a mad or wicked person. A sense of horror is only human. That's why an execution is made a public occasion - because it is horrific."

"But isn't it a barbarity,?" said the Swiss.

"What? That it's public, or an execution?"

"Both."

The purpose of the law is to make an example. An example can only best be made by public punishment. Why make secret something that must be done? Is that not devious or hypocritical? If a judicial system is ashamed of making public its own authority, then why not abolish punishment too?"

"Punishment should always be public, since it expresses the vengeance of society on the offender," said one of the other Arabs. "That has always been the primary purpose of law in all societies. I know that. I'm studying law at the New Campus just down the road from here. Of course the law has other purposes also, such as deterrence and rehabilitation, but in the public consciousness, vengeance is its primary function."

"And nothing awakens the mind to the meaning of life and death so much as the sight of a public execution," said the first Arab. "It helps to purify the conscience. Ending the life of a man - or a woman is the ultimate act of the law. And as such, the authorities are morally obliged to make it a public event. It is an occasion when the law, and society, and the offender are fused into the common purpose of enacting God's holy writ. In that sense it approaches a religious ceremony."

"Can it ever be right to kill a man,?" said the Swiss.

"Can it ever be right to let a man live who kills another,?"

responded the law student. "In Islam we believe in the decree, 'an eye for an eye, tooth for tooth, hand for hand,' not simply because it is the command of God, but because in natural justice there's no better way in fulfilling the call for vengeance. Of course in practice blood money may be paid in compensating the injured party, but you can't take away the underlying right of 'an eye for an eye,' since it marks the degree of the injury and the price to be paid. But when it comes to murder, there's no price that can be paid in compensation. That's why the homicide must die."

"But with respect," said the Swiss, "you have laws and penalties which shock the Western world."

"And long may they do so," said the law student. "Our strict laws and horrific penalties are no argument for their disuse. They're merely a reflection of your own subjective feelings.   If you in the West concentrated your minds on the nature of the crimes to which they applied, then perhaps you could transfer your sense of horror from the penalties to their causes. Wouldn't that give a greater moral sense to the expression of your feelings?"

"I understand your argument but it's still difficult to accept," said the Swiss.

"You must understand," began one of the Americans, "that in the West, over the past hundred years, psychology and the social sciences have changed our entire perception of crime and punishment. Evil can always exists as a concept in the mind, but can its perpetrator, in reality, ever be designated an object of evil? Quite apart from those instances when a crime is committed through an act of insanity, for which the subject cannot be held responsible, every human being is nonetheless a helpless victim of circumstances. Through the determinism of events, and through a power which is both beyond understanding and control, men and women are made to serve as the transmitters of evil which originate from causes external to themselves."

"Exactly," said the law student, "and that's why you in the West have lost all your moral certainties. You no longer believe in human evil. And what are the consequences? Evil is finally explained away as something with no original cause. It evaporates - is just lost in the air. And that's because the social sciences, in which you falsely put so much trust, are not really 'sciences' after all. They're merely a confusion of conflicting theories on which no one can agree."

"And in a moral world you cannot destroy the foundations for belief in evil," interposed one of the other Arabs. "And if you succeed in doing so, you destroy morality itself. There is nothing left but nihilism. Such a society is doomed to self-destruction."

"That is why we in Islam believe in free will," said the law student. "And there was a time when you in your religion, too, believed in the power of free will."

"I believe the only truth to be found in free will is that, it may be said, that those with money and power have it in greater measure than those without," said the Swiss. "But even the rich and powerful are imposed upon by a consciousness which flies in the face of equity and justice."

"We believe in free will because we have to! There's no other basis for explaining the origin of evil - for identifying evil as it really is. Man through God, or the absence of God, alone is responsible for all his actions. He has to be! No excuses are valid. Do you understand?"

"I understand your argument and you've made me think," said the American. "You've left me unsure of what I really do believe."

"If you accept the fact of human evil, you can accept the justice and morality of all the horror of legal punishment," said the law student. "For us who believe in Islam, the Shariah law presents no problems."

"All societies are divided by their own belief systems," said one of the other Americans, "and we have to learn and appreciate the differences between us. What society is perfect? None! What society can claim a final moral authority in teaching another? None!"

"In answer to what's been said on both sides of the argument, I should only like to conclude by saying this," began one of the Americans who had not spoken before: "There are many faults in the legal systems of both West and East, and I believe it would be true to say that the penalties of the Shariah law arouse shock-horror throughout the world, but that that in itself is not relevant. What is relevant is the existence of a sufficiently informed and enlightened society able to effect desired changes and reforms of the law. Now, many and serious faults can be cited in the legal systems of the West, and yet such faults go unremarked upon and uncorrected. There is no excuse for that!

"But in the East, on the contrary, and in due respect to my Arab friends here, there exists neither the knowledge nor the consciousness in society to effect desirable changes in the legal system. Hence, no moral blame can be imputed to the peoples of the East for any tardiness that may be alleged in the reform of their laws. Therefore, we in the West are more blameworthy for the inadequacies of our law, than are the peoples of the East for any shortcomings in their very different systems. Really, none of us should throw stones at people who live in glass houses!"

* * *

After fetching my boarding pass from the airport, the following morning, for my flight out of Riyadh two days hence, I visited the Museum of Archaeology & Ethnography, situated in the Shumaisi district, on my way to Fahad's shop. On moving through the exhibition I was suddenly surprised by the realisation that all other visitors were women - albeit European women - and on returning again to the main entrance, I noted from a prominent sign that Wednesday mornings was reserved for "Women Only." I approached the clerk within the ticket kiosk on this apparent discrepancy.

"We thought no offence would be caused," explained the clerk defensively.

"But aren't you breaking the law,?" I teased.

"Most casual visitors are Westerners," said the clerk apologetically. "Of course, if there had been organised school parties of Muslim women, you wouldn't have been allowed in."

On being driven back to my hotel at lunchtime, I was struck by a curious example of assuaging the strong arm of the law that could hardly have been usefully recommended in any part of the Western world. During this rush hour period, at a busy junction controlled by traffic police, a motorist had aroused the furious ire of the controlling official as he stood in the centre of the junction. A car had advanced forward when it should have obeyed the command to stop in its tracks.

Now oncoming traffic from the diagonal streets would be blocked. The khaki-clad policeman waved his arms, shouting angrily. At once, the driver of the offending vehicle, left his car, ran up to the policeman with conciliatory gestures, and seizing his wrists which he held down at waist level, he kissed him on both cheeks. The policeman relented at this sudden gesture of affection. His anger was defused. He reciprocated by throwing his arms around the offending motorist, and after a mutual hug, the latter returned to his vehicle and drove off without the exchange of another word. Although I had often seen work colleagues in the Middle East embrace and kiss one another with warmth, this was the first occasion on which I saw such a salutation between apparent strangers.

Gradually I was winning over the confidence of Fahad Munof, and his attitude as the manager of the Badanahs' operation in Riyadh became more open in his willingness to explain the workings of the business. Early that evening he was keen to show me where the Badanah stock was stored, and so with Sulaiman in his Mercedes, the three of us drove to an old quarter of the town.

We arrived in front of an ancient two-storey building of sun-dried bricks in a narrow unpaved street. It had a yellow brown unrendered frontage, decorated with a V-shaped frieze on the upper facade in the traditional manner, and as a reminder of its exposure to the elements in an area rarely blessed with precipitation, a jug of water poured over the external wall, would erode the surface. We entered the building through a pair of huge timber double doors attractively carved. My interest was aroused by the ancient house, few of which still remained in a rapidly modernising city which had little respect for its historic past. It had clearly once been the residence of a prosperous family. Once inside the building I had the opportunity to explore the house in the company of Fahad and Sulaiman.

The house was built around a rectangular atrium, each of the spacious rooms having a door and frosted glass windows looking into the central enclosure. There was a cellar and a ground floor toilet built over a cesspit. The room of the toilet was large, approximately nine feet by ten, and the toilet itself was a vitreous enamel panel set into the floor with a hole and indentations to place the feet, so that one relieved the stool in a squatting posture. No windows looked out into the street, and the ceilings of the rooms were high, each with a large suspended fan. There was a staircase which led to the flat roof, surrounded by a high

five foot wall surmounted by parapets. This gave privacy to the
residents if they chose to sleep or spend their leisure hours in view of the
sky. Whilst on the roof, some boys called us from the back of the house
for the return of their lost football, which we threw down to the yard
where they played.

With pride, Fahad pointed out to me where our stock had been
carefully stored, intent on demonstrating that each of our lines had its
specific place, and was readily obtainable in replenishing the retail store
or in delivering supplies as a wholesaler to other outlets. Was
everything to my satisfaction?

"Tell him I think he's got everything in good order," I said to
Sulaiman.

Fahad nodded in agreement and satisfaction.

"Fahad says everything here is his own work," said Sulaiman
translating again.

This was Fahad's realm. The shop, the storage depot, Islam, and
the traditional life of Riyadh was Fahad's world, the extent and limit of
his experience and imagination. Nothing else had meaning or was
comprehensible to this man whose forebears had sprung from the
emptiness of the desert.

It was during my last day in the Royal Capital that I lunched with
Fahad Munof in his home before taking a late flight out of Riyadh. It
was an occasion I anticipated with interest and Sulaiman, who would be
with me, fetched me from the hotel. Sulaiman explained that Fahad had
recently moved into a new flat.

I felt apprehensive when we arrived in what appeared to be a slum
area of the old city, with windowless sun-brick dried houses, and dreary
walls looking down into dark lanes with broken pavements and
overflowing drains, and everywhere strewn with rubbish. We entered
one of these buildings and climbed to the second floor, and although the
staircase was clean, there was the dilapidated appearance of plaster
which had fallen from the wall. Sulaiman knocked on the door and
Fahad answered. He was informally dressed in a skirt and no head
covering. We left our shoes on the public landing (which seemed risky
but there was no other choice than to follow Sulaiman's example) and
we entered the flat, to be conducted into what was described as the

"Men's room."

This was a large recently decorated room of square proportions, the doors painted brown, the walls yellow, and a plain red wall-to-wall fitted carpet gave a spacious impression. There was no furniture in the room apart from a large Thai black lacquer cabinet against one of the walls, on which stood a TV set, a vase of plastic flowers, a brass Eiffel tower, and behind the glass of the cabinet was displayed a *dallah* and set of brass coffee cups.

Along the other three walls were numerous cushions for sitting on and leaning back against the hard surface. Occupying most of the wall opposite the cabinet was a huge printed illustration of the Great Mosque and Kaaba in Mecca - the holiest shrine of Islam. The two small frosted windows in the room were draped with material decorated with an Arabic motif.

Endeavouring to be a good host, Fahad bustled around looking for a suitable video for his English guest, and at last chose an American all-in wrestling film of unbridled sadism. As we sat engaged in polite conversation, Fahad became increasingly absorbed by the contests on the screen, laughing and commenting on their tactics, intent on my sharing in his perverted enjoyment. As a polite guest I had no alternative but to nod in assent to his gestures, and indeed, there was little else on which we could communicate intelligibly.

After a while, Sulaiman and I were conducted into an adjoining and similar room, where we were confronted by the most magnificent spread I had ever encountered in an Arab home. There were bowls of mutton and rice, Tabouleh (finely chopped tomatoes, parsley, shallots and cracked wheat with lemon dressing and mint), plates piled high with all kinds of vegetables and great quantities of watercress and lettuce, liver served in a special sauce, *haloum* (goat's milk cheese), and several kinds of bread. For dessert we had caramel pudding and red jelly, followed by fresh picked yellow dates (which I had never eaten before), apples and oranges. The meal was accompanied by great quantities of bottled fruit and water.

The video was transferred to a second TV set in the dining room, and as we enjoyed all the pleasures of the feast, we were entertained by the spiteful displays of physical force of Swede Hanson, the Incredible

Hulk, the Hangman, the Killer of Mississippi, and others. As we watched several fights without rules or referees, and one in which a contestant removed his leather belt and mercilessly beat his opponent, and another in which the pugilists placed metal braces on their fingers, so they drew a profusion of blood which ran down their bodies, I felt the three of us were like corrupted beings, sitting as Roman nobles with sated appetites in an amphitheatre dedicated to the cause of sadism.

By the end of the meal we had consumed only a quarter of what had been laid out on the dining cloth. We returned to the "men's room" where Fahad served green tea, and a little later, as was often customary, he brought in and swung to and fro a censer (identical with that to be found in any Catholic or High Anglican church) to purify the air. When the video was finished, he placed another in the machine - which unimaginably - was even more distasteful and sadistic than that before. We were now exposed to a display of small boys with gauntlets and metal studs punching and kicking, in a contest without rules, until their faces and bodies were bloodied in the struggle. This, surely, was no fight in any ordinary sense, but instead, a form of pornography far more perverse and corrupting than any erotic exhibition aimed at appealing to the natural feelings of a sexually well-balanced psyche.

What societal values were these that insisted on the covering of the limbs as objects arousing lascivious desire, yet raised no objection to the open depravity of sadistic entertainment? Was it that the call to *Jihad* (Holy War), so deeply ingrained in the consciousness of the Islamic mind, allowed no room for the censure of aggression in the guise of combat notwithstanding its nature or context; or was it that the multiple restrictions of a puritanical society were directed inevitably towards a psychological outlet which eventually was bound to corrupt?

124

CHAPTER 9
The Yemen adventure

"The sword of heaven is not in haste to smite,
Nor yet to linger."

Dante, *Paradiso*, Canto xxii, 1, 16 (Cary's tr.)

After twenty minutes the shower of stones ceased to fall on the condemned figure, which lay prostrate between the two bollards, arms suspended, rope still securing the wrists to the pommels atop the posts.

Two men, dressed in headscarves and skirts, untied the rope, so releasing the figure from the bollards. There was exhaustion in the crowd, and its tension and compactness relaxed, as those from behind pushed forward easily for a better view.

The men in skirts, who seemingly had been assigned a menial task, with expressions of disgust, seized the figure by each wrist, and with painful effort, dragged the lifeless and heavy meat on its back into the centre of the open crescent, leaving a spoor of blood from the bollards to the spot where they flung down the sickening load, and tripped quickly away from the object of their repugnance. Now the figure was in full and better view of the public gaze. The head and upper body was blood-bespattered and bruised with torn flesh, the glazed eyes faced skywards from their sockets, and the body was now identifiable as that belonging to a man of Negroid appearance.

"His head's in a mess," exclaimed an Aussie to a fellow countryman.

"He's really a gonner," came the awed response.

Jostled and sickened by the sight that confronted the crowd, as well as by the oppressive heat of the day, I momentarily felt a feverish spasm, seizing both body and limbs. The thought flashed through me: was I sickening for yet another illness which might paralyse my efforts in completing the assigned mission in the area? I recollected the illness I had contracted in North Yemen, a year or so before, and the hospitalisation to which it had eventually led in another Arabian territory in the Near East. I hoped that no such illness would re-occur, and comforted myself with the realisation that in that event in all probability it had been brought on by a mixture of coincidences: food poisoning, night time insect bites in the desert, the obligatory social act of chewing a foul narcotic, and the drama and hectic events following the exhaustion of business negotiations with the most awkward and unpredictable of prospective customers I was ever to encounter on the Arabian peninsula.

The Yemen was markedly different from anywhere else in the Middle East. It was situated in a mountainous region exposed to a monsoon climate, with a heavy winter rainfall, and a relatively dense population estimated at little short of 16 million. Whilst on the one hand it was enriched with agricultural land, much of it in terraced farming on mountain slopes, producing a wide variety of crops and tropical fruit; on the other, it was impoverished by lack of oil, and more notably by endemic conflict between the People's Democratic Republic of Yemen, in the south and the Republic of Yemen in the north - in addition to banditry and civil strife throughout the entire area. Furthermore, the country had the unenviable adult literacy rate of only 37.3%, as well as the biggest difference of literacy rates between the sexes of any country in the world.

Despite these setbacks, a company decision was nonetheless taken to attempt the penetration of the difficult market of North Yemen. Sana'a, the capital of the Republic, situated almost 7,000 feet above sea level, was not easily reached through the usual air routes. I made a circuitous journey via Amsterdam and Frankfurt, and at the latter stop we took on a bedraggled party of Yemeni deportees, dressed in their *futahs* (or skirts) and untidy headscarves, as they were escorted onto the plane by the German police.

The plane landed at Sana'a airport on a dark night, and as this was a first exploratory trip to the area, I had brought with me several training and marketing videos on our range of products. In arrangement with our prospective distributors, two evenings had already been booked at separate hotels for entertaining business leaders and demonstrating the benefits of our wares. During the baggage search, the videos were declared as tools of the trade, but it was explained that these would need to be examined by the Censors' Department of the Ministry of Information before they could be released. I was given a receipt for their safekeeping and eventual collection by my sponsor, so that in the event of query the responsibility would lie on his shoulders.

As we drove slowly through the dimly lit streets in the back of a taxi, together with my Tanzanian contact, Abdullah Tayeb, the General Manager of Wajeeh & Co., and his boss, Mohamed Nasher, a Sudanese, it was explained that imported videos were not only suspect as pornographic material but also as containing military material which could be of use to an "enemy." Abdullah Tayeb was a well-educated and friendly African of handsome appearance, but he was cautious and apprehensive in the face of every eventuality that confronted us. My explanation for this was that he too, like me, was a foreigner in a strange land. Mohamed Nasher was a corpulent man of few words, and since he was a Sudanese, he wore a skullcap and long white dishdash, which contrasted with the Western dress of his subordinate.

When the taxi was stopped at a military checkpoint, for passport inspection, shortly after leaving the airport, I never gave it a second thought, but when we were stopped on a subsequent occasion in a built-up area, and a bayoneted rifle was thrust through the open rear window, and I noted tank traps and barbed wire across an intersection of streets, I realised that this was reminiscent of crossing points into Eastern Europe. I was glanced at with suspicion by the soldier in his greatcoat and woollen cap, for the night air was cool, and Abdullah explained at length the reason for my being in the country. When we moved on again, I could not refrain from passing a curious remark.

"This country's still at war with the south," explained Abdullah. "And besides, the divisions are not clear cut. There are sympathisers for the opposite cause in both halves of the country. In addition to that, there are heavily armed bandits in the hills taking advantage of the breakdown of law and order."

The Taj Sheba Hotel in the city centre, staffed by Indian personnel, offered every facility and comfort, but this could not detract from an ever-present atmosphere of volatility, and this was not diminished the following morning when I was awoken at 7.0 am by a great shouting in unison of male voices from the street below. I suspected that revolutionaries may have already seized the streets, and were charging the hotel, possibly with the idea of massacring its inhabitants. I leapt from my bed, and standing by the window I was relieved to see that it looked onto a quad surrounded by barracks, and that a company of troops were receiving their early morning drill which included the recitation of patriotic slogans to the glory of the Republic. Every morning I was to be awoken in this fashion at the same hour.

That morning I made my own way to Wajeeh & Co., a fifteen-minute walk from the hotel. Wajeeh & Co. was a wholesale trading business, and their premises in the main street consisted of a modern office staffed by three persons, Abdullah Tayeb, Mohamed Nasher, and a very attractive dark-skinned Indian female secretary who was elegantly dressed in Western attire. Over the following days, the abrupt and distant manner in which she was treated by her employers - which would only have been interpreted as rudeness in the West - never failed to surprise me. Her presence as a womanly being seemed hardly to exist in the eyes of her employers. There was no veil or chador, as would have been compulsory in neighbouring Saudi Arabia, and her demure figure was exposed by a knee-length skirt and sleeveless top.

At around noon, when the office closed until early evening, the two men excused themselves, pulled out prayer mats from a cupboard, turned towards Mecca, and began their silent formalities of prayer, whilst the secretary and I descended the staircase and out into the bustling street. For some distance I followed her, as we went our separate ways, but I dared not break the strict Islamic taboo of speaking to her in a public place. She wore no marriage ring, and in the office, when she served tea or produced files for protracted discussions, our eyes never met. Her fashionable Western dress made her an anomaly in such an environment, and this was emphasised all the more by a distant manner and a certain self-consciousness and melancholy. I was curious about her background and domestic arrangements, but realised it would be improper to pry into these matters through my business associates who treated her so gruffly.

Abdullah Tayeb and Mohamed Nasher, who came from very different regions on the African Continent were not time wasters. Both had little time for small talk, or the kind of socialising usually regarded as vital in developing business relationships in the Middle East, and over the following days, I was to learn little about their personal lives. Both had been established in the Yemen for a number of years, and the Tanzanian who was responsible for receiving foreign visitors, soon revealed that he disdained certain aspects of Arab life.

The only fact I was to learn about Abdullah is that he had a wife and five children trapped in Aden - three boys and two girls. The girls' school had been bombed two weeks previously, and so temporarily their education had been cut short. I had this information on the day he received a letter from his wife, routed via Jeddah or Djibouti, for direct postal and telephonic communications no longer existed between the two halves of the country. He was trying to rescue his family from the isolated enclosure of Aden, but bemoaned that this was difficult.

During the meeting of that first morning, the three of us sat down and reviewed the problems of business with the Republic, and such was the length of our discussion, that we never even began to consider the qualities or prices of our product range. The Yemen was at once the most primitive and modern of states on the Arabian peninsula. Whilst on the one hand it had the poorest and most ill-educated population, on the other, it had begun seriously to develop a manufacturing base, and could boast several of the most modern milling and other plants in the world.

The idea of importing and selling our products direct to retail outlets could be dismissed from the start. Essential licences for raising the necessary currency would never be granted. We would need instead to target influential government officials in certain ministries to pull the right strings, and pave the way ahead for bringing our products into the country through desirable back-door channels. At this stage prices were irrelevant, and to discuss them would be a nonsense. This was partly because there were at least eight different exchange rates, and the right arrangements needed first to be identified before prices could be formulated. The end-buyers would need to be government ministries, hotels, or factories purchasing our products as essential requisites for their smooth operation.

"Do you have any government officials in mind,?" I asked tentatively.

"Yes, a very important official who's a friend of the President," answered Mohamed Nasher. "A Captain Juhani - a close friend of ours."

"He'll be coming to this office tonight to meet you," added Abdullah.

"Of course he'll need baksheesh in addition to commission payments," continued Mohamed, "and we don't really know what his requirements will be until we sit down and discuss them. You must understand that government officials control business in this country. All government employees are businessmen. That's because they're so poorly paid they couldn't live on their salaries alone."

"We'll just have to cross each bridge as we come to it," I merely commented. "But what about the collection of our videos from the Censors' Department?"

"Captain Juhani will fetch them from the Ministry. He's also our sponsor," assured Abdullah.

That evening at 7 o'clock I arrived at the office to be met by my two associates and a third person lounging on the spacious sofa between them. The three were in the midst of a lively discussion. The third person wore a *futah*, exposing his hairy legs, a *jambia* (or curved dagger) stuck in his belt, a soiled jacket, and a filthy brown headscarf. Cheerful greetings were exchanged, and a fourth glass of tea was placed by the secretary on the coffee table in front of us. The third person was introduced as Capt. Juhani, but what most surprised me was that such an unprepossessing individual should be identified as a high-ranking government official. He was at the same time lively but rolling from side to side as if in an inebriated condition, but his most marked characteristics were watery bloodshot eyes and what first appeared as a bulging tumour which had grown within his cheek.

It was only when he interrupted his conversation with silent chewing that I realised his mouth was filled with a thick green mushy substance. This was the first time I encountered *qat* - the amphetamine or narcotic curse of the Yemen - a substance and habit forbidden throughout the rest of Arabia. In his lap, loosely packed in newspaper in maize leaves, lay a green bundle of covered twigs, and every few minutes he would pluck one or several small leaves, and deftly throw them into his mouth to be added to the cud of the messy vegetation.

Capt. Juhani wanted to be helpful. Our range of products ideally suited the needs of his country - that was clear! However, he would need a 12% share of the landed cost of our products before he could authorise the importation of our products or before they were released to Wajeeh & Co. This was necessary since not only did he have to smooth the palms of the port officials, but he had to pay the established back-handers to the licensing authorities in raising the hard currency. All this was established custom. To facilitate this our FOB prices needed to be raised by at least 70%, and a printed price list should be produced in proving to the authorities that such prices were universal or standard. I assured him that my company had no objection to producing any prices he required, since we already had twelve levels of standard FOB prices in suiting different situations throughout the world, but I expressed reservations with regard to endorsed invoice declarations certifying the basis of such prices.

After three hours Capt. Juhani suggested we should adjourn and continue our discussions in the greater comfort of my hotel. Mohamed and Abdullah exchanged a sceptical glance at this suggestion, but I interrupted their response by assenting to the idea - not knowing what would follow. Capt. Juhani drove us to the Taj Sheba in his 4-wheel drive landrover, and soon after as we were seated in the lobby of the hotel, a heated exchange took place between Capt. Juhani and the Indian waiter. Soft drinks - and only these appeared on the menu - was not an option as far as Capt. Juhani was concerned. A bottle of Whiskey and four glasses were called for. The explanation of the waiter was unacceptable. Mohamed and Abdullah maintained a stony silence. The head waiter was called over. He explained that the supply of alcohol was illegal and that anyway they had none.

After he had moved away, Capt. Juhani whispered that we should move to my room. In the private rooms anything was allowed if your purse was right. Now it was my turn to cast an apprehensive glance at my associates. Abdullah began to raise objections, but Capt. Juhani rose from the deep recesses of his armchair, and waving him aside, said we should complete the groundwork for our negotiations that night. I agreed and led the way to my room. Room service was called and the same problem encountered as in the lobby. Capt. Juhani wanted to see the hotel manager, but the latter merely repeated that the hotel was unlicensed although reputedly the first hotel in the city.

By this time Capt. Juhani was both depressed and irritable, and began to express doubts as to the viability of our business proposition. At last Mohamed rose from his chair, reassuringly patted the captain across the shoulder, and took two bundles of 5-riyal notes out of his deep dishdash pocket - well over £100. He knew a place nearby where Whiskey could be obtained. Juhani at once put on a brighter expression and he and Mohamed left for the secret destination to obtain the forbidden bottle.

As soon as the couple had left I turned with a stern expression to Abdullah, exclaiming, "I don't think I like the idea of his drinking alcohol in my room."

"Don't worry - that's quite out of the question," returned Abdullah reassuringly. "His mind's already blowed on *qat*. If he gets hold of a bottle of Whiskey, he'll drink it, wreck your room and drop dead drunk until morning."

It was decided we should eat in the restaurant. Mohamed returned alone two hours later.

"Where's Juhani,?" asked Abdullah.

"He's a happy man," returned Mohamed. "He's got the Whiskey and now he's consuming it in his car. Soon he'll be unconscious. I'll drive him back to his residence as soon as we've finished our meal."

* * *

The following morning when I met Capt. Juhani and my two associates at Wajeeh & Co. I was relieved to see that he had made a complete recovery from the night before. I was also pleased to see him in a fresh attire. Gone was the *futah* and dirty headscarf, and instead he was dressed in the military uniform of his officer's rank. Instead of the *jambia* he carried an automatic in his belt. I was concerned about our videos. They were still with the Censors' Department. I reminded Capt. Juhani that they would be needed that night for the reception at the Sheraton. He assured me he would be on time and that the evening would be a success.

The four of us drove around the city, calling on various ministries, and meeting officials who would arrange the distribution and use of our product range. Capt. Juhani was a fast driver, well-known and respected throughout the city. At every traffic police junction, and at every sentry box before the ministries and patrol posts, we were saluted and waved through. Even at red traffic lights, the police halted oncoming vehicles to give us right of way, and the captain blew the horn of his landrover in alerting our approach.

Shortly before noon elderly women appeared in the streets carrying baskets piled high with paper bundles. Capt. Juhani wound down his window and bought his daily ration.

"The gold of Yemen," whispered Abdullah with a nudge and a nodding wink. "The *qat* farmers are the new millionaires. This country used to be famous for plantations of Mocha coffee. Those days are gone. The *qat* plant is a much better cash crop. The leaves must be plucked daily and chewed fresh, and so with their high price, there's a constant and high cash flow for the industry."

On another occasion Abdullah explained the social significance of *qat* chewing as a leisure activity amongst most circles of men, and the ostracism of those Yemenis who refrained from the habit. Several years earlier a former President of North Yemen had questioned the desirability of the drug habit and suggested the possibility of its prohibition. Within a week of his presidency he was shot dead. Was this the only country which chewed *qat,*? I asked. No, in Tanzania and Kenya, it was also a widespread habit.

A magnificent buffet was laid out on side tables in a reception room of the Sheraton Hotel that evening, and about fifty businessmen, half of them Europeans, filled up the rows of chairs before a flipchart and lectern. The time came for the function to begin, but Capt. Juhani had not arrived with the videos. The minutes passed by and I introduced myself individually to the guests. At last, after three quarters of an hour, I felt obliged to make an apology. I was surprised by the equanimity of the guests in such a situation, but a French manufacturer sitting in the front row smilingly explained that such muddle and non-compliance with arrangements was not unusual in the country. I decided to give a verbal presentation of our products, and after another three quarters of an hour, the guests were invited to take refreshments.

Two and a half hours after the scheduled time, Capt. Juhani cheerfully arrived with bleary eyes, carrying a small bag. He had three instead of five videos and the identifying labels had been torn from all. On beginning to play the videos we discovered that only one was ours. One was a demonstration for Michelin tyres, and another which was almost pornographic, and caused great amusement, demonstrating the value of a firemen's frame for catching people leaping from burning buildings, showed an attractive girl jumping from a window, the fall blowing her dress beneath her shoulders. Capt. Juhani was neither put-out nor apologetic over this confusion in bringing the wrong films to the meeting.

The following day we toured factories in the area, and that night an order was drawn up for a £10,000 order. However, such an order was purely theoretical. It could not be acted upon until a licence had been issued and the actual hard currency made ready by the bank. Now came the task of oiling the palms of a hierarchy of government and bank officials. When I made a reference to the existence of corrupt practices, Abdullah stopped me short by saying that corruption in the Yemen was nothing by comparison with that in his own country, and that he far preferred the business practices in Yemen compared to those in Africa. All was relative!

My second presentation was arranged for the following day at the Taj Sheba Hotel. Would the four other videos be supplied in time? Capt. Juhani never came to the function and the remaining videos were never found. They were permanently mislaid somewhere within the storage area of the Ministry of Information.

But Capt. Juhani had another project in mind in furthering our business plan. It was suggested that Abdullah and I should accompany him on a trip by road, to the Red Sea port of Hodeidah, and that his boss, Col. Wazir, should join the merry party. Abdullah momentarily drew back at the suggestion, but then it was realised we could not very well decline the invitation. This would be a combined social and business event. I hesitantly accepted the proposal, but reminded Abdullah that I had to be back in Sana'a in time to take the once weekly flight out of Yemen to Abu Dhabi where I had important commitments. Capt. Juhani assured me that that was no problem. We would be away for one night. Abdullah confided that he would have preferred to take a flight as the mountain road to Hodeidah was infested with bandits who descended from the hills and attacked travellers with no consideration for life.

We left at noon in the 4-wheel drive, and Capt. Juhani and Col. Wazir were in high spirits, having just purchased four packets of *qat* that they laid out on the front seat between them. Abdullah and I sat sullenly in the back. Juhani handed a packet to Abdullah, which he reluctantly accepted, and several twigs with leaves for me to "try." I chewed two or three leaves only, with no side effects, but found the substance disgusting. My only embarrassment was that out of politeness I was obliged to retain the mushy vegetation in my cheek until after arriving at the hotel in Hodeidah before spitting it out into the toilet.

Shortly after leaving Sana'a we were stopped at a checkpoint, but waved through as soon as the uniforms of the two officers were recognised, and we passed many other armed patrols before reaching our destination. At first the journey took us higher into the mountains, along precipitous ravines and hairpin bends, and through ancient villages and small towns displaying such incongruous hoardings proclaiming, "Rothmans," "Canada Dry," and "Sinalco." The scenery was dramatic as we drove above terraced farmsteads descending into deep valleys, and approached ageless apartment blocks, five, seven and even ten stories high carved out of the naked rock, their windows dark and uncharacterised by any sign of human life. Did these originate from the time of the Queen of Sheba, I asked myself, and the great civilisation which marked this region three thousand years ago?

The hours went by and the sun began to set, and after driving through the Haima pass, there was a heavy rainstorm, and we descended alongside a gushing river and waterfall, and then we passed by banana plantations, coconut trees, and fields with many fruits and vegetables. Eventually we descended into the heat of the Tihama coastal plain, and into an environment quite different from the mountainous region of the north east. Here there were straying camels, rich agricultural land, and conical straw houses reminiscent of those in Africa. At 7.30 pm, after seven hours, we arrived in Hodeidah.

I was booked into the Ambassador Hotel - supposedly the best hostelry in Hodeidah - a dark, dank, foul-smelling place with green walls and lavatory style white tiles, and a black concrete floor. The others booked into the cheaper Bristol Hotel, some distance away. I had no window in my room, since there was no outside wall, but a noisy box unit air conditioner for ventilation, and a forty watt bulb hung from the ceiling as the only source of light. I threw myself onto the metal framed bed and slept until the arrival of my business associates at 10.0 pm when we ate together in the third rate restaurant, but my appetite was broken by the ubiquitous smell of broken drains.

The following day was marked by conflicting decisions, confusion, frustration, and finally, the most uncomfortable journey I was ever to take in my life. The morning passed smoothly enough when in the company of the two military officers, Abdullah and I toured the ultra-modern Italian built plant of the Hodeidah Red Sea Flour Mills Co., several miles outside the city, at the end of which we succeeded in doubling our theoretical order to £20,000. By midday, because of time pressure, it was decided to spend another night in the port town, and to be nearer my associates, I moved into a room in the Bristol Hotel, which was worse even than the room I had just vacated. There was exposed electrical wiring, a toilet without a seat, brown water gurgling from the taps, an air conditioner which failed to work and threadbare carpets.

Abdullah and I dined together in an otherwise empty restaurant apart from screeching cats fighting over tit bits of food left on plates carelessly piled up on a sideboard. It was arranged that that afternoon the two military gentlemen would drive us around the town and point out the sights - but meanwhile, they had disappeared. Abdullah seemed depressed. Our food was served, and the minute steak I had ordered broke up beneath my fork, as if already rotten, although inside it was raw. The chips and rice, as well as the meat, was cold, but in such a place with the affable but uncomprehending young Indian waiter, who had earlier misunderstood several of our instructions, there seemed little point in complaining. Only a glass of beer could assist the appetite.

"I don't expect we'll be seeing Juhani and Wazir for some time," remarked Abdullah breaking the gloomy silence. "I guess they've gone off to chew *qat*."

"Do you really think so,?" I replied naively.

Shortly after the meal, both head and stomach were aching. I decided to exercise by walking in the town rather than lying prostrate on the bed. The heat was intense, and the streets empty, and all windows of the low-built houses heavily shuttered as I strolled towards the coast in the hope for a refreshing sea breeze. The only signs of life were several packs of miserable dogs, their tails between their legs, trotting from one rubbish heap to another in search of food, and the occasional goat tearing apart and chewing discarded cartons. I strolled a mile or so along the empty beach, and saw an Indian family fully clothed bathing in the sea, before returning to the hotel.

Abdullah was in a tizzy when I approached him in the hotel lobby. Juhani and Wazir were nowhere to be found. It was assumed they had gone off to a *qat* party, and there was no knowing when they would return or be in a sober frame of mind to make sensible decisions. Abdullah suggested we should fly back to Sana'a that night - not bothering to wait for the other two. Early that evening we strolled through the crowded streets to the travel office, passed many beggars and those crippled with rickets and leprosy - some with limbs and faces hideously eaten away. It was the only occasion I encountered lepers on the Arabian peninsula.

At the travel office we learnt that the first flight out of Hodeidah was not until 9.15 the following morning. This was not satisfactory! Because of my stomach pains and general sickness I was now more determined than Abdullah to return early to Sana'a.

"Then let's take a taxi," I exclaimed, not knowing the adventure this would lead us into. We returned to the hotel, and I drank strong tea without milk or sugar, and I was doubled up in pain. Abdullah went to the reception to enquire about taxis to the capital.

"We have to go to the Sana'a taxi rank in the town centre," he explained on return. "Only specially licensed taxis are allowed to make the journey, and they have to leave from that one centre where they issue the authorisation papers."

The thought of an additional journey added to my feeling of exhaustion. Abdullah could speak but not write Arabic, and so he dictated a note to the concierge to be left for Juhani and Wazir. Fifteen minutes later we piled our luggage into the back of a taxi for the short journey to the terminus. The Sana'a taxi rank was situated in a large open noisy space amongst hundreds of parked cars and crowds of pedlars moving to and fro in selling their wares. No sooner had we stopped at the rank - and before we had given any instructions - a taxi assistant had seized our luggage and thrown it into the back of a muddy Peugeot already packed with passengers.

"I'm not travelling in that," I cried instinctively, pointing to the decrepit looking vehicle.

"Come on, climb in," responded Abdullah pushing me towards an open door.

"There's no room," I protested as I squeezed in making room for my business associate.

The taxi assistant closed the door behind us. Eight passengers were squeezed into the large vehicle, and I was squashed between a chain-smoking Yemeni and Abdullah. As our luggage was already packed in the back of the vehicle there was little point in further protest. Two hags at once thrust their arms through the open windows, demanding money with open palms. The young Yemeni men, who comprised the passengers, sat quietly, but two responded by giving alms, which seemed to incense the beggars to demand contributions from those others sitting trapped. Several pedlars appeared, one offering soft toys, another perfume, and yet another watches - a dozen strapped onto his forearm, but amongst the noise and confusion, the passengers remained tight-lipped and silent.

At last an official appeared, demanding passports and identity papers, in preparing documentation for the journey. At first a register needed to be drawn up, with full names and addresses, and then authorisation papers had to be issued for each individual. This completed, the taxi driver climbed into the car and asked for his fares. The passengers, who up to this point had maintained a discreet silence, broke out into argumentative pandemonium. This lasted for several minutes, and when agreement was reached, there was a noisy exchange of notes until all was settled.

"It's still a fraction of the air fare," whispered Abdullah by way of consolation.

The moment came for departure. The driver turned on the ignition but nothing happened. He made several more attempts but still to no avail. My feelings were of exasperation, but the Yemenis remained silent as if unconcerned by the delay. The driver stuck his head out of the window and shouted desperately towards the rear. Several taxi officials, pedlars, and even the old hags, pushed the vehicle forward. The engine spluttered but still it would not start. Shouts of encouragement and heaving and puffing came from behind the car. Now we were accelerating, but it was all human power that drove us forward, until suddenly the engine spluttered into life, and as a cloud of exhaust fumes rose behind us, we heard a distant cheer.

After some miles we stopped at a military post, and after the inspection was over, again the car was stalled. Without further ado, we jumped out of the vehicle and push started the car before the driver had time to request assistance.

"We'll never get to Sana'a at this rate," I exclaimed to Abdullah as I helped to push the great weight forward.

Several more miles were behind us, and then to my surprise, we turned off the road for re-fuelling. Surely he could have done this before, I thought to myself. But worse was to follow. We stopped by the petrol pump but the engine was kept running. The driver was fearful of it cutting out yet again, and if any further risks were involved, then such was the will of God! My alarm was raised further when as fuel was pumped into the vehicle, a young man sitting at the back, adjacent to the petrol cap, lowered the window flicking hot ash from his cigarette. What insanity was this,? I thought, but protest was impossible, or coming from a foreigner would be interpreted as insolence.

Abdullah explained the following day, that several years previously a law had been passed forbidding the construction of new petrol garages anywhere in town centres or built up urban areas. This was following a number of forecourt explosions due to the carelessness of smokers. The authorities had therefore drawn the conclusion that it was easier to amend building regulations than to prohibit an undesirable habit even when it presented a major fire hazard to life and property. This was a case of defending "liberty" or "personal rights" whilst remaining blind to a far greater evil.

As we were about to drive off after being detained at the next checkpoint, a flat tyre was noticed on the rear offside wheel. Another fifteen minute delay! As we stood around the stranded vehicle no one thought it worthwhile to complain, or even to remark on the unlucky coincidence of yet another breakdown.

The driver was now determined to make up for lost time, and we drove at great speed across the Tihama plain towards the mountain range which lay ahead, but after some thirty miles, the engine spluttered ominously and came to a halt. We were fortunate to have broken down in the high street of a small town, but unfortunate in that we had encountered a major fault and so a protracted delay. The bonnet was raised and there was much fiddling with pieces of wire to affect a satisfactory repair. After fifteen minutes we all left the vehicle and sat down on the sandy road. My stomach pains were now acute and my mouth parched, and there were flies and insects in the heat.

I complained to Abdullah about the impossibility of the journey, suggesting we should hail another taxi or hitch a lift from one of the numerous trucks passing by. Abdullah replied that our paperwork only allowed us to travel in this taxi with its particular number plate. If we changed vehicles we risked arrest as suspect bandits.

"I'm prepared to take that risk," I responded.

It was hard not to admire the Eastern equanimity of the other passengers. They sat uncomplainingly on their haunches in the sand, with passive expressions, as if nothing untoward had occurred. But neither did they seek to advise or assist the driver, apart from one individual who had pretensions to mechanical expertise. In the West, by contrast, there would have been much excitement, recriminations, threats to sue, and advice from all directions as to how the driver should solve the problem of getting his passengers to their destination. But here in the East all was "inshallah" - all up to the will of an ever-merciful God.

After an hour's delay I wandered a hundred yards along the street looking for a stall that might sell bottled drinking water to satisfy my thirst and ease my aching stomach. As I left the shop I saw the car slowly moving forward. I ran ahead. The car turned to pick me up, and minutes later, we were again speeding forward towards the mountain range. There was silence in the car as we rose zigzagging in the hills. None dared speak for fear that a false word or an accidental expression of optimism might prove the nemesis to yet another breakdown.

During the following hours we were stopped at a number of checkpoints. The Yemenis were body-searched for handguns but I was always the object for greater suspicion. My luggage was searched whilst theirs was not, and on one occasion my passport was taken away to the guard room for a tense ten minutes. When the soldiers returned, I was told that the Captain wished to see me. Abdullah accompanied me to a small concrete hut illuminated by a flourescent light, so that if necessary, he might act as interpreter. A small man dressed in a *futah* and grey headscarf, a *jambia* stuck in his belt, was reclining on a rug and a pile of cushions. He was surrounded by several companions resting on their haunches, and as he chewed *qat* and glanced at me through his bleary eyes, he questioned me as to why I was in the country and the purpose of my present journey. After several minutes, his curiosity satisfied, he dismissed me with a friendly gesture.

As we rose higher in the mountains, close to Sana'a, it became intensely cold, for there was no heating in the car. At the military posts the soldiers were dressed in heavy greatcoats and balaclavas, swinging their arms around their bodies for warmth, as they stood by the roadside, their bayoneted rifles slung around their shoulders. At last we turned a bend, and far below, over a wide plain, we saw an array of many lights stretching to the distance. Sana'a was in view!

I felt less physical discomfort during the following two days but it was a temporary respite from a developing malady. On the day following my return to Sana'a I arose at 4.30 am to catch the 7.30 am weekly flight to Abu Dhabi, via the diversionary route of Kuwait, not reaching my destination until 2.0 in the afternoon. By then I had a fever that I dismissed as a heavy cold. Two days later I was in Dubai, and despite the intense heat, I was obliged to wear pyjamas in addition to winter underwear to ward off the "cold temperature." I dosed myself with paracetemol, was unable to eat solids, and experienced more comfort in the bright sunshine than in the cool of my room.

The stomach pains returned, and despite plentiful bowls of soup and black tea, there was no sign of recovery. On the flight to Amman, I was doubled up in pain, and no medicines offered by the stewardesses seemed to ease my predicament. On the taxi journey from the airport we had to stop by the roadside where I was violently sick. I was surprised by the humanity and sympathetic attitude of the Jordanian driver in the face of such an unpleasant interruption to a busy day, for he showed no impatience or irritation at having to carry a sick passenger.

At the hotel I collapsed onto the bed, and in my exhaustion, was willing to faint away and die within the next few hours. The telephone rang, and my prospective business partner, a Palestinian whom I had never met before, was on the other end of the line. I had just enough strength to explain that I was ill and unfit to meet him.

"Stay there and I'll fetch you," he responded with concern. "I'm taking you to the best doctor in Jordan!"

Half an hour later I checked out of the Intercontinental, and Ibrahim Rasheed drove me to the Queen Alia Hospital on the outskirts of the city. On arrival the eminent doctor was ready to receive me, and I was examined and blood tests taken. Malaria was suspected, but fortunately it was a less malignant virus, and I was put on a drip feed in a private ward. The following morning my malaria tablets were confiscated, not merely because they were unnecessary in the region, but because blood tests had shown that in present circumstances they were destroying my white blood corpuscles.

Over the following days, in the peaceful environment of the new hospital managed on American lines with its international staff, I gradually recovered. As I lay in bed and looked out of the window, I was presented with a strangely Biblical scene: rugged hills with flocks of sheep accompanied by their shepherds - a scene which might not have changed in any detail in two thousand years. Due partly to a relaxing environment, and also possibly, due to my drugged condition, I was inspired to write two poems recording impressions of the Yemen: one describing Hodeidah and the onset of illness, and the other a narration of the journey to Sana'a.

On leaving the hospital a week later, I was told I was the first European patient since the formal opening three months earlier by King Hussein, and I was happy to fulfil the request on returning home of sending a testimonial and personal letter of thanks.

CHAPTER 10
Uncertain of the future

"But in their deaths remember they are men;
Strain not the laws to make their tortures grievous."

Joseph Addison, *Cato*, Act iii, Sc. 5.

A white-coated figure emerged from the crowd and crouched down beside what seemed the blood bespattered corpse. First he felt the pulse. Then he took out a stethoscope from his pocket, and carried out an examination which seemed to last an age. At last he rose to his feet, walked over to the man in the brown thobe, and whispered a confidential instruction.

With reluctant steps and bowed head, kicking the dust before his feet, the man in the brown thobe strolled slowly to the pile of stones, and moving the rocks from side to side in searching for a suitable object, to the horrified gasp of the multitude, he lifted a jagged and heavy rock. Returning to the prostrate figure, he lifted his right arm and hurled down the missile. A spasm shook the prostrate figure and a sound like that of a butcher's cleaver hewing through meat and bone resounded throughout the square, as the executioner turned on his heel, daring not to glance at the outcome of his ghastly handiwork.

Again the doctor approached and crouched down beside the figure, feeling the pulse before using his stethoscope for any sign of heartbeat. Again he approached the executioner. For a second time the latter strolled lazily over to the pile of stones, and to the accompaniment of a sound from the crowd which seemed to exclaim with a single voice, "Oh, no,!" he took up a second rock which he again hurled down onto the skull of the condemned man. For a third time the doctor carried out his meticulous examination.

At last he nodded to the ambulance. Two paramedics pulled out the single stretcher from the hearse-like vehicle, and carried it over to the battered corpse. Four men lifted the body and dropped it unceremoniously onto the stretcher, then carried their heavy load to the ambulance that was loaded with its grisly cargo. The two paramedics climbed into the front seats of the vehicle, and with siren blaring, the ambulance drove off to the morgue or place of burial for the final disposal of the corpse.

As the speeding vehicle left the crowded expanse of Deira Square, so ended another episode in the Kingdom which had begun with a crime and concluded with the punishment of its perpetrator. Such an occasion, and such a death in the sight of thousands, could not but concentrate the mind of the beholder. This was a crime-free society - or relatively so - for that was its reputation amongst residents and visitors alike. Certainly its streets were safe from robbery and violence - surely a gain to be acknowledged in any community in our modern age of worldwide social unrest and rising crime.

But perhaps there were other crimes and other vices, lurking in dark corners, which possibly might cast a more disturbing shadow over the orderly and harmonious reputation of this desert land. It might be argued that the frequency of capital punishment in itself contradicted the assumption of a society relatively free of crime; or it might be contended that these exhibitions of punishment were a necessary and effective deterrent to crime; or again, that the severity of punishment was so extreme that it exaggerated the nature of the crimes committed. Where lay the truth or the proper balance for such varied arguments?

If prosperity relieves the pressures on society, in leading to the diminution of crime, then the Arabs of the peninsula are indeed a fortunate people. By comparison with the West, the restrictions of their society might seem oppressive, but such restrictions were traditional, imposed from within the religious culture and adhered to by all. Their strict living had not proved a bar to their prosperity as either the accumulators of wealth or as lavish spenders. It was, besides, a society of easy wealth. The Gulf Arab was a rentier who lived on the profits of land, urban construction, and the business enterprise of a huge expatriate population.

Few people in history had had lesser need for the advantages of a welfare state, yet the Gulf Arab not only enjoyed such benefits but special arrangements, which in certain circumstances, would honour his debts. He may have harboured fears about the distant prospect of the exhaustion of oil resources, and the political implications of a remaining expat population in the event of that - but those were thoughts for the future. Meanwhile, that expat population, too, enjoyed good earnings and material prosperity, and so there may have been no society with a lesser reason to sink into crime.

The Westerner might interpret the Arab's own explanation for his good fortune as a convenient dissimulation. The Arab was loathed to account the derivation of his wealth to the purchasing power of an advanced and alien technological civilisation, and although he acknowledged the world's dependence on oil - for how could he do otherwise? - he took little pride and wanted no credit for the revolutionary social changes effected by the gold beneath his desert sands. The Arab chose to stand aside with cold indifference - unawed by the upheavals, be they good or bad, of the 20th or 21st centuries. He had his own explanation for his prosperity and good fortune, regarding it with the equanimity of inevitable fate. His good fortune was the gift of God alone!

This endowed him with a complacency pervading his conception of the world, and it was a complacency with little basis in morality. Is the gift of good fortune, or wealth, to be necessarily seen as reflecting the deserving or moral good of its recipient? Such was certainly the belief of primitive humanity in the age of magic; as it was later the basis of primitive morality in early religion; and later still, with belief in predestination, it was the foundation for both Calvinist morality and the Protestant work ethic.

But good luck or serendipity is always the outcome of accident, and because of this, surely no moral cause should be attributed to an occurrence that has no more virtue than the luck of the lottery. Surely a moral good can only spring from the intended initiation of its cause. Good acts reflecting on their doers may only be achieved through good intentions also. In a world seeking to be rational in freeing itself from falsehood, superstition and hypocrisy, there can surely be no other acceptable approach in explaining deserving or undeserving fortune.

Such a passive view of humanity that accounts deserving fortune as either granted or withheld according to chance or the predestined will of a deity leads to an indolent perspective of the world and to idle attitudes.

It is a view, however, which accords with the traditional culture of the Arab, mercilessly exposed as he was in the past, to the infinite space and changing conditions of the desert, not knowing the replenished state of the approaching well nor the occasion for his next feast. He knew that his dependence lay with God alone!

For occupation he knew none but trading and driving camels. He may have been a hard bargainer, skilled and cunning in his struggle for survival, but buying and selling set the limits of his experience in the practical world. This ideal was a passive life: to sit behind a table and wait for passing custom - and trust in fate to the outcome.

Meanwhile, the outside world had formed a harder carapace in all its aspects. Confronting the desert may have borne its tribulations, but confronting the seething mass of humanity in the face of diminishing resources was harder still. Passivity and mere trust in God was no path to survival, as the world had already learned. A pro-active attitude, and the positive exertion of the will, was now a necessity for all. Hard work, the achievement of skills, and higher education, these were the aims of peoples, not only in the West, but in the Indian subcontinent, the Far East, and everywhere afflicted by population pressures.

Consequently, over past decades, millions had made their way to the Arabian peninsula to accumulate earnings for the betterment of families at home. Through changing demographic conditions, and an irreversible and inevitable process, there was emerging in Arabia a society divided by conflicting moral attitudes: there was the expatriate attitude that individual effort and skills should form the basis for life's rewards; and there was the attitude of the locals that rentier activity was in itself a sufficient justification for wealth and income.

These attitudes were crystallising in the awareness of growing uncertainties in the future, and were not diminished by the changing educational patterns and broader occupational activities of the Arab population. The one consolation to be discerned in this threatening situation was that both Arabs and expatriates were dependent on one another in equal degree. This alone could ensure the continuation of mutual partnership in preventing the open expression of clashing views.

It was evident, due to circumstances for which none were to blame, that many lived easy even undeserving lives, free from the burdens of work; whilst others, hardworking and deserving, lived under the shadow of an uncertain future. It is unnecessary - if not immoral - to affix blame to misfortune or good to good fortune. No occurrence need necessarily be explained in terms of justice or injustice. It need only be noted that injustice is in itself inequity - irrespective of circumstances.

With these thoughts in mind I recollected Denny Mohen and his family, and in a small way, by a logical train of events, I had in some way been made responsible for further undermining his vulnerable situation. Denny Mohen was the General Manager of our agents in Bahrain. He was a university educated Indian from the southern state of Kerala, with a subtle sense of humour and a generous understanding of the wider world.

But he was hindered in belonging to a category, not infrequently met with amongst his race, who are so intent on pleasing, that they dare not express an opinion without the assurance of its immediate acceptance. In preliminary conversation he was therefore tentative in proffering facts or suggestions that might possibly be contradicted, and in the event of inconsistency, and in an attempt to please, he was not afraid of immediately reversing a previous statement - however absurd the impression created. This brought difficulties in business discussions in eliciting both the truth of a situation or his opinion as to a line of action to be taken.

Consequently, it was necessary to feign a self-effacing attitude, talk in indirect terms, and express uncertainty at every step, in wheedling out his real thoughts. He could either act in authority, as over his manservant (misleadingly described as a "clerk"), or as a subordinate, but he could not act comfortably as an equal. He chose to regard me as someone in authority, and this at once raised difficulties in communication in cementing a successful business relationship, since on first arriving in Bahrain, I was ignorant of the detailed marketing situation and dependent on a guidance which was lacking. In addition, he adopted an unnecessary secrecy about the management of the business as if safeguarding a realm exclusively his own. At a later period, when I better understood his difficulties, I was to see his diffidence in a different light.

All these difficulties, it is only fair to add, might have been accountable to the particular nature of the old-established firm for which he worked. Bowes-Davison (as we shall call the company) was one of the few remaining traditional British confirming houses, managed on the old imperial model still extant in the Gulf. It had been established in Bahrain for well over a century, having settled in the wake of benevolent British influence. Bowes-Davison was a shadow of its former self, having contracted with the retreat of British commercial power.

It had long since disposed of its European staff, and had resorted to the employment of cheaper more malleable labour from the Indian subcontinent. The firm was managed from a cubby-hole situated in one of the older office blocks in the City of London, and its avuncular and ageing director would pay an annual visit to the emirate and other branches in the Far East, "pat his staff on the head" in thanking them for "holding the fort" for yet another year, before returning again to the safety of his London office. The style of the firm was slow and relaxed yet rigid and authoritarian, with all the consequences that might be expected from such a mode of management.

Denny Mohen sought to fulfil the role of the ideal executive as expected of him by his employer, and in succeeding in this, he entered into a partnership contributing to the irreversible decline of the confirming house.

There was a symbiotic relationship between the employer and his subordinate, and it was difficult to discern as to which of the two was the more dependent on the other. It was the type of relationship, which in a former age, had once been characteristic and universal between Empire builder and helper in the Indian subcontinent. But now it was a relationship that could only end in unfortunate circumstances.

Such a respected and old-fashioned firm, with its comfortable and gentlemanly mode of management, sat comfortably - for the moment - in the Emirate of Bahrain, for if it had found itself in Dubai, for example, it would have folded quickly in the face of tougher competition. But Bahrain was a gentler place. It was usually the first choice for residence of European expatriates obliged to work in the Gulf. It had become a British protectorate five years after the fall of Napoleon, and following a series of agreements with the ruling sheikhs, support and protection was offered in exchange for outlawing local wars, piracy and slavery.

Furthermore, during the 19th century, the imperial power had intervened on several occasions in defeating attempts to assert dominion over the islands by the Sultan of Oman, Turkey, Persia, Egypt, and perhaps most significantly, the Wahabis of neighbouring Arabia. The ruling princes of Bahrain were Sunnis (little influenced by the extreme puritanism of the Wahabi sect) but the majority population was Shiite, and this was a contributory fact to tension with Iran - the latter country having held the territory for almost two hundred years until the close of the 18th century.

The Arabs of Bahrain were accounted by European expatriates as "friendlier" and "nicer," and more understanding of Western ways, than their counterparts elsewhere in the Gulf. Consequently, many European companies - and especially banks - centred their Gulf headquarters in the emirate, and these were welcomed by the ruling Sheikhs in view of diminished oil resources. Meanwhile, alcohol was available in the international hotels, and the business environment was less abrasive than in Dubai or Abu Dhabi.

It was perhaps fortuitous that my first arrival in the Gulf coincided with a visit to Bahrain. Denny met me in the arrival area of the modern airport on a Thursday evening, and after introducing me to his wife and three-year old daughter, Shandy, we made for the exit. I was struck by the warm air and refreshing breeze of the dark night. It was at the beginning of March.

"The weather's been bad," said Denny's wife as he went off to fetch the car. "We've had a lot of rain - and it's windy and overcast."

I looked at the road surface and noted it was dry with a covering of light powdery sand.

Denny returned with a dirty battered old car, and after loading the boot, we climbed in, and drove off away from the island of Muharraq, across the causeway, and into the capital Manama situated on the north eastern tip of Bahrain island. In ten minutes we arrived at the Delmon Hotel, and after ascertaining the booking, it was arranged he would fetch me at 2.0 pm tomorrow. Due to an unfortunate accident it was an appointment that was only just to be met.

The hotel was comfortable and obliging, and the porter who insisted on carrying my luggage, refused a tip. I strolled through the dimly lit streets in the late evening; noting the open air coffee shops where Arabs smoked hubble-bubbles and played board games; passed by small shops selling a vast variety of merchandise; and was surprised by the broken pavements and construction sites at every turn of a corner. At 4.30 am the following morning I was awoken by the muezzins' call to *Fajr* (dawn prayer) from mosques all around the city. It lasted for some fifteen minutes, and seemed to awaken all the birds in Manama, for they set up their song until the final breaking of dawn.

It was natural I should spend the following morning by the hotel pool, sunbathing and swimming, but on entering the pool by a metal ladder, shortly before noon, the step gave way, and I was alerted to a sharp pain which foolishly I ignored, and it was not until ten minutes later, on leaving the water, that I discovered my foot was bathed in blood. I dressed immediately and hurried to the reception. The assistant manager was called and expressed his horror. This was clearly an incident that was not allowed! He drove me to the Salminula Medical Centre, a large state run hospital, where I received a tetanus injection and three stitches.

Then followed the documentation that was a protracted formality. The hotel manager falsely declared that I was a guest at the "Hilton Hotel." Three clerks were needed in entering the details into a massive ledger: the first for holding the book, the second to hold the pen, and the third to instruct the second what to write.

A week later the stitches needed to be removed, and this was done at the Rumailah Hospial in Doha. On arriving there with a colleague we were met by scenes of confusion. Numbers of outpatients, mostly Pakistanis were locked out of a waiting area and were banging violently on a door. Their patience was clearly exhausted, and they were not to be appeased by an orderly within, who momentarily unlocked the door, telling the crowd to wait a little longer.

On my arrival, however, the crowd gave way, assuming that as a European I was naturally entitled preference irrespective of the nature of the ailment or injury. I refused to jump the queue, for following us into the courtyard were six Pakistanis carrying a groaning man in a blanket that was saturated in his blood. He had just fallen from the fourth floor of a building site. I knocked violently on the same door, which was opened by the same orderly, who was overcome with humility and profuse apologies as soon as he saw me. On my insistence the badly injured man was immediately admitted into the doctor's surgery, and I was attended to a little later.

Despite a bound foot, the outing on that first afternoon in Bahrain was an enjoyable social occasion. Denny's wife and little daughter were no less friendly and hospitable than Denny himself. We toured the northern part of the island: saw the Portuguese fort by the seashore; then a herd of camels belonging to Sheikh Hamad, the Emir's brother - and I paid "backsheesh" for the privilege of photographing the animals; then we visited the Budaiya Experimental Station, a botanical garden. From there we strolled to the shore, and looking out to sea, we saw the grim prison island situated on a rock, housing those condemned to life, including many Iranians and followers of Ayatollah Khomeini who had attempted to incite an uprising in Bahrain in restoring the island to the northern power across the Gulf.

As we drove across the stony desert I was apprehensive that we might be stranded in the event of Denny's dilapidated car breaking down in the empty wilderness. We crossed to the other side of the island, passing the palace of the Emir, then the palaces of several relatives, and then the palace of his mother. We stopped to look at an old oil well - one of the few remaining "nodding donkeys;" and finally we drove to a remote hilly area, where we sat on some rocks and enjoyed refreshments. As Denny's wife served Indian snacks and tea from a thermos flask, I watched another group in the far distance picnicking and playing football.

Denny recounted something about his family background, explaining that Kerala had the highest percentage of university educated people of any state in India, and that his family belonged to the ancient Christian community. Some days later, whilst seated in his office, we were visited by his local Mahratta priest who had been working in Bahrain for the past three years, and during a long chat over tea, he described how Christianity had been established in Kerala by St. Thomas the Apostle in 72 AD. Last year he had received Dr. Runcie, the Archbishop of Canterbury, in his church in Manama.

As Shandy skipped happily in front of us, Denny explained that her name in his native language, Malayalam, meant "Peace." Denny's wife worked full time as a clerk for a construction company and so Shandy spent her days at a nursery school. Both Denny and his wife spoke with disparaging humour about the Arabs as an indolent people with little initiative.

The premises of Bowes-Davison consisted of an open wholesale loading area and platform, three feet above street level, reached by a flight of steps. It was situated in a narrow lane in the heart of the busy commercial area. When the premises were closed they were secured by heavy steel roller shutters. There was also an upper floor with further supplies of stock.

Bowes-Davison was a place of remarkable inactivity. All day long, Denny's young clerk, Gupta, would sit on an upright chair by the entrance looking out into the noisy street. He was always very obliging, and whenever I arrived at the premises, he would rise to his feet with a beaming smile, move his head from side to side in that curious fashion unique to Indians, and place a chair in its exact position for me to be seated comfortably at the office table. He would then hurry off to make tea or fetch cold drinks. He could neither read nor write, and his only function was to serve drinks or run errands, and it was apparent he had considerable difficulty in understanding Denny's instructions on those rare occasions when he was put into activity.

Surely this was an example of over-employment! I was surprised when Denny revealed that Gupta's wages were paid from his personal resources. Gupta had only been eight months in Bahrain and resided in crowded accommodation with several other families - all from Kerala. He came from the same village as Denny, and although he looked only eighteen years of age, he was already twenty-five. I expressed further surprise on learning that he had a wife in India.

"They're all married in this part of the world," laughed Denny who understood the prejudices of the West.

It was left to me to design a programme for my days in Bahrain, for Denny seemed apprehensive about suggestions of his own. I said I should like to visit customers. During the following days we visited a number of very small shops, always being invited to sit and chat for any period between twenty minutes to two hours, and in this way we accumulated a number of low value orders. Most our customers were small Indian retailers, but there were two observations that worried me: firstly, we made no visits to the big stores or groups; and secondly, Denny had no working knowledge of Arabic.

After further independent research it soon became apparent that Bowes-Davison were quite unsuited to representing the interests of our company if we sought to maximise our market share on the island. This was because as a confirming house they purchased and consolidated goods for export within the UK, fixing their own margins for prices and profits until the point of retail sale.

Because of higher tax rates in Bahrain, as well as the preservation of dated business methods when compared to those of the other emirates in the area, there was lesser price sensitivity, and so Bowes-Davison were able to promote a type of operation they could not possibly have maintained, for example, in Dubai. When I finally told Denny that we must find a way of penetrating the larger retail outlets, I sensed his anxiety, but he did promise to explore the possibility.

Begging was more prevalent in Bahrain than anywhere else in the Gulf. This was not because the Arab population were any poorer than elsewhere, but possibly because of the preservation of older traditions, and a slower more indolent attitude to life. Beggars, both men and women, were seen crouching on their haunches everywhere in the souk area, the women like black pyramids, for even their outstretched hands were hidden by the long drapes covering their forms. A casual visitor to Manama might easily have assumed that this was a place of poverty, but I was soon to be disabused of such a false impression.

Whilst sitting in Denny's office one morning, an old man entered, and without so much as a word spoken, held out his begging palm beneath Denny's face. Denny took out his wallet and handed over a note, as I gasped in astonishment at what struck me as rascally impertinence.

"He comes every week for his allowance," explained Denny.

"But he never even acknowledged what you gave him," I answered.

"That's typical of their behaviour," laughed Denny. "As almsgiving is obligatory in their religion, they feel they don't have to make a show of gratitude."

Denny explained it was illegal for beggars to go from shop to shop or from office to office, but they did it all the same. Thursday was the main begging day, and every afternoon on that day, the office of the wealthy merchant across the street was visited regularly by several dozen beggars, and each would receive his or her allowance, or *Zakat*, which describes the money to be spent on the poor.

"All beggars receive enough for a comfortable subsistence - and some are wealthy," said Denny. "Not long ago a beggar was prosecuted for soliciting from shops, and the police found he had taken the equivalent of more than £300 in a single morning. He was heavily fined."

Later in the morning, as we walked through the souk, Denny pointed out a legless man sitting in a box-like cart pitifully holding out his hand for alms.

"That man has two wives," began Denny. "He has a large American car with special controls, and he lives in a spacious house on the outskirts of Manama. Every morning he drives to the centre and parks his car; then two of his small sons, about eight and nine years old, push him in that cart to his established begging spot. There's really no need for begging in Bahrain. There's generous social security as well as homes for the disabled and sick."

On the last evening of my first visit to Bahrain I had an enjoyable evening as the guest of the Mohens in their flat within walking distance of the souk. They lived on the third floor of a modern building, the room being high and airy with huge fans suspended from the ceilings. The walls were bare concrete and the floors covered in linoleum. The front door led directly into the living room and I was introduced to two other male friends, also from Kerala.

We four men sat and talked at the table where we were later served a meal of simulas, chicken, and rice and curried seasonings. All the while Denny's wife and Shandy stood by the entrance to the kitchen, looking on the men from a distance, serving food and drink, and occasionally, joining in the conversation. Denny produced an unopened bottle of Whiskey, removed the cap, poured out half a tumbler, and set it before me.

"Aren't you having any,?" I asked embarrassed by the quantity of something I could not possibly be expected to consume.

"We don't drink alcohol," replied one of the other guests.

"But we know that British people cannot live without Whiskey," said Denny's wife from the kitchen.

I dared not admit that I never touched Whiskey, but by way of alleviating an embarrassing situation, I was able to raise a discussion on measures for different spirits, and after ten minutes on this topic entailing the tactful strategy of a circuitous conversation, Denny at last took the hint and returned most of the precious liquid to its original bottle. Ice was then added to the remainder and I enjoyed the drink - and a second glass too.

The conversation covered Kerala, the geography of India, literature, and Western philosophy. One of the guests enthused over the writings of Bertrand Russell, and this gave rise to a lively discussion. The other guest was a member of the British Council, regularly attending their meetings in Manama. Towards the end of the evening there was an exchange of addresses.

"You must visit me in England sometime," I said.

"That would be quite impossible," they responded.

"Nowadays you can't even get a visitor's visa," said Denny.

I felt ashamed of an ignorance giving rise to such a foolish suggestion.

CHAPTER 11
Families divided

"The object of punishment is, prevention from evil; it
never can be made impulsive to good."

Horace Mann, *Lectures & Reports On Education*, Lecture 7.

Over the following few years I saw the changes in Denny's
family, but I also noted the pressures which were crowding in.
Denny and his wife had a second daughter, but by the time that
Shandy was six years old, she was already bound by an onerous regime
of study.

She attended a private school in Manama, and during one of my
visits she was in the middle of a three-week intensive examination
period covering twelve subjects, including English (the language of the
school) and Hindi. Every night she was kept up late with her text and
exercise books, and her pleas to watch TV cartoons were rejected firmly
in the cause of promoting her examination success.

Then there was the problem of accumulating dowries for the
future. This was a more urgent question, however, for a cousin then
sharing Denny's flat. I had met the cousin and his wife on a previous
visit, and on returning to Bahrain half a year later, I learned that both had
returned to India - she permanently, and he for a temporary period. He
worked as a clerk in the Bahraini Ministry responsible for issuing visas
and passports, and the couple who had a baby son were obliged suddenly
to return to India to attend to family matters after only eighteen months
of marriage.

Her reason was to look after her parents for a two-year period - so
necessitating a two-year break between husband and wife. His reason
was more complex. As an only son, he found himself burdened with the
sole responsibility of earning dowries for his three sisters, and it was that
which had brought him to the Gulf. Each sister needed a dowry of
150,000 rupees (£10,000), plus £2,000 of 21 carat gold. In addition each
needed to have her own plot of land, but this had already been allocated

from the inheritance. Dowries had already been earned for the two elder sisters, who had been found husbands and married off.

There now only remained the third sister. The reason for the cousin needing to return to India was to find a suitable husband for this last sister, and this entailed press advertising, interviewing prospects, taking up references, and looking into medical records with regard to hereditary defects, etc. Having found a prospective husband from a respectable family, an introduction could then be effected.

As marriage in modern India was a voluntary and private arrangement, the prospective parties were allowed to meet and talk with one another in the presence of other family members, and if the couple failed to form an attachment, they might part without resentment between either of the families concerned. If, on the contrary, the couple agreed to marriage then an engagement would be announced. Denny's cousin would then return to Bahrain, earn the balance of the dowry for a year or so, before returning again to India for the final marriage arrangements.

Denny's dowry arrangements for his own daughters - a far more distant prospect - were vaguer than those of his cousin. He would only admit that each girl required "at least" £4,000, and although the dowry system had been officially outlawed by the government thirty years earlier, in practice it was no less in force at the present time than it had ever been. No girl could expect to find a good husband without a dowry, or any husband who would be approved of by his parents in entering into an otherwise financially barren arrangement.

The dowry system, therefore, still entailed the greatest financial cost in the life of any Indian involved in the institution of marriage, irrespective of whether he or she was the intended married partner or else a third party in assisting to bring about the nuptials of a near relative. Hence tens of thousands from the Indian subcontinent came to the Gulf with the primary motive of accumulating marriage dowries.

There was, however, a strange reversal of this system within the Gulf amongst resident expatriate families of the subcontinent. A man wishing to marry the daughter of an Indian or Pakistani whose family was resident in the Gulf, had to pay a dowry to the father of the daughter. Such a custom must naturally have arisen from the imbalance in the female population.

But Denny's immediate mind was not on a dowry for his daughters. He would shortly be faced by another considerable expense. The great movement of population from the subcontinent to the Gulf, accompanied by the huge transfer of private financial capital to India through the remittances of individuals, had caused inflation in certain parts of the latter country including Kerala. Denny's father therefore urged his son to build his own house as soon as possible, rather than delaying such work until after his return to India.

Denny's father (a farmer) owned eight acres, and had three sons and two daughters. Family arrangements would be as follows: the youngest son would inherit the farm as was customary, but the land would nonetheless need to be equally divided between the three. In the village an acre of land had been purchased for Denny to build his house, and the building of a two-storey three bedroom home would begin towards the end of the year - providing a licence for the purchase of cement could be had in time, for cement was a commodity difficult to obtain in Kerala. The house would be designed and built to maximise space on the plot for the cultivation of food resources, and the cost of the house would be limited to £13,000 as Denny could afford no more. Once work had begun, all immediate supervision would be entrusted to his father. This financial outlay was now the primary object of Denny's efforts in earning and accumulating capital.

Although Denny wished to remain in the Gulf for another eight or nine years, as with many Indians, he had no illusions about the vulnerability of the area. In the event of a sudden political crisis, he was fatalistic about the possibility of an immediate return to India at any time. He often spoke about the instability of the region, the extension of the Iran-Iraqi conflict, the implementation of the threat to block the straits of Hormuz, or the outbreak of religious violence between the Shiites and Sunnis in Bahrain itself. Nothing was certain!

On the other hand, there was the consolation that the Indian expatriate community was essential to the economies of the Gulf States. Arab locals were just not fitted to taking on tasks requiring diligence or specialised skills. Denny's wife had recounted, for example, that the Bahraini hospitals had taken on twenty-five Arab women as trainee nurses but that only five had persevered to complete the course. The hospitals on the island were staffed by Indian nationals assisted by a few Europeans.   How could the Arab authorities expel the expatriate population on whom they so heavily relied?

If expatriates, as temporary guest workers, assumed no political rights, or were often denied the opportunity for formal association, they were nonetheless held together on an informal basis by a quickness of wit and a sensitivity to political events, and easy communication was assisted by the advantage that many had relatives and friends in several parts of the Gulf. Denny, for example, had a brother based in Dubai, employed by the Danish Dubai Dairy Co., and the post entailed frequent travel throughout the Gulf.

The separation between husbands and wives for protracted periods, of those from the Indian subcontinent in the lower grades of employment, was not without its psychological strains, and these had often been discussed in the Indian press. Eastern patience and fatalism could only be pushed so far! The need for human warmth and contact could not be withheld for an indeterminate period. The common pattern of events was that men entered into marriage with young girls, living with them for three months or so, before embarking for the Gulf for longer term employment. Such periods of absence were only broken by annual leave which at most would be for four to six weeks, and because of the high expectations of most girls from married life, many developed mental disorders which were not helped by having to live with parents or parents-in-law.

If some of these girls received the news of the recession and its consequences as an end to their marital loneliness on the earlier return of their menfolk, this was not the response of expatriates striving to work and accumulate savings for the future. The recession not only generated feelings of insecurity but brought about its actuality. It resulted in several of the Gulf States introducing legislation which was not merely callous and arbitrary but even spiteful. Denny was touched with foreboding for his brother, for example, on describing to me a new law in Dubai whereby foreigners would have their permits cancelled automatically after ten years residence, so amounting to deportation.

On the other hand, the fears of the local Arab population could be well appreciated when they were outnumbered several times to one in their tiny states along the seaboard of the Gulf. The authoritarian (even if usually benevolent) administration of the Gulf states, the secretiveness of their rulers in their daily lives; and the withholding of rights for free association, may have been motivated out of necessity rather than the will to power. Nonetheless, their obsessive display of power sometimes bordered on the absurd. I well remembered one occasion on arriving in Bahrain. All outward flights had been delayed for two hours. The event was the return of the Emir after two days absence in Doha (thirty-five minutes flight away) after attending the annual GCC (Gulf Co-operation Council) meeting.

All entrances and exits to the airport had been blocked, and the military with machine guns at the ready were posted on every corner. As I stood looking out of the windows of the arrival terminal, I could see the red carpet and guard of honour in their splendid white uniforms drawn up in three ranks in preparation to welcome home His Highness. As soon as the Emir's 727 landed on the tarmac, a 21-gun salute began firing at five second intervals, the reverberation of each shot shaking the airport building. His Highness Sheikh Essa bin Salman al Khalifa then descended from the aircraft with his entourage, and the salutations began - an incessant kissing episode between senior ministers, courtiers and other government officials.

An American standing nearby the window, was so overawed by the scene, that he took out his camera to record the event for posterity, only to be seized immediately and hustled away for questioning. That night I took the opportunity to watch the dramatic event on the English language TV news bulletin, twenty out of thirty minutes being devoted to the Emir's historic return, as if it warranted a significant place on the world stage. To the accompaniment of martial music he was seen leaving Doha, then arriving on the tarmac in Bahrain, and finally, sitting in his palace together with senior ministers. The emperor of China could hardly have had a more impressive homecoming!

If the above ceremonial was an isolated or rare event, it would not need to be noted, but the TV news coverage on almost any evening of the year, throughout the smaller Gulf states (as well as in Saudi Arabia), featured the comings and goings of sheikhs as leading news items with regular monotony. Such was the regularity of these events, that every film sequence could be anticipated with an almost absolute certainty: viz., descent from the aircraft; inspection of the guard of honour; sitting comfortably on sofas back in the palace; and sometimes, phoning another ruler to extend an invitation for a return visit. World news was then condensed as an afterthought into the last few minutes of the bulletin.

During one of my later visits to Bahrain, Denny spoke about the secrecy of Arab life, and how on the rare occasion, an interesting tit-bit of information would be leaked to the outer world. He told me of an occurrence, gleaned from an acquaintance involved in the family episode, of a man who had recently bought another man's wife and four children. The transaction arose out of the vendor's financial difficulties, and apparently, such deals were not uncommon (even if kept confidential) in Arab circles. I told Denny that such transactions were not entirely unknown in England until the 19th century, and that their occurrence was similarly motivated through financial misfortune. Such a story had even played a part behind the inspiration of a major novel by one of our greater writers towards the end of the 19th century.*

The family lives of local rulers, however, was shrouded in almost total secrecy, the numbers of their wives and children never being publicly revealed. The veil was only partly lifted when the son of an emir was appointed to a Ministry or other official appointment. The review of a Cabinet list was the closest one might approach to studying the family life of a local ruler, especially when some fifteen ministries were equitably divided between four or five elder sons of an emir.

External political problems, however, were not to prove the final threat to Denny's financial security in the emirate. Increasing business pressures were to play that role. Bowes-Davison, as an organisation, was no longer fitted to operate as the export representative of any serious manufacturer. Denny's efforts in introducing our products into the larger stores and modern supermarkets all came to naught. It was not his fault. The fault lay in London with a company unprepared to change. Bowes-Davison, that "great name" and confirming house from the

---

* *The Mayor of Casterbridge*, by Thomas Hardy, published in 1886.

imperial past was prepared to do no more than rest on the laurels of its former reputation. Denny's hands were tied by the pricing margins within which he was forced to operate.

Meanwhile, I had no alternative but to explore other outlets and accept order from other parties. I was open with Denny in explaining the changing marketing and sales strategy, and he never batted an eyelid. I believe he anticipated the possibility of such an outcome even before we met. He was not so myopic as to close his eyes to the realities of the market place, and I now interpreted his apprehensive and evasive attitude in the earlier years as due to foresight rather than as a reflection of indifferent ability or an attempt to mislead. After all, he could not have been expected to buck the system of his employer.

Any awkwardness I might have felt through these unfortunate developments was diminished somewhat through intervention from an unexpected quarter. Our company shared the same agents in Bahrain as also in Saudi, namely, the household goods brand leader I had first encountered on the Badanahs' stand at the Jeddah Spring Fair. Dick Wadsworth, the aggressive Product Manager from Chicago, had visited Bowes-Davison in Bahrain and was horrified by what he saw. Clearly, they must be thrown out! The bloodletting was left to Rob Haworth who managed the overall Middle East operation from his office in Amman. When the agency was relinquished the Bahrain office of Bowes-Davison lost 30% of its business overnight.

When I found another agent to take on our own company's products - as I was forced to do through the logic of good business - Bowes-Davison lost another 15% of their turnover. Hence, within several months, the business of this "highly respected" firm was reduced by almost 50%. How much longer could it now survive? It was not long before I was to know the answer.

During my final sojourn in Kuwait, on that last and fateful visit to the Middle East - with its memories never to be erased - I was to meet a competitor, one evening, at the buffet bar of the Holiday Inn. We were soon in conversation and sat together, and as he had flown in from Bahrain that very afternoon, it was not unnatural that in the course of the discussion mention was made of Bowes-Davison.

"Haven't you heard? They've closed down the branch," he said.

I felt as if I had been struck by a blow.

"We were never notified," I responded.

"It was all hush-hush," said my competitor. "The stock was sold to Jashanmal & Sons, and the company closed overnight."

"What happened to the staff?"

"They only had two employees: a jack of all trades and an errand boy who could neither read nor write. I haven't heard what's happened to them."

"It's fortunate we made alternative arrangements in good time for another importer," I said.

Several days later I was in Bahrain. The shutters were down and a notice of closure fixed on the former premises of Bowes-Davison. No one knew the whereabouts of Denny Mohen in the adjoining businesses on either side. I went to Denny's flat only to find the property "To let." It could only be assumed he had returned with his family to India.

Was no other position in Bahrain a possibility? It must have been a heavy blow to his financial hopes for the future. I was never to know the end of the story. But in real life is there ever an end to any human story?

CHAPTER 12
A celibate in Doha

"Wealth is an application of mind to nature; and the art
of getting rich consists not in industry, much less in
saving, but in a better order, a timelessness, in being at
the right spot."

Emerson, *Conduct of Life: Wealth.*

It is a sorry situation when after years of study to qualify in a specific occupation, and after successfully graduating at the end of a course, it is then found unfeasible (for one reason or another) to practice a chosen career, or to utilise hard won knowledge and skills.

Such wasted time and effort is more difficult to bear if the alternative employment taken up seems menial by comparison. Throughout the Gulf such a mishmash of employment to the accredited skills of other occupations was commonly met with amongst non-European expatriates.

This was the case with Mr. Gamdi, the sad-looking Egyptian, with whom I worked over the years in promoting our products in Qatar. But not only was Mr. Gamdi depressed by a mismatched profession, but more so by a posting far from home and by a family situation which could scarcely have been satisfactory.

Qatar, and its capital Doha, were dreary places. My first visit to the emirate followed on from that to Bahrain. I was not met, as had been arranged, by Mr. Emad Radhwan, the General Manager of the Contemporary Department Store, and almost as soon as I reached the empty arrival hall I sensed that something was wrong. The airport was uncannily quiet. There was a ghostly atmosphere. I tried to change some money but the banks had already closed for the day at 1.30 pm. I waited around for twenty minutes but not a vehicle approached the terminal. A fleet of six taxis were parked outside, the drivers sleeping on the back seats of their vehicles.

An elderly bare-footed man dressed in a white dhoti, who appeared to earn his living by touting for fares on behalf of others, approached me to assist. Minutes earlier he had been sleeping on the pavement outside.

"I'm waiting for someone," I said dismissively.

"Who?"

"Mr. Emad Radhwan."

"He's a famous person," said the man in the dhoti. "He won't be here until six o'clock."

As it was only just past 2.0 pm I would have four hours to wait. But the proffered information was anyway meaningless. I tried phoning the Contemporary Department Store, but there was no reply from any of the numbers listed. I waited another hour and tried again. Still no reply. This was odd being the leading store in town - even though it might still be the siesta period. I mentioned my difficulty to an Arab local using an adjoining phone.

"You won't get the Contemporary Department Store," he replied. "One of the family have died and the store's closed for a week."

This was astonishing information. It was as if Selfridges had closed for a week on the death of one of its directors.

I took a taxi to the New Doha Palace Hotel, to find that a message had been left for me by Emad Radhwan an hour earlier. Since I had not already arrived at the hotel, he assumed I had cancelled my trip to Qatar. He left no contact number for a return call and his name was not listed in the telephone directory. I went to the hotel manager who consulted his own private directory and he succeeded in extracting a home number.

Mr. Radhwan explained that the company had gone into mourning following the death of a partner from cancer in a Swiss hospital. His body had been returned to Doha for burial and guests had arrived from all parts of the world for the funeral. I expressed my condolences, and then surprise at this resulting in the total closure of the business.

"You were lucky to get into the country," said Mr. Radhwan. "It was only because you had a British passport that you were allowed in. If you'd been French or German, you'd have been refused a visa and put on the next flight back to your last destination. All week I've been inundated with telephone calls from the airport from frantic businessmen complaining they've made a wasted journey. But what can I do about it? The business is closed and visas can't be issued. That's the law."

It was arranged that a Mr. Abdulla Assaf, the relevant department head, would fetch me the following morning for a tour of the town. When he arrived at the appointed time, I immediately recognised from his khaki military style suit, that he was an Egyptian, and it transpired that most the staff of the Contemporary Department Store were also of that nationality.

Mr. Assaf was profusely apologetic over my not having been met at the airport, and he reminded me that out of respect for the deceased, who was a "famous merchant" and a brother of the proprietor, it would not be possible to discuss business matters until the following day. He was a small well-proportioned man with crisp yet gentle manners, a well cut moustache, and immaculately turned out in a newly pressed suit. He was a friendly and competent guide in showing me the sights of the town, and when I photographed him in front of the Grand Mosque, he stood erect with military precision, his hands pressed to his sides. I was later to learn he had been a colonel in the Egyptian army.

Doha was very different from Manama. On the one hand it was a city of low built flat-roofed one or two storey houses, and if they had windows facing the street, then these were heavily barred or shuttered; but on the other hand, there were broad, noisy and busy streets in the town centre. The traditional style souk area was smaller in Doha, but there were far more modern glass-fronted shops than in Bahrain.

Qatar was a Wahabi state and this was everywhere reflected in the plainness and lack of decoration on buildings or in street furniture, although it should not be suggested that life was anywhere near as restrictive as in Saudi.

We drove passed endless construction sites, along the well-designed corniche, and stopped by the Grand Mosque opposite the Amiri Palace. The Amiri Palace was a vast and hideous structure, twice the size of Buckingham Palace, with forbidding purdah walls and high heavily shuttered windows designed for admitting light but not for looking out of, and a flat corrugated roof sprouting a forest of TV aerials.

Mr. Assaf could tell me nothing about the life of the Emir, or as to the number of his children, wives, or concubines. As we stood observing the palace, over-awed by its size and the mystery of the activities which occurred within, we were alerted by the deafening din of a police escort of motor cyclists, followed by a convoy of huge black-windowed limousines leaving the Amiri Palace for an official function.

One of those vehicles was carrying His Highness Sheikh Khalifa bin-Hamad al-Thani, the ruler of Qatar. Lastly, we visited the National Museum, an interesting exhibition in a building of modest proportions which had once been the home of the present Emir's grandfather. How much simpler life had been in those not so far distant days - small dark rooms with almost no furniture other than cushions and a coffee pot on a *gursi* or brazier, and in another room for the schooling of the young princes, a wooden stand decorated with mother of pearl for holding the *Koran.*

Early the following morning I was fetched by Mr. Gamdi (I never knew him by any other name), a tall well-built handsome Egyptian with wavy hair and a sad expression. As we drove to the Contemporary Department Store, which was opening for the first day after a week's closure, he explained that he was the salesman responsible for our company's products. On arrival at the store I was taken to the offices on the second floor, and I felt impatient and a little annoyed when both of us then had a two and a half hour wait before being led into the office of Mr. Radhwan, the General Manager. Meanwhile, we were seated in the sales office, used by three or four representatives, and during this intervening period, endless canned drinks and glasses of sweet tea were served.

A lively and attractive Englishwoman came into the office, introducing herself as Miss Sutton, the Yardley representative for Qatar. She enthused about the country, comparing it favourably with Bahrain.

"I don't like Bahrain - it's too British," she exclaimed. "It's so cliquey. Everywhere there are circles and clubs intent on keeping people out rather than including them in. That's why I left Britain - to get away from snobbery. Here it's free and easy. There are frequent parties for expatriates and there are beautiful beaches just outside the town. There's a more modern atmosphere here than in Bahrain - and business methods are far more advanced."

"But you can't drink here," I responded.

"Oh yes you can, if you're a European expat. You can get a special licence for alcohol - provided it's consumed on private premises. It's so friendly here. Give me Qatar any day!"

She then bustled around the office and began teasing Mr. Gamdi about his poor command of English. How could he expect his customers to understand him if he spoke like that! Mr. Gamdi made no response to the gibes. He might have replied that as the greater number of his prospects were Arab and not Indian traders there was little problem with language.

At last Mr. Gamdi and I were led into the office of Mr. Radhwan, who was another Egyptian, and Mr. Abdulla Assaf was also present. Apologies were made for the long delay that was due to protracted negotiations with a French company for the sale of men's suits.

"Well, what shall we do,?" began Mr. Radhwan dismally. "Your prices are too high and stocks are moving slowly."

After a monologue in this vein for several minutes, I suggested that it might be better if they relinquished the agency, calmly mentioning (which I knew to be the ultimate threat) that I was sure the British Embassy could suggest a few alternative names to take over from the Contemporary Department Store.

"Then what do you think we should do,?" said Mr. Radhwan at last.

Realising the price parameters within which we worked, I decided to suggest the impossible, but I knew that this alone would either make or break our future relationship with the Contemporary Department Store.

"If you take a full container load from us, I'll give you a one in twelve free promotional offer," I said.

"Will you be coming to Doha again,?" asked Mr. Radhwan.

"Yes."

"When?"

"In six months - every six months."

"Good, because we don't like doing business with people who call once and are never seen again."

During the next hour the three of us drew up a mixed consignment for a twenty foot box, which culminated in an £11,000 order - more business than we had received from the emirate over the previous three years.

On visiting the souk that afternoon with Mr. Gamdi it was clear that our products had not been properly serviced. They were often grubby, badly displayed, and sometimes damaged. One small souk trader showed us an item he had sold twelve times: on each occasion it had been returned as useless.

"Then why didn't the idiot withdraw it from stock,?" I exclaimed.

"He says he hoped to sell it to someone flying out of the country," said Mr. Gamdi.

"That kind of dishonesty doesn't help our reputation," I remarked.

"He says he doesn't care about the reputation of suppliers, because he always sells competing stock," Mr. Gamdi translated back again. "He says he's only interested in selling."

The elderly souk trader had a dirty lazy appearance as if he didn't care much about anything. I told Mr. Gamdi that he would need to inspect and withdraw faulty stock and the Contemporary Department Store would need to write this off from profits on sales.

That evening Mr. Gamdi took me to a restaurant in an international class hotel owned by the family who controlled the Contemporary Department Store. We were soon absorbed in a conversation about his personal life. His one desire was to have a family as he loved small children. I showed him the photos of my own children, and he looked at them admiringly, again saying he wished he had children of his own.

"Then you must get married," I said.

He said he was already engaged and that that was the reason for his being in Qatar. He had studied and qualified as a mechanical engineer in Egypt, explaining that such work was very poorly paid in his native country. He needed to earn and save up a lot of money, as in several months he would return to Port Said to marry. The parents of the two families were close friends, and the prospective bride was in her last year at medical school.

Marriage, however, would not mean they would live together in the near future. She would return to medical school followed by a year's service for the state as a doctor in a small Egyptian village as was obligatory on attaining final qualifications, and he, meanwhile, would need to return to Doha for another four years. His earnings as a salesman in the Gulf far surpassed any salary level he could hope for in his own country. The need for money overrode everything.

"But why doesn't your future wife come to Doha,?" I asked.

"She'd never get a visa," he replied.

Mr. Gamdi portrayed a dreary impression of his life in Doha. He shared a flat with three other young men and they were all responsible for their own cooking and laundry. He found it difficult attending to such household chores. On Fridays he went to the Mosque for prayers, and afterwards, played football with friends. He seemed to have no other hobbies or amusements, although occasionally he went to the cinema.

On my next trip to Qatar I stayed at the hotel owned by our agents. The son of the proprietor, who supposedly was to inherit this considerable business empire, had little interest in running the concern. He was instead studying psychoanalysis in England, and at great cost, his professor had been flown out to Doha during the holiday period, so that student and teacher might continue their confabulations in the more endearing environment of a sunny clime.

Every afternoon, whilst lying by the poolside, a balding Englishman with a high-pitched voice, a self-satisfied smile and rolling blue eyes, would stroll with an almost affected gait into the recreational area, a towel slung over his shoulder. Minutes later the student would arrive, and the two would recline on adjoining sunbeds, as the five or six of us around the pool, would be entertained to a monologue on psychoanalytical theory, only occasionally interrupted by a reverential student with a diffident question.

It was during one of these days, early in the evening, that the professor was introduced to the student's father and controlling power behind the business empire. Shortly before dusk, in the lobby of the hotel, an elderly man in dark glasses and gold rings on most of his fingers, was wheeled into the lounge area, to meet the distinguished academic. Little could be seen of the features of the business mogul, as his headscarf was pulled towards the front of his face, and little could be discerned from his body language, as he sat immobile like a tailor's dummy, clutching onto a walking stick. Introductions were effected by the respectful student.

"Delighted to make your acquaintance," exclaimed the Englishman taking a gnarled hand, grinning all the while, and bowing awkwardly as he cut a ridiculous figure.

It was not possible to hear the reply that came from the ailing figure in the wheelchair.

"Quite so! ... Oh yes, remarkable, remarkable,!" continued the academic with that ingratiating grin unique to the English race. "Such lovely weather! ... So sunny! ... Oh, I do like to tan myself, ha, ha! ... Very privileged to be here, I assure you."

It was impossible to guess what these oddly assorted men really thought about the other, but if either could have understood the ideals or life philosophy of the other, would there have been room for mutual respect between them? The student, on the other hand, might one day really develop the consciousness of a Westerner - how could it be otherwise in view of the enlightening subject matter of his chosen study?

On subsequent trips to Qatar I stayed at the magnificent and recently constructed Doha Sheraton, built in the form of a pyramid on the shoreline of reclaimed land to the north of the city, each room with a spacious balcony. On one such visit I wandered into a Palestinian wedding reception, being invited to join the guests. The bride and groom (who was a director of the Syrian bank) sat on thrones at one end of the banqueting hall, and I was seated at a table with guests of both sexes. Although Palestinian men and women could socialise together to a limited degree, dancing was a strictly segregated activity, and later in the evening, in the friendly and joyous atmosphere, I was dragged by several Arabs onto the dance floor and taught their traditional steps, to the cheers of the assembled crowd.

Mr. Gamdi had already been married three years when I met him on the last occasion, and still there was only a distant prospect of husband and wife living together. The recession was delaying the desired accumulation level of his savings for a future home together in Egypt. Nuptial bliss was only possible for a few weeks during annual leave, and for the rest of the year Mr. Gamdi led a celibate life in an all-male environment, for there was little social mixing between expatriate Muslims and Europeans. The cultural differences and inhibitions of the majority of Muslims were too strong to warm to the inviting (or corrupting) hospitality of their European co-workers - especially if they were bound by the moral obligation of wives in distant places.

Such were the feelings of the long-suffering Mr. Gamdi, who could only take pleasure in the thought of a better and more meaningful life when the oppression of want had been lifted in an indeterminate future. It was a condition of life that would have been intolerable to any modern Westerner spoilt by both affluence with no memory of past poverty, and by a hedonism which had overcome the inhibitions of an earlier era.

But an enduring patience, and the denial of immediate pleasure for future benefit, was still a virtue inherent in the peoples of the East, and this was both a consolation and a necessity in the face of relative penury.

CHAPTER 13
Apartheid between the sexes

"The divine wrath is slow indeed in vengeance but it makes up for its tardiness by the severity of the punishment."

Valerius Maximus, *Annals*, Bk. 1, Ch. 1, Sec. 3.

There was a low murmur amongst the crowd and slowly it began to disperse, as soon as the body of the convicted man had been removed from Deira square.

Closer to the execution spot five or six men, their faces contorted, were wandering amongst the remaining carnage, spitting on the bloodied stones. Clearly they were the aggrieved relatives of a victim of some horrific crime. I strolled towards the bollards before the Governor's Palace. Thousands of bloodstained stones covered the roadway, and close to the bollards lay pieces dashed from the criminal's skull - but white rather than grey in colour.

"It's good, good,!" exclaimed several men in a tone of anger at my approach, and pointing contemptuously to the bloodied stones.

Perhaps I had worn an expression of moral perplexity that they felt needed an explanation. Wandering amongst the stones were several fathers holding the hands of their eight and nine year old sons whom they had brought along to witness the execution. I was curious as to the offence that had been committed. I approached and questioned a young man spitting with such hatred on the soiled roadway.

"He murdered a small child," replied the man with passion, and he made a gesture with his hands to indicate there had been a sexual assault.

"And who's that old man,?" I asked, indicating towards a bearded figure with tears rolling down his cheeks as he spat on the stones.

"That's the grandfather," replied the young man.

I asked no more. I had no wish to. Here was a family expressing its final sense of grief and resentment on the concluding episode of a horrific crime and the judgement of law. I now realised that here was an example of the true vengeance of society on the worst of offenders -

when the law and the aggrieved party were united by a feeling of common purpose in the infliction of punishment.

This was the way the law had always been in pre-statist tribal societies, when both men and women had been allowed the free flow of their natural passions in the determining and execution of justice. It was still partially so in the Islamic East. It was no longer so in the progressive West, where a multitude of factors, abstruse and debatable, false and true, had intervened in the judicial process in building a divide between the aggrieved party and his or her natural desire for vengeance.

Was vengeance the will of the savage, as argued in Western thought, or did it still remain in reality the essential and underlying source of justice? How much hypocrisy was hidden in the rational moral motives of Western man, and how much truth was hidden in the expressive anger of judicial systems older than our own?

There was so much misunderstanding between peoples in the modern world preventing the achievement of desired concord amongst nations, and this was often exacerbated by the degree of cultural differences. But all such misunderstanding arose from either ignorance or prejudice alone. In a world fast becoming a "global village," such ignorance or prejudice could now be accounted a moral failing in the character of those concerned. Such failings arose from too great an absorption and reliance on the immediate conditions of life.

It was reflected in the provincialism and pettiness of a particular environment. Its moral fault lay in the narrowness of the individual in idealising his own community in blocking out a consciousness of the other lesser known world. Known and cherished objects, friends and values, were used as a cocoon of safety and comfort in acting as a barrier against all that was strange and alien. When such individuals, therefore, by chance or necessity, were removed abruptly - and maybe only temporarily, from such an accustomed environment, the shock was so great to the system that it remained sometimes forever in their memory as a trauma of unimaginable proportions.

It was in the light of such thoughts that I recollected the unhappy experiences of my colleague, Larry McEwan, in Saudi Arabia. Larry had a desk bound job as an Export Product Manager, but it was thought he might usefully be relieved from his office duties for a ten day stint to assist me on the Badanahs' stand at the Jeddah Spring Fair. On an earlier occasion he had already assisted me in Bahrain without incident. But Bahrain was not Saudi Arabia.

Larry raised no objection when the idea was mooted. Larry was a heavily built easy going chap, outspoken and sometimes quick-tempered, fond of his pint of bitter at lunchtime and after work, and with a dry sense of humour - but not sufficient to overcome the tribulations he was to face in the desert Kingdom.

He gave no more thought to spending ten days in Saudi Arabia than if he was to move from Basildon to Billericay for the same period of time. He would take it all in his stride as being part of the job - or so he thought. His first mistake - for it led to a disastrous incident - was his insistence on the choice of airline. I had already booked on Saudia Airlines but this was unacceptable. His given excuse was the factor of "safety," but I knew he was only using this as a cover for another motive, for the chosen airline happened to be "dry."

"I'm not putting my life at risk by going through the experience you had," he insisted.

"But that was several years ago, and I've often travelled on Saudia since," I answered.

"I don't trust those bloody Arabs to pilot an aircraft," persisted Larry.

"They're not piloted by Saudis," I answered. "None of their crews are Saudi staffed. It would contravene their laws of illegal seclusion to do so. As international agreements require that aircrews must comprise a mix of men and women, Saudia are always staffed by foreign nationals. On the last occasion I travelled, half the crew were Korean and the other half British."

"I've never heard anything so stupid," concluded Larry. "I'd feel safer on British Airways. I've got to think about the wife. She wouldn't like me to travel on a foreign airline."

The "experience" to which Larry referred occurred two years earlier on a flight from Heathrow to Jeddah, stopping at Geneva. As the Tri-Star approached Geneva there was much turbulence, and as I sat near the galley area where several of the crew were assembled, I overheard one stewardess say to another, "I hate coming into Geneva!" On landing we were told there was a "mechanical" fault, and as this incurred a delay, we would be escorted into the terminal. On descending from the aircraft, I was surprised to see an engineer atop a ladder at the rear of the plane, hitting the upright tailpiece with a mallet.

An hour later the plane took off again, but after ten minutes and before we had reached a comfortable height, there was aloud explosion from the port side that shook the craft. Moments later, the slow calm voice of the American pilot, came over the communication system: "I'm sorry ladies and gentlemen but we've encountered another small problem. Our port side engine is causing difficulties and we'll be returning to Geneva. However, for safety reasons we'll be taking a circuitous route to relieve the overload in our fuel tanks. We'll be landing in Geneva in twenty minutes. Please keep your seat belts fastened as we shall be going through some turbulence."

As I sat on the starboard side, I had no view of what was occurring beneath the left wing of the aircraft. The engine was already in flames. The plane was losing height as it flew through black cloud, occasionally broken by the sight of jagged snow-topped mountain peaks on either side of the aircraft. Momentarily, a brown expanse of water was visible far below, as a break in the cloud revealed the lake of Geneva.

A valve was released in the starboard wing and a long stream of aviation fuel was ejected into the atmosphere. The plane bumped violently as it passed through air pockets. There was a stillness and total silence amongst the seated passengers and aircrew. There were tense and pallid faces, and some of the Arab passengers pulled forward their headscarves and began to pray. Others closed their eyes in feigning sleep. With a feeling of stoicism I was prepared for final annihilation.

As the Tri-Star landed again at Geneva, a fleet of fire engines and ambulances sped alongside the runway in readiness for an emergency. The incident entailed a twenty-four hour delay in diverting two Saudia airplanes from other routes. Although the incident was unreported in the Swiss press, Saudia Airlines were to take their own particular precautions for the future. On every subsequent occasion when I was to travel on the airline, irrespective of whether it was an internal or external flight, as the aircraft set off along the runway, a deep reverential monologue in Arabic would be broadcast over the communication system. This was a recitation from Mohammed's Travellers' Prayer taken from the *Hadith.*

Finally, Larry had his way. As the two airlines alternated on the Jeddah route every other day, I cancelled the Saudia flight for a BA booking a day earlier. But Larry's woes were not to begin in Saudi Arabia. They were to begin at an altitude of 35,000 feet, possibly somewhere between the Sea of Marmara and the Taurus mountains. His fate was sealed at the Check-In when we chose our seats. As I was a non-smoker and he a chain-smoker, this presented a problem.

The BA Check-In girl told us not to worry - something could be arranged to accommodate the wishes of us both. She was charming over our predicament. Any problem could be overcome! I would be seated in the middle row in the non-smoking section, and Larry would be seated directly in front of me facing a dividing compartment wall. Although he would not, strictly speaking, be placed in a smoking section, it was nonetheless, a seat where no one would be so "unreasonable" as to object to his occasionally taking out a cigarette. Everything seemed satisfactory as we made our way to the departure lounge.

The first part of the journey was relaxing and uneventful, although Larry was determined to tank up sufficiently in compensating for the prospect of ten "dry" days ahead. Every time a stewardess passed down the aisle, he would raise a hand for another bottle to be served. I hardly gave it a thought when during the first half of the journey, a tall burly man several times stood in front of Larry, engaging him in conversation. Because of the engine noise it was not possible to overhear what was said. Perhaps the stranger was an old business acquaintance. Then came lunch, accompanied by plentiful quantities of wine, and finishing up with several glasses of cognac. At last, Larry sat back in comfort, and lit up a cigarette, blowing out clouds of smoke.

Again, the heavily built man approached Larry. I could now see that his intentions were far from amicable. There was an angry exchange. Although it was impossible to follow the altercation, by watching Larry's lips I noticed that he finally delivered the ultimate expletive. All hell broke loose! The tall man picked up Larry's coffee cup, throwing its contents over his adversary's shirtfront. At once fists were flying. From my perspective, from the back of Larry's seat, it was reminiscent of a Punch and Judy show, for one moment Larry was visible bearing down on his opponent who disappeared from view, and the next moment, the situation was reversed.

Suddenly, a man larger than both the contestants, loomed up behind them, and holding up a plastic card, exclaimed authoritatively, "Break it up, you guys! I'm from the FBI. You're both under arrest!"

The fight ended as abruptly as it had begun. The aggrieved party returned to his seat, and the American, meanwhile, disappeared as if into thin air, never to be seen again. I was apprehensive over the next few hours as to the possible outcome of this air-rage. Would the pilot radio ahead to the control tower at Jeddah alerting the authorities to arrest one of his passengers? I had visions of standing in a square as Larry McEwan underwent a public flogging. Nothing was impossible!

As Larry and I queued up for passport inspection at Jeddah airport, early that evening, the aggrieved party sidled up behind us. Moments later the two were exchanging words in an undertone, and embarrassed and as if to dissociate myself from their presence, I took a step aside.

"I'm only a poor salesman," burst out the aggrieved party at last. "I'm only trying to make a living. I hate this bloody country. It churns me up inside every time I have to come out here. But a job's a job! I've got no other alternative."

"Next time, don't throw coffee over me, that's all," responded Larry.

The Spring Fair, as expected, was a busy event demanding every moment of our time. The presence of other Westerners on the stand, of Dick Wadsworth, John Crawley, Rob Haworth and Pierre Legouis, was a welcome relief for Larry from the tensions and oddities of this foreign environment. It was not sufficient, however, to prevent him from a perpetual outpouring of complaints. Firstly, there was the heat, and the sweat streamed off his body.

"Just think cool and you won't perspire," I advised. "I'm not sweating and so why should you? It's only because I refuse to think about the heat. Try to concentrate your mind on other things."

All the Badanah family were at the Jeddah Fair, and even Fahad Munof had been flown in from Riyadh, and still he eyed me with that curiously suspicious look.

"Why's Nazeer dressed in white bath towels? Is he trying to prove something? He looks a right proper wally," exclaimed Larry on one occasion.

"He's dressed in the traditional *Irham*. He's going on the *Hajj* next week - pilgrimage to Mecca," I explained. "It's part of the preparation."

"It looks as if he's just stepped out of the shower and forgotten to dress," remarked Larry.

"What's that disgusting drink that bearded old man serves out in egg cups to anyone in the hotel lobby early in the morning,?" asked Larry on another occasion.

"That's coffee," I answered.

"It doesn't taste remotely like coffee," said Larry indignantly. "It doesn't even look like coffee - more like a thin brown soup."

"It's flavoured with cardamon, to cover the brackish taste of the water," I explained.

"If that's supposed to be traditional, it's a tradition best forgotten," concluded Larry.

The Fair was, in reality, a glorified bazaar, packed from morning till noon and from dusk till ten at night, with retail shoppers - the vast majority being women moving around in small family groups. I was surprised by the frequent appearance of Saudi Arabs of Mongol appearance."

"They come from Kazakhstan," explained Nabeel Badanah. "Or rather, their ancestors did. They came as refugees from religious persecution after the Russian Revolution."

There was much bargaining for the purchase of our products. Larry and I stood behind one particular counter, and often a group of hooded and heavily veiled women would confer with a small child in their midst, and moments later, we were approached by an eight or nine year old girl, who in fluent English and grinning all the while, would try to knock down our prices. When they failed to reach a deal they would leave and return in half an hour or so to alter their bargaining position, and it was difficult to resist their charm and young attempts at business negotiation.

Even after several days in the Kingdom it was still difficult for Larry to realise we had left the confines of Essex. Walking along the street one day, he burst out, "Just look at the state of that pavement. I could have broken my leg on that. Now if this was Basildon, the Council would be sued. It's disgraceful!"

No explanation could have answered his reasonable resentment. It was only possible to laugh.

On the second evening we all went for a meal at Mousa's villa on the outskirts of Jeddah, and for a swim afterwards. We drove up to the gateway of a compound and the driver sounded his horn. The gatekeeper, an elderly Yemeni, opened the huge doors, and as we drove through, we saw the gatekeeper's lodge: a chair and table, and the pallet on which he slept. His was a twenty-four hour job, answering the call of all who entered or left the compound.

The car drove into a huge area paved with polished marble. Within the compound were three houses, one for each of the brothers in the Badanah partnership, and between the houses was a spacious swimming pool. A broad flight of black polished stone steps led up to the entrance of Mousa's house, and once inside, it was like the foyer of a London theatre. We removed our shoes and entered the majlis, a long room brightly illuminated with a row of crystal chandeliers. When later we passed through a pair of double doors into the dining area, we were confronted by the decor and era of Louis XV at the height of the rococo. Here was the dining room of Versailles reconstructed to the last detail - or at least it was a brave pretence to do so.

"What have we here? Sitting at a table for dinner - whatever next,?" exclaimed the cheeky Frenchman, Pierre Legouis. "You're getting modern ideas Mousa. Where are you leading us?"

As we sat sipping tea in the majlis after the meal, Larry kept up a polite grin, but I could see he was uncomfortable.

On being driven to our hotel during the lunch break the following day, and whilst the muezzins' call was heard throughout the city, we saw Mousa and Nazeer in a crowded street, lining up with others into three ranks on a carpet behind a prayer leader.

"What are they doing,?" exclaimed Larry. The two partners had only left the exhibition hall a minute or so before ourselves.

"They haven't time to reach a mosque," I replied. "They have to pray in the street."

"And they've broken their journey and left the car for that,?"

exclaimed Larry in bewilderment. "This praying is so disruptive! Why can't they just be like us, and kneel down by their beds at the end of the day?"

That night Rob Haworth had to leave for Amman and as the car which was taking several of us to the location for our evening meal passed nearby the airport, and a plane flew low overhead, Dick Wadsworth exclaimed in a half satirical tone, "There goes Rob! I wonder what he's got to go home to?"

This led to some joking and opaque speculation about Rob's sexual orientation, for Mousa had still not succeeded in persuading him to enter into the joys of nuptial bliss.

"Does he live with anyone,?" asked Pierre.

"Search me," said John Crawley. "I know nothing about his domestic arrangements,"

"I expect he lives with his mother," said Larry in a deadpan voice.

A peel of laughter filled the car - from all that is except for the Arab driver. The ironic speculation over Rob's domestic situation was lost entirely on Ali Badanah. He somehow took the remark as a general slur on motherhood rather than as an imputation on a taboo topic. He merely frowned, exclaiming in a disapproving tone, "In Islam, we respect our mothers!"

Before I was fully dressed, early in the morning of our fifth day in Jeddah, there was an impatient knocking on my room door. On answering it, I was surprised to be confronted by a flustered Larry McEwan.

"I'm taking tonight's flight back to Heathrow," he declared.

"You can't do that," I answered, "we're short handed."

"I've had enough of this place. I've had it up to here," he said raising his hand to his chin.

"There're only five more days to go," I insisted.

"I'm fed up with drinking sweet tea and lemonade all day long. All I want in life is a pint of bitter. Listen, last night I phoned the MD and got his clearance to go back."

"How could you have done that? The office has been closed since last night."

"I phoned him at his home," said Larry.

"You shouldn't have done that. You went over the Department head," I exclaimed angrily.

"I tried to phone Guy Wallis, but he was out for the evening."

"You can't leave just like that," I insisted. "What excuse did you give the MD?"

"I told him I'm not a bloody shop assistant. It's not in my job spec."

"You'll need an Exit visa to leave Saudi Arabia. That won't be so easy," I said. "No one can leave without an Exit visa."

"What's that?"

"It'll take two days to get."

"Surely you can pull a few strings," said Larry in desperation. "I'm fed up with everything in this country, and most of all, I'm fed up with the Badanahs pontificating on how I should conduct my life. Nabeel even had the cheek to tell me alcohol was 'evil.' Where do you draw the line with these people? I mean, not one of them's even presentable and so they can't talk. And I'm fed up with mutton - and I'm not going to eat another bowl of rice. And as for Mousa, he talks religion non-stop all day long. They're fanatics, these people! He's even been trying to convert me to his own religion."

"They do that all the time," I said.

"What's he think he's playing at,?" exclaimed Larry. "He'll never convert me. I'm Catholic!"

"I don't expect he knows what a Catholic is."

"All I want is to get out of here."

"Then we'll need a credible excuse," I said. "We'd better say your wife is sick - or better still, your son is dangerously ill. He'll understand that. That's the story we'll use. But only the Badanahs can apply for an Exit visa."

That night Larry flew out of Jeddah for Heathrow. As I waved him off from the departure area I had never seen him in a happier frame of mind.

At the end of the Spring Fair I remained three more days in Jeddah to complete company business. When I wrote a thanking letter to Samir Badri for the gift of the hubble-bubble, I enclosed a photo of the magnificent implement in use - of a bearded artist friend drawing on the water pipe, before a coffee table with three cups and saucers. For some reason the photo had been framed and placed on Fallah Abdullah's desk.

One evening whilst several of us were seated in Fallah's office, he took up the photo, and being an observant and curious person, he pointed to the photo, enquiring as to whom the third cup and saucer belonged.

"My wife," I replied.

"You mean she was sitting with you,?" said Fallah clearly shocked by this revelation.

"Yes - and my friend's wife was present too," I assured.

"I thought Englishmen spent their time in clubs with other men," said Fallah.

"They do that too," I answered.

This led to some mumbling in Arabic between the others present. Although they must have known it was customary for men and women in the West to sit together - something made evident in any Western film - they found it difficult to accept this on a personal level that a friend and supplier should actually participate in such questionable social activity. Social mixing between the sexes was so taboo, that they seemed to be indicating that such behaviour was hardly credible amongst "nice" people - irrespective of cultural background.

* * *

It was also during the few days following the Spring Fair that I caught a glimpse of life in Saudi from another perspective. A GP friend from my home town who was breaking up with his wife had recently taken on a two-year contract with a medical practice in Jeddah. I was interested to learn how he was adapting to life in the Kingdom. He was in high spirits when he fetched me from the hotel to show me his flat and life in the well-protected compound. He had been two months in the country and was especially proud of having obtained a Saudi driving licence in only four weeks.

He lived in a large compound managed by Arabian Homes, and many smaller compounds, each surrounded by a high wall, were situated within the greater area. Doug Hall lived in a compound of eleven luxury flats surrounding a swimming pool and attractively laid out garden. His own flat comprised two small rooms overlooking the pool, and he proudly showed me the wine-making equipment he had surreptitiously installed in the kitchen area, assuring me that he and his friends were never short of alcoholic beverages for their frequent parties. After a swim he took me to the shopping centre situated in another compound - all compounds being entered through a steel door and the display of a pass.

There was also a small library, a bowling alley, a gym and sauna, and a restaurant where we ate. He had already established an active social life within the closed European community, which was as far apart from that of the Saudis as if on another planet.

"I've joined a French course at the French Embassy - and there's a really great choral society at the American Embassy," he said beaming with enthusiasm. "We've just started rehearsals for Mendelssohn's *Elijah*. It's a pity you couldn't be here for the concert."

He had already been invited into several American homes and regretted the inability to return their hospitality due to the smallness of his flat. The majority of patients visiting his practice were Europeans, but there were many other nationalities - including even Arab women. I reciprocated his hospitality by inviting him to lunch at my hotel the following day.

"How can you possibly adapt to going back to life in England after all this luxury,?" he exclaimed over-awed by the lavish surroundings, as we helped ourselves to the impressive buffet at the Marriott Hotel.

"It's not easy," I replied. "The culture shock of returning is as great as the culture shock of arriving. That's life! Nothing is really right."

I did not confide with Doug at the time that because of circumstances outside my control this would probably be one of my last trips to the Middle East.

* * *

Hussein was the most fastidious of all the Badanahs, and he was responsible for managing the family business in the Eastern Province, and that was my immediate destination some days after the end of the Jeddah Spring Fair. I had first met Hussein when he came to meet me at Jeddah airport, shortly after the near crash over Geneva.

He had heard the story not from my lips but from the airline on the failure of my flight arrival the previous day. On that occasion he was overflowing with sympathy and concern for my safety, and filled with the miraculous wonder of a "merciful and loving God" who had chosen to spare my life.

The Eastern Province was centred around the two coastal cities of Dammam to the north, and the newer city of Al Khobar, some eight miles to the south; also the inland city of Dharan, some four miles to the north west of Al Khobar, which comprised the airport, the University of Petroleum & Minerals, and the vast secluded compound of the Arabian American Oil Co. (ARAMCO).

The Eastern Province was the oil-rich region of Saudi Arabia, a place of hectic activity and constant change and construction, the desert littered with oil towers and other steel-built industrial structures, the night sky lit up by a forest of flares burning off crude oil pumped up from the depths of the earth. It was also an important military centre in defending the Gulf, and the presence of American heavy weaponry was evident to anyone passing through the airport of Dharan.

Previous visits to the province had left me with the impression that our products were not being actively promoted. I was unsatisfied with Hussein's marketing efforts, and I had therefore begun to explore other outlets for the sale of our products. Providing I sold direct to retail outlets, and not a wholesaling intermediary, no embarrassment would be caused to the Badanahs operation. Nonetheless, I needed to tread carefully. The Badanahs remained our valued agents, albeit on a non-contractual basis, and liaising closely with Hussein was a first priority in visiting the area.

Hussein was a son of Nazeer, aged twenty-three, and as with other relatives of his generation, married to a first cousin (a daughter of Mousa), the couple having two children. He was a slight figure, looking younger than his years, and his fastidious behaviour and inhibited attitudes, not merely seemed to reflect an obsession with rule-keeping for its own sake, but a constant fear of all the evils lurking beyond the frontiers of his own experience. He was scrupulously conventional in everything he undertook, and it seemed he was not so much fearful of committing sin as being infected by its presence irrespective of his own volition.

He had already provided me with an example of this. He was studying Business Administration at the University of Petroleum &

Minerals and would be obliged shortly to spend six months in a practical capacity within an industrial organisation. He would be offered an opportunity to work in England or America, but this he was loathed to do (he had previously spent six months in England) on the grounds that the outside world is "filled with temptations" where people are "corrupted by drink and other undesirable habits." He had therefore lodged an appeal to the University authorities for a posting within ARAMCO.

It was these things, reflecting a sterile imagination, which led me to believe that there was little chance of his one day playing a part in modernising the Badanah enterprise. In a world moving faster than our ability to adapt our attitudes, the machiavellism of Italian guile was more important than the fastidiousness of German rectitude if long term survival was to be the end purpose of success.

On arriving in Dharan I made my own way to the Meridien Hotel in Al Khobar, where I had already arranged to meet Hussein later that evening for a coffee. On signing into the hotel I soon realised it was noisy with a wedding reception. A member of the famous Tamimi family had just been married, and as was customary with Gulf Arabs, there would be a male party in one hotel, and a female party (attended by bride and groom together) in another. The Meridien was hosting a party for the female guests.

On taking my luggage from Reception to my room on a higher floor, I did something that an Arab would hardly dare to do, but in my hurry, I never gave it a second thought at the time. I entered a lift with five or six women who came up from a lower floor - possibly returning from the ladies room to re-join their party. None were veiled and all wore colourful dresses, their hair uncovered, laughing and chatting happily. They showed no embarrassment at my presence, probably because I was a Westerner. On reaching my room, I suddenly recollected what a young Arab had once told me about his awkwardness in London. He said he had never been able to bring himself to enter a hotel lift already occupied by a woman. His inhibition, or adherence to the law, did not simply stop on arriving in a different geographical location.

Hussein arrived in good time and we sat comfortably in the coffee bar, but his attention was soon alerted to the fact that a wedding reception was being held on one of the upper floors. Occasionally we caught distant glimpses of noisy groups of girls running from the lobby to the lift, or even chasing one another up the staircase. It soon became apparent that these distractions were disconcerting, and momentarily, he would fall into glum silence before resuming conversation. I was lost as to how I should respond to his feelings, but when at last he spilt his coffee into the saucer, I knew it was time to leave, and I made the suggestion.

"Yes, I think it would be better," he replied primly. "They shouldn't really allow those women into the public area. It lowers the tone of the place. It's embarrassing for guests."

It was decided we should eat. When Hussein asked me to choose a restaurant from several different national cuisines I plumped for Chinese. As we drove to the restaurant in Hussein's spacious new Buick with its noiseless engine and old-fashioned dashboard, he raised the question of illegal seclusion.

"The hotel is really not acting in the spirit of the law when it allows women to run wild like that," he complained. "I suppose it's because it's under foreign management. That's the trouble with all international hotels. They don't understand our customs."

All the while I nodded in agreement, for politeness gave me no other option. To have contradicted such profoundly felt convictions would have been deeply offensive. Such matters were not up for discussion.

"Is it possible for you to meet any other woman - apart from your wife,?" I asked casually.

"Oh yes," he answered. "I'm allowed to greet my sisters-in-law - to shake hands only. I can see them unveiled in the home - providing their hair is covered. But to talk with them? That wouldn't be allowed."

"How about your nieces?"

"As small children, that's no problem, but as soon as they reach puberty I can greet them - but only if they're veiled," said Hussein. "It would not be allowed to meet or talk to any other women - and that's how it should be. It would not be possible to enter any room in my house if a female was there. I would have to call my wife to remove the female first."

"That must cause problems," I said.

"In Saudi Arabia we have big problems with young female servants," said Hussein, "firstly, because it's unacceptable because of what they are intrinsically; and secondly, because it's improper to have an unveiled woman in the home. An unveiled woman means any foreign woman, and Saudi wives have a difficult job in keeping foreign women under proper control. They need to be very strict because foreign women don't understand our culture. For example, they don't understand the laws of illegal seclusion. They even have the idea sometimes they can go outside and talk with men. That's why Saudi wives must keep foreign women locked up in the home. It's for their own safety - quite apart from protecting their moral welfare."

"What about older women?"

"They can be tolerated in the home because they don't pose a moral danger."

"And what about male servants?"

"If they're elderly and have been known to the family for a long time they may be tolerated."

"What about castrated servants? Do you have many of them in Saudi Arabia today?"

"We don't carry out castration any more," said Hussein, "although there are still a number of elderly eunuchs around. Today castration is purely a voluntary act. It's only found amongst Guardians of the Holy places in Mecca - so that carnal desire may be kept in check."

On arriving at the restaurant, we found ourselves the only patrons in the sumptuous surroundings, and once we were seated, Hussein continued pontificating on the status of women. He repeated what I had often heard before: that early marriage was important in preventing immorality, and that his father had been sixteen and his mother fourteen when they were married, and that now they were blessed by nine children aged between twenty-six and one and a half.

"And all from the same mother,?" I asked.

"Yes," replied Hussein. "My mother's only forty-one and my father's forty-three. Now, in the West such a family would not be possible because you marry so late. I feel sorry for women in the West. They have to go out to work. That's disgraceful - and very unfair on the woman. It exposes her to every kind of danger. Here in Saudi we cherish and protect our women. We respect them. That's no longer so in the West."

"But - ," I began.

"Listen, I've lived six months in England with an English family. I understand these things. I know what life is like in the West. Everywhere there's divorce and misery. In Islam, divorce is the easiest thing to achieve, but in Saudi we have less than a one per cent divorce rate. What is it in England? Thirty per cent? Do you know what the greatest evil is in the world today?"

"Tell me!"

"Social mixing between the sexes. All the evils in society: greed, robbery, rape, murder - and all misery and unhappiness, is due to social mixing. And do you know the reason for that?"

"What is it?"

"Because it creates lust and desire for something none of us can have. And that in turn leads to frustration, vice, crime and misery. That's why we have a better life in Saudi. We've created a moral society. We try to be a good people."

"The greatest criticism in the West of Islamic society is polygamy," I ventured, since he had taken me so far into his confidence.

"But polygamy is necessary. It belongs to human nature," retorted Hussein. "Many men have a need for more than one woman A man can love several women equally. But the reverse would be impossible. A good woman can only be committed to one man."

"But in one night, a woman can satisfy more men than a man can satisfy women. That's a physical fact. It could be used as an argument for polyandry as we once had in ancient Britain."

"That's reducing women to mere prostitution," retorted Hussein. "All the more reason for their protection from vice. And as for justifying the satisfaction of sexual need, it cannot be considered according to the short time-span of hourly intervals because that doesn't allow for proper love. It must be considered according to the longer time-span of the night."

"But do women feel the same way towards polygamy as their menfolk?"

"Certainly! In Islam women accept polygamy. It belongs to the law of God. But a man must treat his wives as equals. If he favours one above the others, then there's trouble."

"Isn't it difficult to avoid favourites?"

"Maybe, but a man must keep his feelings to himself."

"Then he's forced to be dishonest"

"But justice is the first priority. Now if a married man was to have a forbidden relationship with a woman, then his wife would be rightly offended. It would not merely be disreputable but a crime. That's why adultery is the worst of crimes and punished by stoning - as it should be. If, on the other hand, a man's allowed several wives, no offence is given and there's peace in the household."

All the while Hussein was bolting down the food served in front of us, and with little sign of savouring its delicate flavour. At the time I never asked myself the reason for his hurry, only accepting it as the Arab's usual mode of eating. He had declined the use of chopsticks, and was not persuaded by my argument that the use of a knife in eating was a "barbarity" in the eyes of a cultured Chinese. Suddenly he jumped up from the table, exclaiming, "I must get to a mosque to pray."

He paid the bill, and we made for the exit, only to find the door was locked. The waiter and other staff had meanwhile disappeared into the back of the building. Hussein began to panic.

"Can't you use a prayer mat,?" I suggested.

"I could, but it's twenty-seven times better to pray in a mosque," he replied. "God is always a better listener to those in the mosque."

He disappeared into the kitchen shouting for the waiter. I should have asked him how the calculation of "27" was precisely reached but I never did. Our absorbing discussion had made him lose track of time.

"We have to lock the door at prayer times - it's the law," said the Chinese restaurant manager appearing with a bunch of keys.

We drove round the town looking in desperation for a mosque, and when at last it was found, Hussein disappeared for fifteen minutes, leaving me in the car to ponder on the certainties comprising his philosophy of life.

CHAPTER 14
Twilight of the European expatriates

"Hard is the task of justice, where distress
Excites our mercy, yet demands redress."

Colley Cibber, *The Heroic Daughter*, Act iii.

The Westerner with aspirations to super-efficiency who settles in the Gulf with Arabs for colleagues, and then expects to apply his European mind-set to that different culture will be frustrated at every turn. In the spheres of both thinking and action he will crash against a barrier, which although invisible, is as resistant as steel.

If such a person also has the dogmatic and abrasive personality of a Scot, who expresses his convictions with a downright bluntness out of force of habit and love of truth rather than rude intentions, he is especially destined for a rocky path. Such a person was Jim Angus, an engineer in the oil industry, and the General Manager of a company in the Eastern Province engaged in diverse activities.

There are many in the Protestant northern hemisphere who are very free in their use of the terms "truth" and "lying," as if these were absolute or self-evident concepts, rather than subjective notions with many subtle layers of interpretation, as well as differing meanings according to the analysis of the bare facts of a situation. After everything is considered, it might finally be found, that the people of no nation is either more honest or dishonest than another. This is because every nation has its own modes of honesty and dishonesty.

Such problems in communicating the truth are best demonstrated, perhaps, through the decision-making process, when a "Yes" or "No" has finally to be reached. It is a fact that in group discussion in the Eastern hemisphere when opinion is split, and irrespective of whether the topic be theoretical or concrete, it is difficult or impossible to force a decision one way or the other.

In such situations the words "Yes" or "No" are seen as expressing the crude logic of Western thought riding roughshod over good manners and the sensitivity of those participating in discussion. In such negotiations none wishes to be seen to offend another. Of course decisions must be reached, but it is the explicit expression of a final absolute which is offensive to Eastern ears. In the East, subtlety is the route to unanimity. Whilst the Westerner sees such subtlety at best as unnecessary procrastination and at worst as "lying" or "deceit," the Easterner (from the Bosphorus to Japan) sees the imposition of a sharp "Yes" or "No" as the coarse barbarism of an unmannerly people. In the Middle East the word "Frank" is not simply a synonym for any Westerner (and not merely that of a Germanic tribe who invaded and occupied Gaul), but for any person, bold and outspoken, with little sensitivity to the feelings of those whom he addresses.

Ahmed Ishaq was the director of Ishaq Engineering & Trading, and I had met him once before in exploring the possibility of a business relationship. On completing my discussions with Hussein Badanah, I telephoned Ahmad to learn he was allegedly "trapped" in Germany. Half an hour later I was fetched from my hotel by Jim Angus who had taken overall decision-making of the company placed at his discretion, during Ahmad Ishaq's absence. He had only been a year in the country, but I was soon to learn he was like a bear with a sore head.

"Ahmad's the biggest shit in the Eastern Province," exclaimed Jim as we drove along. "He should have returned last week, but he's lost his passport in Germany. That's the story anyway. I wouldn't be surprised if he's had it seized by a pimp in a Hamburg brothel for the non-payment of 'favours received.' That's where he is. I'd put nothing past him. I hope he doesn't find his passport and never comes back. He's impossible to deal with."

Jim was alone in Saudi with a wife and family back home in Aberdeen, and the immediate cause of his ire was that he had been promised three weeks leave four months earlier, with the prospect of the family meeting up for a holiday in Cyprus. This had not come about as Ahmad had not authorised the necessary issue of an Exit visa, and of course, Ahmad was meanwhile the holder of Jim's passport.

"I've been phoning my wife every fortnight, to cancel and re-book the holiday," complained Jim, "but Ahmad has broken every promise he's made. What can I do about it? Is it any wonder that forty per cent of European expats abscond after the first twelve months because they can't stand it here?"

"He's afraid of losing you," I suggested.

"Then he's going about it the wrong way," said Jim. "Where's the trust? Nobody trusts anyone here."

"You should have been like a Finn I once met in Bahrain," I said. "He worked in Jubail but only agreed to stay in Saudi on the condition of holding a Business Visitor's visa. This meant he could retain his passport and leave the country at will, which of course is not possible with a Residence visa. All he did every three months was take his family to Bahrain for a few days when he got his sponsor to renew his Visitor's visa at the Saudi Embassy."

"That was smart," said Jim. "No one's got any sense of responsibility in this country."

He recounted how on taking over the job he found the fleet of relatively new cars to be in an appalling state of disrepair: none had been serviced and the interiors had been ruined by cigarette burns and careless treatment. One employee had even damaged nine tyres in four months simply by driving at full speed across rough desert terrain.

"I insisted on having the fleet serviced - it was vital for safety," said Jim. "Recently I spent several weeks in the desert making out a report on the maintenance of oil well equipment. When I returned to the office to discuss the report in detail with Ahmad, it was impossible to pin him down. Always there were interruptions with people wandering in and out of the office. 'Come back tomorrow,' he'd say, and when I went back he'd forgotten everything we'd discussed before. 'Look I need your signature for essential expenditure,' I'd say. 'Come back another day, I'm busy,' he'd answer.

"Eventually, I told him we've got to sit down early one morning without interruption and talk this whole thing through. We fixed on a day and a time. What happened? I turned up one Saturday morning and was told he'd flown off to Germany. That was two weeks ago. He hadn't even told anyone he was going off anywhere! The man's impossible!

"And another thing, they're all bloody liars out here. They lie to one another all the time. I'll tell you one occasion: a warehouse had been built, and in the plans eight skylights were supposed to have been installed but there were none. After much argument they installed two.

When we met again I said, 'Two is not eight.' It was then pretended there were only supposed to be six. There was a prolonged discussion and each of the Arabs began lying to the others. It was senseless! They were talking nonsense. At last, I got so fed up, I rose from the table shouting 'Eight,' and stormed out of the room slamming the door behind me. Then they installed the eight skylights that should have been there in the first place."

In the course of our discussion mention was made of ARAMCO, and when it was learned I had not seen the complex, Jim Angus suggested we visit the place on our way to his office in Dammam. Jim showed his pass in addition to the car sticker allowing entry, and we drove into the heavily guarded compound. It had all the characteristics of a mid-American town: attractively built timber and brick houses with spacious lawns, box bushes, wide avenues and a profusion of vegetation. We saw teenagers riding around in shorts on bicycles, men and women sunbathing or watering gardens, and shopping precincts which might have been transferred from Phoenix or Cincinnati.

"The great days of this place are over," said Jim. "At one time it had a population of 80,000, but with cut-backs in oil production and government measures to phase out the high ratio of Western employees in favour of Muslims from the Indian subcontinent, it's now down to 35,000. It's no attraction to Brits any more - they're only paid a quarter of the salary of Americans for the same work.

"Nominally all departments are now managed by Saudis, but in point of fact, they manage in name only. They're technically incompetent. When the King comes to make an inspection, the managers are told by the controlling engineers, 'For God's sake, touch nothing! No fiddling fingers on switches or buttons, or you'll blow the place sky high!' I can't believe the King can really be so stupid as to entrust this place to Saudis. But it's Prince Abdullah who's the real power behind these changes. If he ever takes over this country, then it's really goodbye to the blue-eyed boys.

"There've been some scandals in this place in the not-so-distant past. Last year they broke up a ring of American teeenage high school girls on the game. They were charging 600 Riyals (£170) for blow jobs in the back of limousines. They were so successful they decided to extend their operation outside the compound. That's when the Saudi police pounced and made the arrests. It needed the US ambassador, and negotiations at the highest Ministerial level, to get the girls off the hook - if you'll excuse the half-pun - and keep the entire episode strictly hush hush.

ARAMCO's still a paradise for plain janes though. You see the ugliest women walking around this place hanging on the arm of a Tarzan or a Mr. Atlas. Most women are nurses at the hospital here - or else they're working at the hospitals in Dammam or Al Khobar. ARAMCO is their European haven for picking up a boy friend. I know a nurse in Dammam, and she's told me a few stories. Over the past years there's been a spate of women visiting their doctors with unknown gynaecological problems, and their doctors have referred them to the hospital. And do you know what it was? Their husbands were returning from sex trips to the Far East and giving their wives a dose of the clap."

"I'd have thought that would be the least they'd be giving them," I remarked.

"Too true with Aids about," agreed Jim. "But the real problem is that the medical authorities daren't let out the truth behind the real condition of their patients. All they could do is offer cure and treatment. They daren't confront the menfolk of these women - as they'd be legally bound to do in the West. If they did, it would be more than a question of embarrassment. It would in fact amount to confronting them with adultery, and you know the penalty for that!"

As we drove towards Dammam Jim remarked on the recklessness of the driving, and this led to his reflecting on what he described as the crazy attitudes and laws arising from road accidents.

"I tell you what I hold most against Ahmad Ishaq," said Jim. "It's not his stupidity, his laziness, or even his deceit. It's his total lack of any sense of justice or objectivity. Let me tell you a story. A little less than a year ago there was an accident in Riyadh involving one of the Ishaq company cars. An Egyptian was driving one of our own Brits to a meeting when he drove slap into a truck. The Egyptian was lucky. He was killed outright. Now the Brit - who was a fellow engineer - had only been in the country a few weeks, and he had a wife and kids back in England. He had a broken neck and was paralysed from the shoulders down.

"The car was uninsured - of course. That's typical! Taking out insurance in this country is still regarded as a policy against God. That's why they never use their seat belts, and get offended when you strap yourself in as a front seat passenger. Anyway, Ahmad arranged a collection for the dead Egyptian's family, and that together with what the company put in, amounted to £40,000 - in Egypt enough to make his wife and kids wealthy for life. Now Ahmad refused to give a penny for the Englishman. He vetoed, even, the idea of raising a collection."

"Why should he do that,?" I asked.

"Because the Englishman was held responsible for the accident. If he had never been there, going to where he was going, the accident would never have happened. That's their twisted logic in this part of the world."

"I've heard that argument before when it comes to road accidents," I remarked.

"Heaven help any Westerner who gets involved in a traffic accident," continued Jim. "If a taxi driver carrying a Westerner crashes into a bus, there's as much chance of the passenger as the driver being arrested and thrown in gaol. The passenger shouldn't have been where he was at the time of the accident. The driver only has to say his attention was momentarily distracted by the Westerner, and there you have a guilty verdict. Anyway, the family of this poor bastard never received a penny in compensation, and to add insult to injury, it cost his wife a fortune to have him sent back to England by the hospital authorities. Now tell me: What kind of religion is it that promotes those kind of values?

"Now you can understand why I insisted on getting the Ishaq fleet of cars properly serviced. But I still don't know if they're insured. Ahmad just refuses to answer one way or the other. How can you work with a man like that?"

* * *

Jim Angus had drawn a depressing picture of life in the Eastern Province from the perspective of the European expat, and if some of the faults for his personal difficulties lay in the failure to assimilate local cultural values, this was not sufficient to explain away the dreadful fate of colleagues and acquaintances.

Assimilation could not go so far in wearing down the perceived rough edges of a foreign culture. Substantive disabilities or the perception of unfairness is distressful to anyone from anywhere in any place, irrespective of cultural factors which may be used to explain if not to excuse a situation. There is a certain commonsense in factual situations which attracts the universal understanding of humanity. It is this which cuts through the false sociological excuses of cultural clutter.

As I went up in the hotel lift to my room, early that evening, a Filipino bellboy was at the controls. He looked at me curiously, possibly because he saw I was exhausted after a hard day, or possibly because he noted my, I LOVE SAUDI ARABIA, sticker on my briefcase, and he gave a friendly smile.

"Do you like Saudi Arabia,?" he asked.

"Oh, yes," I replied by way of trying to avoid a conversation.

"You only say that because you don't have to live here," he responded with a sad smile, and he left the lift before I had reached my floor.

The sticker which I had bought at Jeddah airport only three days earlier was already becoming a bit of an embarrassment. I had bought it half as a joke and half as a public relations exercise, and its second purpose did prove of some value.

By the hotel poolside, the following day, my impressions of the worsening status of resident Europeans were to be further reinforced. The recession in the Gulf was biting harder and expats were at the sharp end. I met an English resident who was also separated from his family in the UK. As with those from the Indian subcontinent, Westerners too were increasingly offered employment in the Gulf on the condition that they came out as "Celibates." As earnings from any source, in the face of increasing world unemployment, was a first priority of those with family commitments, such posts for "Single men" were now quickly filled. The desperate need for money overrode the risks of undermining family life.

"Financial stringencies are so tight out here, that companies are simply ceasing to pay salaries to their European employees," said my poolside companion. "I know one company where they were paying their British employees three months in arrears, and then one day they said, 'We can only pay you one month's salary for your three months' work.' All the Brits, except one, accepted this arrangement as a *fait accompli* they were anyway unable to challenge, and immediately returned to the UK. My friend, on the other hand, decided to stick it out and fight, and a month later the company went bust, and so he didn't get a penny.

"The boredom out here is just soul destroying. There's just nothing! Still, there are Brits coming out here and working for a fraction of what they'd have earned two years ago. The good days have gone! It's the bare necessity to make a living - and nothing more - that brings out people nowadays. In a way I suppose it could be argued that the Arabs are now getting their own back for the mishaps of the past."

"How do you mean,?" I asked.

"The big construction companies really ripped off these people in the early years," explained my companion. "The faulty building work was atrocious. It cost these people billions! You had cracks appearing in reinforced concrete, and tower blocks collapsing everywhere. They were mixing the local saline sand with cement, and after several years it just disintegrated. Now they import shiploads of sand from Britain and elsewhere for building work. But the swindles and incompetence have created a deep-seated resentment. These people want the Westerners out. They've had enough! And who can blame them? So that's how we're paying for the sins of the past."

Due to a set of developing circumstances, beyond my own control, I sensed that my own days in the Gulf were drawing to a close.

CHAPTER 15
The writing on the wall

"He that's merciful
Unto the bad, is cruel to the good."

Thomas Randolph, *The Muses' Looking Glass*.

L ater in the afternoon, following the public execution in Deira square, I was reclining on a sunbed with an exotic fruit cocktail, by the spacious swimming pool of the Intercontinental.

The relaxing environment of the hotel with its attentive waiters bustling to and fro with drinks and appetising snacks; the gentle warmth of the winter sun in the declining day; and the prosperous ambience of a luxurious location, was a welcome change from the event of some hours earlier. If Deira square was but three miles measured in terms of space, in terms of time, it seemed to turn back the clock by 2,000 years.

But suppressing the memory of events of earlier that day was not to be. They were imprinted on the mind - never to be forgotten. Soon I was in conversation with a middle aged German businessman who for six years had been resident in Al Khobar. I described what I had seen that morning.

"I couldn't have watched it. I'd have been physically sick," said the German meditatively. "I saw an execution once in Al Khobar. It was just as you described - the crowd went wild. I was hit with a headrope. Two men were beheaded for sodomy. It was a messy business. They needed four or five blows with a scimitar. I'ld never go again. But if you go back to Europe and tell people what you've seen, no one will believe you. They'll think you're some crazy guy making up stories. No one knows anything about this country. It knows how to keep its secrets."

As we spoke two or three Arabs in their early teens, ran passed us diving into the pool, throwing up a splash that showered our sunbeds.

"Sexually, this country's in a mess," said the German. "Look at those boys. They've got the whole pool, but they're trying to attract our attention. They're not supposed to be here. They're rent boys. They think it's safe to pick up a European. At home, in Al Khobar, I sometimes go to the Sunset Beach for Celibates, but I talk to no one. Soon I'm surrounded by Arabs who just sit staring at my body. These people are repressed and they've no natural outlet for their instincts. All their emotional in-put goes into religion. That turns them into fanatics. What hope is there for this country?"

"They're increasing their standards of education. Look at the new universities and all the facilities they're investing in," I said. "Isn't that the beginning of change?"

"Not necessarily," replied the German. "The acquisition of knowledge doesn't make for change in itself. Segregation between the sexes is as strict as it ever was. There's no movement of ideas in this country. And because of that there's no possibility for social development."

"Do you think they should try to introduce some kind of parliament or representative system,?" I suggested.

"It would be impossible. It would collapse under its own weight. There's no tradition to build on for a party system. The country's locked into a time warp. The Americans are no less afraid of change here than are the Saudis themselves."

"Then leaving aside the question of democracy, there must be some kind of underground reform groups around," I said. "After all, even the most totalitarian regimes are faced by opposition of some kind."

"There are such groups, but the problem is, they present a worse alternative than what already exists," replied the German. "They're all differing brands of Islamic fundamentalism, and if they came to power, they'd offer a dictatorship hardly less ruthless than those in Libya, Iran or Iraq. Life would be unpredictable, business confidence would collapse, and in no time there'd be economic want and poverty. The present regime may be authoritarian but at least life is reasonably predictable - providing you keep your nose clean. Most enjoy good material standards, and there's a fair degree of freedom for business."

"But change is bound to come sometime."

"It will - with the force of economic change, but not through planned reforms," said the German. "That's what's so terrifying. If this society implodes in on itself there'll be nothing left but anarchy. There's no way this country can be Westernised through gradualism. The stepping stones are just not there."

"And what are those economic forces for sudden change?"

"Either a major oil crisis - worse than in 1973 - or when the oil runs out. I mean, how can you maintain a vast expat Asian population and huge cities on empty desert sands without oil wealth? There's no scope for a subsistence economy. Desalination plants are already an expensive luxury when you consider the subsidies entailed."

"There's one viable possibility for the future of this country," I said, "and that depends on perfecting the technology of the long distance transportation of electrical power. If solar power is sufficiently developed, Arabia could become the power house of environmentally clean and cheap electricity for the northern hemisphere. Just think of it: cheap power for heating, factories, domestic use, and even road vehicles designed for a new millennium. If that could be achieved then Arabia would generate sufficient capital for extensive afforestation and agricultural projects as yet undreamt of - as well as desalination plants on a grand scale."

"That might save the country for its longer term future," agreed the German. "It might even allow time for the gradual development of a modern mind-set, which if not Western might at least be moving in a parallel direction. If that was achieved, it would benefit us all."

As I reclined on the sunbed sipping the yellow green cordial of indeterminate tropical fruits, I reflected that in all probability this was the last full day I might ever enjoy in the Middle East. This time tomorrow I would already be on the return flight to Heathrow. Through a set of circumstances outside my control, partly accidental and partly inevitable, I had fallen into the entangled web of a political intrigue being fought out amongst the senior management of the company. I wanted to enjoy the last warm rays of the sun, and for the last time watch the red orb descend in the West over the darkening desert. I was touched by a pang of sadness.

There were friends and business acquaintances I might never see again, and as I anticipated a loss I had never before contemplated, I was overwhelmed with feelings of regret. I regretted the failure to reciprocate fully friendships that had been offered, and I regretted offence, which occasionally, had inadvertently been given. Was it possible I was filled with sorrow at finally leaving a country so often detested by those from the Occident? I realised that a love hate relationship was emerging from the complex feelings and diverse experiences of the past six years. Detestation was merely the negation of understanding. It could not endure beyond the point of final departure.

It was individuals who comprised the character of a nation - not just an abstract collectivity - and it was the memory of individuals in all their diversity, in virtue and weakness, which completed the picture of a people. The genuine warmth and hospitality of the Arab people - and the generosity of their hearts - could not but leave a lasting impression on those who had enjoyed their kindness and friendship.

They exuded a genuine benevolence towards friends and acquaintances not often met with amongst peoples in the hectic modern world. They allowed time in their lives for contemplation and meaningful socialising, qualities rarely encountered in the modern West with its increasingly superficial values. These were people I might never see again. I was not looking forward to returning home, and to the tensions it so often brought after a long foreign trip.

The conflict within the company, back at Basildon, struck at the heart of industrial policy. It arose from differences between the Marketing Department in conflict with the Managing Director's office and Export Sales. Two unpleasant individuals controlling the Marketing Department, both relative newcomers to the enterprise, the one recruiting the other, had wormed their way into the company and were now engaged in a conspiratorial intrigue. Their unpopularity with the rest of the management team stemmed from their self-imposed isolation, their unwarranted assumption of superiority, and their desk-bound ivory tower approach to innovation and change.

They were chary of listening to the evidence or opinions of other departmental heads, and appeared afraid of liaising in any effective way. Their *modus operandi* was to enter into a huddle with each other, formulate a detailed line of action, and then impose it on a department head without prior discussion. They felt the need to justify their remuneration through the invention of unending excuses to interfere with established systems and lines of communication, not to improve but merely to experiment in a meddlesome way. It was this which exhausted the patience of those at the sharp end of practical business - of those who confronted the competition and negotiated with prospective customers.

The grounds for a much more serious conflict, effecting every part of the company, were set in motion when at last it was urged that selected products should be factored in from Germany and Japan, so enabling the closure of several production lines at the Basildon plant. Rumours filtered down, even to the shopfloor, that one third of staff could be made redundant as a result of alleged "improvements." When the marketing boys encountered a barrier to their ideas in the Managing Director himself, they then turned to secret discussions with the parent company across the Atlantic. The fight was now on in earnest!

"We don't want the hassle of shopfloor employees," argued the Marketing Manager. "Why should we waste valuable hours listening to a Works Council?"

These sentiments were favourably received by the American holding company.

"It's easier to buy in products from abroad than design our own," said his colleague. "Besides, we haven't sufficient investment capital to produce radical new lines. Our margins must be maximised for investors' profits *not* for innovation."

These sentiments, too, appealed to the Corporate office across the water.

Inevitably, I was dragged into the dispute, but my stance remained purely objective and pragmatic. The previous year I had taken several samples of these proposed German and Japanese products with me around the Middle East. Everywhere the response was negative.

"Do you know the first thing a browsing customer does when he picks up one of your products,?" exclaimed Fallah Abdullah in the Badanahs' office. "He looks for the origin mark. If he sees 'Made in Japan' he won't buy - not at your prices."

"And people out here aren't interested in German products unless it's a known brand," interposed Mousa.

"This country's full of Japanese and Taiwanese products,"

continued Fallah. "But they're half your prices. And you can't ride on the back of a brand name."

"British made products still have a magic out here," said Mousa. "'British' and 'good quality' are seen as one and the same. Remember, most of the buyers are probably from your old British Empire. They still feel a loyalty to what that means."

"And so, Mr. Robert, in this competitive environment, we have to tell you that these products would be unsaleable out here,"concluded Fallah.

The competitive struggle for market share was indeed becoming intense. On that particular trip to the Middle East I was shadowed by two Japanese representatives during my days in Jeddah. It seemed they even anticipated the exact timing of my calls on each outlet. As soon as I entered a shop or general office, they were there, and with impeccable manners and smiling politely, they rose from their chairs and bowed.

They were even sitting in the Badanahs' office, sipping tea, as I negotiated business for the forthcoming half year, but as they were already established suppliers to the Badanah Brothers, there were no grounds on which I could object to their presence. In later conversation with the two Japanese, I learned they were resident representatives of their manufacturing organisation, travelling throughout the Kingdom in servicing and selling their products. There was no way in which my company could invest in personnel in ensuring that level of market penetration.

The response to these proposed new products in the smaller Gulf states was more negative even than in Saudi - especially when talking with Indian buyers. All these facts were naturally included in written reports produced at Basildon, but I was unprepared for the counter-measures of Marketing in attempting to block the circulation of the reports themselves. Oral instructions came down that no copies of reports should be sent to the MD, but as he asked for them anyway, in addition to requesting a personal meeting in his office on my return from a trip, such lame attempts at censorship were doomed to failure.

It was easy to perceive that I was seen as a thorn in the side of the Marketing boys, but it was neither possible nor desirable to act in any other way than I did. My task was to increase export turnover by any reasonable means, and this included the submission of objective reports as well as conveying energetically a point of view to other managers.

The spread of the conflict was outside my control, and the fact that the factoring in of foreign made products and the closing of a production line, became a topic of discussion on the factory floor, was none of my doing. I was surprised, therefore, on making my way to the Quality Control laboratory, one day, to be stopped on the factory floor and questioned by a Works Council representative. I was even more surprised by his impression that I was already in the thick of a dispute.

Since he had already been so widely informed by other sources, I saw no reason why I should withhold further information in helping to fight a common cause to which most of us were committed in the company. Was the purpose of the company to exist as a highly efficient, competitive, and productive organisation for the longer term; or was it to exist for the short term purpose of lining shareholders' profits - even if this meant de-industrialisation? Those were the simple choices. Some days later, when leaving the office late, I was even stopped and engaged in conversation by the security guard on the future of the company. Everyone had the jitters from senior managers down to employees on the factory floor.

When at last my name was no longer included on notices for crucial policy meetings, I knew the writing was already on the wall. This was shortly followed by the withdrawal of secretarial facilities on the grounds of "cut backs." It was fortunate I had an efficient keyboard ability and could operate all the office equipment. One day the Marketing Manager's Secretary came into my office and began rummaging through the files in my cabinet.

"The word's gone out to look for any incriminating material - any errors in facts or figures," she said in a confidential tone. "Marketing are looking for anything to stick the knife in."

"Were you told to tell me that,?" I asked with a smile.

"As a matter of fact I was," she admitted, overcome by my percipience. "But that doesn't mean I still don't think Ken Ashley's a big turd. If I don't do as I'm told I'll be out of a job. I don't like these big games when one manager tries to stick the knife into another, but what can I do?"

Before embarking on what I sensed would be my final trip to the Gulf, I was determined it would also be my most successful in terms of sales. Fortunately, over the previous year, I had carefully laid the foundations for several new arrangements in the smaller Gulf States. There were agencies that would be relinquished as larger and more modern firms took their place. At the time I was also aware that however successful such a trip might be it was hardly likely to reverse the trend of events in ending my connection with the company. To fast forward events, I might add that shortly after leaving the company 50 or so redundancies were made in the name of "improvements." Some two years later the company was taken over by another conglomerate, and with further "improvements" the head office and main manufacturing plant at Basildon was closed and quickly demolished with 500 redundancies. By this time the two "nasties" referred to earlier had already left the company. The operations of the firm were then consolidated at their advanced technological plant 100 miles to the north. Final "improvements" were made in July 2000 with the closure of the UK plant and it transference to China with 300 redundancies.

In returning to the situation as it then existed in the Gulf, it might be noted that any severing of a business relationship in the Middle East required the utmost diplomacy. It was necessary that the other party should be placed in a position to be seen as desiring a break and it was advisable to feign as the hurt party trying to prevent the occurrence of such a break. It was then imperative to invent a variety of stratagems in saving the agency, after which one would regretfully admit one's failure to succeed. In this way there would be a face-saving for the other party, for the victor (as it were) would then be obliged to extend a farewell gesture of benevolence.

As it happened, events were to ease my task in relinquishing the agencies in bringing into fruition new arrangements. My second stop after a highly successful visit to Jeddah - and I would be returning to the Kingdom at the end of the trip - was Kuwait. Saad Aakef, the fair-haired Pakistani General Manager of Al Qasim & Co., was in a state of turmoil when I visited his office.

Business had become increasingly difficult over the past year due to huge unsold stock reserves in the non-food sector (possibly partly due to unwise buying policy in assisting Hamad Zohair to purchase a new wife); the continuation of the Iran-Iraqi war, whereby it was impossible to re-export to these two important and traditional markets in the north; and the recent difficulties in dumping merchandise in the other Gulf markets due to the decline of dhow traffic plying the seaway because of fear of bombing. All these difficulties were exacerbated by the banks ceasing to grant credit, due to widespread bankruptcies; and by the collapse of the Kuwait stock exchange the previous July.

Saad had therefore decided to re-organise the company into what he described as, a "profit centre" in the fast-moving food sector. What had happened to Hamad Zohair?

"I'm afraid we couldn't continue to employ him," replied Saad. "We had to release him together with five other salesmen."

A little later we moved over to the office of Jamil Al Qasim, the Managing Director. He was a quiet retiring man of few words, who sat back in his comfortable chair behind a desk, listening intently to what was said. Saad continued to list the problems in marketing our products.

"In view of the competition we face today, your products are just not sufficiently saleable or fast-moving," said Saad. "Now look at the versatility of the Japanese. Every six months they produce entirely new ranges, and their quality is now equal to yours. Consumers are catching onto that. If you're to be viable in the future, you'll have to reduce your prices. In the sophisticated market place of today it's volume that counts, and heavy TV advertising has become a necessity. Now we don't sell your products in sufficient quantity to justify such advertising. But with the Japanese competition, they have all the TV advertising they need."

After listening to this catalogue of woes I exclaimed at last, "Do you want to relinquish the agency then,?" to which both men replied an abrupt, "Yes!"

At once there was a relaxation of tension and an exchange of compliments. Al Qasim had held the agency for twenty years and Kuwait was our largest Gulf market after Saudi. Saad offered to take me to Kuwait Towers for lunch, but I politely declined the invitation on the grounds of a more pressing engagement. Tea was brought in, and on Saad's instigation, the three of us were soon involved in a political discussion.

"The Americans are to blame for many of our troubles," bemoaned Saad. "They've been playing a great chess game in the region and it's all gone wrong. First they ridded themselves of the Shah because he wanted to create a balance of power in the area. A month before he was overthrown, he had been due to visit Moscow. Whilst Ayatollah Khomeini was supported by US armaments supplied via Israel, Iraq was supported by Saudi Arabia, although King Fahad has at the same time always remained a puppet of the US. That's why the War never comes to an end, and is so senseless in its destruction. US arms merchants are supplying both sides.

"Everywhere the Americans stir up trouble, form alliances, and then leave their friends in the lurch. We've seen it in Vietnam, in Pakistan, and shortly we'll see it in the Philippines where they're withdrawing their support from President Marcos. It's all because the Americans have no historical sense - no understanding of other nationalities. And that's because of their political power structure. It's the big corporations that nominate US presidents and put them where they are. No wonder they're politically uneducated.!"

On leaving the premises of Al Qasim & Co. a little later, I came to the conclusion that most of their troubles were probably due to the gross incompetence of their General Manager, Saad Aakef. Clearly they had bought excessive stock and over-stretched their financial limits. Their sophisticated computer system with all its supposed benefits had failed to alert them in time to the approaching crisis. All Saad's talk about the weakness of the Kuwait economy and the political games of the Americans was merely a smokescreen - and not merely intended for my consumption.

Here was another sharp-witted manager from the Indian subcontinent running rings around his Arab sponsor! I had little trust in the business acumen of Jamil Al Qasim. He gave me the impression of someone out of his depth in his own company, who had become pitifully reliant on his Asian lackeys, and if not too careful, would soon be bankrupted himself. I felt I had relinquished the agency none too soon.

That afternoon I was with our prospective new agents, Motwani Rejesh, a substantial Indian-managed and owned company which had been established in the emirate since 1946. All its executives were young, American-University educated, and used modern marketing methods. After a day spent in field research with one of their sales managers, an agreement was reached, and a substantial initial order taken.

On my last evening in Kuwait I was fetched by one of the Rajesh brothers, and together with an American from Stuttgart, Wisconsin, who supplied rice to the company, we were taken to the family home of one of the directors. We sat in a spacious living room, and I was surprised when the Indian servants, who were hovering around, served Whiskey with soda and ice.

"I thought Kuwait was dry," I exclaimed.

"It is, but everyone drinks here," said one of the brothers.

"They've been tightening up the law," explained another. "At one time Western residents were allowed to bring in a litre of spirits for their personal use. Now they've stopped that loophole."

"And they're enforcing the anti-alcohol laws more strictly than ever before," said a third brother.

"Then how can you drink,?" I asked.

"It's a monopoly controlled by the Royal family," answered the first brother. "All containers with alcohol are shipped directly to the Royal family, because only those are exempted from customs inspection. But alcohol is costly. A bottle of Whiskey costs 25 Kuwaiti dinars - that's about £60. The Royal family make a fortune from the trade! They'd never stop it."

Soon I was in conversation with the American, who like me, travelled twice yearly to the Gulf. When he explained that on his next trip he would be taking his wife at the firm's expense, I expressed surprise at such generosity.

"The company feel responsible for the marriages of their employees," he answered. "Do you know that three out of four marriages of travelling export executives fail within the first two years of their taking up the work?"

"I didn't know that, but I can well believe it" I said. "The strains are tremendous. Women are so suspicious."

"Too true they are," responded the American. "As soon as the front door is closed and the plane is flying, they think we're fornicating from the first day to the last."

"And there's nothing you can do to reassure them to the contrary," I said. "They think we're compulsive liars escaping to some kind of freedom."

CHAPTER 16
Women and progress

"Vengeance is not cured by another vengeance, nor a wrong by another wrong; but each increaseth and aggregeth the other."

Chaucer, *The Tale of Melibeus*, Sec. 31, 1, 2475

Abu Dhabi was the wealthiest and most powerful of the seven United Arab Emirates, not only because its land area dwarfed the other six by comparison, but because of its oil-generated riches. Its Emir, H.H. Sheikh Zayed bin Sultan al-Nahyan, was also the President of the federation. Abu Dhabi and Dubai had always been rivals, their respective capitals having comparable populations, and in the not so distant past, they had frequently been at war with one another.

The only other UAE emirate of significance was Sharja, a fifteen-minute drive to the north east of Dubai. Sharja was the only place on the Arabian peninsula where a serious attempt had been made to establish a tourist industry, but when the emirate took out a substantial loan from Saudi Arabia, and the condition of that was to go "dry," the developing tourist industry was stopped in its tracks.

Sharp contrasts divided the rival cities of Abu Dhabi and Dubai. Whilst Dubai was an ancient trading port with low taxes, laissez-faire in its attitude, and friendly to merchants; Abu Dhabi was modern and aggressive in its business methods, but bureaucratic. The city was laid out on a grid plan of long broad streets, and whilst the two main parallel streets of Sheikh Hamdan and Zayed the Second were lined on both sides with modern office tower blocks, the space between them was a shanty town of one and two-storey shacks with corrugated roofs, comprising the housing, business premises, and fourth rate hotels of those from the Indian subcontinent. Whilst numberless goats wandered around the alleyways looking for food, camels were kept in many a narrow back yard.

But Abu Dhabi was also known as the green city of the Gulf. There were flowerbeds and lawn areas shaded by palms down the central reservations of major streets, and numerous roundabouts were ablaze with the colour of tropical plants. In addition to sprinklers, hundreds of men were employed throughout the day in hosing the fertile areas. The ruling Sheikh had also invested huge sums in afforestation projects, a Finnish company having been contracted to supervise the planting and care of palm trees along the motorways to both Dubai and the inland city of Al Ain.

It was alleged that this huge increase in vegetation had transformed the climate of Abu Dhabi city over the past decade. One evening whilst in the office of a business contact, he opened the window exclaiming, "Ten years ago this would have been impossible because of the heat. Today I open the window and there's a cool breeze. There's been a big fall-off in the sale of air conditioners over the past few years. We also get more rain than we used to."

There was a large Indian enterprise in Abu Dhabi, Kumar & Co., which I had visited on several occasions, and I now hoped they would take over the UAE agency from Ramesh & Sons in Dubai. After settling into the hotel, I was fetched by one of the directors, Mr. Harminder, and we drove to his flat in a modern block, where his wife served us with tea and refreshments. I was surprised to note that most of the furniture was covered with sheets.

"We have to protect the furnishing from flakes of plaster from the ceiling," explained Harminder's wife who worked for another company. "It's especially bad after the rain. The rain seeps through the flat roof and then passes down the inside walls throughout the entire building."

"You can't imagine the damage," said Harminder. "All the woodwork is warped - both door and window frames. The building's in a bad state of repair - and you've seen the plaster falling away in the outside hall."

The couple had lived for seven years in the building, since construction was completed, and paid an annual advance rent of £15,000 - although this expense was borne by the company. I suggested they should approach the landlord to carry out necessary repairs.

"That wouldn't be possible," replied Harminder. "The landlord is the Sheikh of Ajman. There's no way we could complain. It would invite immediate eviction."

That evening in the office of Kumar & Co. I met the Jordanian General Manager, Adib Nasri, who was very distraught over a serious family matter. Because of his distressful domestic situation, it was not possible that night to discuss business, but the following day we fully investigated the marketing possibilities, entered into a long term arrangement, and I came away with a high value order.

Adib's domestic problem concerned his brother who had been in prison for a week, and the conditions in that particular prison were appalling, with twenty to thirty men in a room with no airconditioning and no proper facilities. The prisoners slept on the floor with no mattresses or blankets. Adib's brother had been arrested as his papers had not been in order. His visa had expired and he had changed his job which was now illegal. The arrest had occurred following a routine police raid on shops and offices to inspect the identity papers and permits of everyone in the area.

That morning Adib had sat in court as some two hundred cases were heard of foreign prisoners on remand for faulty papers. Most had already been in prison for two or three weeks before their cases came before the court, but some had been confined for as long as three months. Adib's mission that morning had been partly successful, and this had been helped by the fact he was an Arab speaker. Prisoners without knowledge of Arabic were often confronted by fearful problems arising from the protracted delays and mounting costs of translating documents on a two-way basis. Adib had succeeded in immediately freeing his brother on the payment of 500 dirhams (about £85), but he had not succeeded in preventing his deportation back to Jordan.

"There was also an adultery case this morning," said Adib. "It was an Englishman who had caught his wife with another Brit. Both the accused had already been in prison for several weeks. The judge asked the husband if he wanted to drop the case. If he wouldn't, and the case went to trial, and there was a guilty verdict, the wife would be stoned to death."

"They wouldn't dare stone a European to death. The scandal would reverberate around the world," said Harminder.

"That's why they'll keep deferring it until the husband agrees to drop the case," said Adib. "But meanwhile, the wife and her lover remain in gaol."

"And so what happened,?" I asked.

"The husband said he wanted to free his wife but not the co-respondent. Then the wife yelled out in court saying the man should be freed as well. But the husband wouldn't agree to that."

"Then what?"

"The judge said they can't free the one without the other. They either drop the case as it is, or go on with it as it stands. There was a lot of shouting and then the judge adjourned the case for another two weeks."

"Did you see other Europeans in court?"

"Not this morning. But there are dozens of Europeans rotting away in the overcrowded gaols of Abu Dhabi. Most are serving sentences for drink and driving offences. There are no breathalysers here, but if you're stopped and smell of alcohol, that's enough for a conviction."

"Abu Dhabi may have its disadvantages, but it's still the best place to live in the UAE," assured Harminder. "There's a greater degree of political security here - although it has to be admitted there's a lot of tension between the emirates. The smaller emirates think Abu Dhabi should make a greater contribution to the federal purse, but she stubbornly refuses. Last year Abu Dhabi and Dubai were on the point of mobilising against each other, and Sharja, which likes to ingratiate herself with more powerful neighbours, sided with Abu Dhabi.

"Meanwhile, in the palace of Dubai the two sons of the dying Sheikh Rashid are quarrelling over the succession. Whilst one son is pro-Dubai in supporting the traditions of local business, the other is pro-Abu Dhabi, and wants to raise taxes and introduce a more bureaucratic state. If you read the papers, though, you'ld know nothing of these conflicts. Everything is presented as rosy and peaceful between all the rulers. But if you're in business here - especially if you're a foreigner, it's wise to search out the real facts. Nothing is really certain about the future. There may come a day when we all have to clear out."

My final trip to the coastal emirates was hectic and exhausting, and before visiting Dubai and Oman, and lastly, Saudi Arabia, I decided on a diversion to the oasis city of Al Ain, 140 miles inland. A battered and filthy taxi drove me along the desert route of dual carriageway edged with wire fencing protecting the thousands of saplings from the ravages of goats and camels. Miles of punctured hose-pipe for watering the vegetation ran parallel with the road in addition to stand-pipes situated every few hundred yards.

There was a strange silence in the empty but spacious Intercontinental Hotel, and as I looked out from my fourth floor window at the forest and greenery extending to the distance, if it was not for the coarseness of the grass immediately below, the view might have been that of a north European town in high summer. Al Ain was situated at the foot of the Western Hajar mountains on the borders of the emirate of Abu Dhabi and Oman, and as it was a mere 2 ½ hours drive to Muscat, it had a reputation as both a trading and smuggling post between the two states. When I went to the poolside only one other person was there.

Early the following morning I arranged with the hotel to hire a guide (or taxi driver) to be shown the sights of the town, and minutes later, a wild looking Pakistani from Peshawar on the north west frontier, arrived to place himself at my service. His unshaven unkempt appearance, his bandit's moustache, and his baggy Afghan trousers gave him a forbidding appearance, but he was good-natured and reliable and entirely honest. Although he supposedly spoke English, his knowledge was negligible, but he did have a working grasp of Arabic in addition to his native Urdu.

We visited the local museum, and then the livestock market where goats, camels and Indian as well as Western cattle were auctioned and moved from pen to pen. We then want to the Zoo which was closed for cleaning, and was anyway only open for two days in the week, but from what we could see on the outside, it was situated in attractive park-like surroundings and housed over 300 species - an aquarium having been recently added to the exhibits.

Finally, we visited the Buraimi Oasis situated in the so-called Free Zone just across the frontier in Oman. It comprised a thickly wooded and shaded area of giant palm trees, shrubs and grass, in a hollow of several square miles, criss-crossed with paths set on a higher level bounded on both sides by mud walls and fast flowing streams in ditches. Much of the area was divided into privately-owned garden plots, sometimes with houses, accessed through brightly painted multicoloured iron doors through the mud walls.

As I walked along the winding paths with my Pakistani guide, not knowing what we were to meet around the next corner, we saw several men with soap and sponges, their futahs tucked beneath their thighs, as they stood waist deep, performing their ablutions in fast flowing water. A little further on we saw a group of small children playing happily in a more shallow stream.

On reaching the hotel again, I decided to leave for Dubai as soon as practicable. I negotiated a price through the hotel porter for my guide to act as a chauffeur. Then as I went to my room to pack and the guide drove off to tank, the porter wrote out a pass for police purposes authorising the taxi to make the journey from Al Ain to the neighbouring emirate of Dubai.

Much of the terrain during the 100 miles drive to the north consisted of dark red dunes, suggesting the colours of the setting sun, but as this was in the middle of the day, the hue was intrinsic to the sand. We passed through several small towns and villages, and verandah-fronted cafés with corrugated roofs, and the Al Ain Dairy farm with green fields and a herd of Friesians sheltered under an open barn.

After two hours I was happy to espy in the far distance the towering office blocks of Dubai emerging from the desert. My heart expanded with a sense of joy, for in my experience, Dubai was not only the most pleasant city on the Arabian peninsula but also the most pleasurable.

There were only two places on the Arabian peninsula (that I knew of) where it was possible to meet and socialise with women in a relaxed environment, and both were in Dubai. The first was a rooftop swimming pool, overlooking the Creek, shared between an international hotel and a block of luxury flats, and whilst in Dubai, I would always spend four or five hours during the siesta period, reclining on a sunbed, swimming, and when the inclination and opportunity arose, spontaneously engaging other patrons in innocent conversation. In this sunny leisure centre it was possible to meet bikini-clad women from anywhere in the world.

After several weeks of living in an all-male environment, where women were unseen and certainly unspoken to, I was eventually overcome with a feeling of depression at this prolonged deprivation. The restrictions of Arab society outlawed all the natural pleasures of feminine company except for those of the bedroom. In such an artificial society even the most innocent socialising between men and women was condemned as immoral. Because of the strictly enforced laws of illegal seclusion, two consecutive weeks was the maximum I could endure in Saudi Arabia, without being seized by claustrophobic depression through the denial of this particular form of human warmth. For these reasons, arriving in Dubai was always accompanied by anticipations of pleasure.

The sociable environment around this particular swimming pool was not so much created by the hotel guests as by the occupants of the luxury flats. A clubbable ambience was created by a group of women who regularly tanned themselves on the rooftop area. They were led by a middle aged French speaking Lebanese woman who seemed to act as both a chaperon and socialite. Sometimes they had friends staying in the hotel, but that apart, their presence was sufficient to offer an opportunity for easy conversation amongst all who spent their leisure hours around the pool.

On one occasion I met an English girl, resident and working in Dubai as an importing wheeler and dealer. She moved with confidence in Arab circles, had entrée to the Palace of Sheikh Rashid, and showed me the sights of Sharja. On another occasion she used her influence in obtaining an NOC (Non-Objection Certificate) for my entry into the Oman. One of the most beautiful women I ever met was a friend of the French Lebanese and a guest in the hotel. She was a black Egyptian with the delicate features of a Nefertiti, the figure of a sylph, and her thick braided hair fell to her waist. She had a seductive charm and frank manner, and her command of English was better than that of most men with whom I negotiated business in the Middle East.

The second location where it was possible to meet women in Dubai was at a nightclub belonging to the same hotel, but the entrance to the club was not accessed through the hotel lobby, but from an adjoining plaza where a lift was taken to the 16th floor. Hotel guests were automatically made members of the club, but women unaccompanied by men were only allowed entry on certain nights. As the club was intended for Westerners it was unsuited for Arab women, but it was often patronised by girls from the Far East who were usually employed in secretarial or hotel work.

As four-fifths of the patrons were men, the majority being roughnecks from neighbouring oilrigs, their main preoccupation was to sit up at the several bars consuming lager until the early hours. I usually chose to sit at one of the tables around the dance floor as this afforded a better opportunity to meet the women guests. It was pleasant to talk with the happy and laughing Thais after several consecutive weeks of all-male company, and sometimes they would playfully grasp the right hand, looking for a ring on the third finger. Their thoughts were often on the search for a husband and they were wary of being played with.

Later that night, on the last occasion I visited Dubai, it so happened that I encountered an Egyptian girl working for the Dubai customs. She was effusive in the outpouring of her thoughts, and if I was struck by her commonsense attitudes it was because of the secularism of her mind-set. How this contrasted with the often dogmatic, narrow, bigoted, and intolerant prejudices I had been forced to listen to from the lips of Eastern men over the previous weeks!

Here was a girl from an Islamic culture with a natural humanism that seemed to have driven out or suppressed the inclination for religious thought. She was untainted with that ubiquitous fanaticism of the Middle East, and her calm and peaceful personality reflected a balance and Golden Mean rarely met with amongst Arab men. As we sipped our cocktails, conversing against the rising volume of the disco music, I suggested we should escape the noise, a gesture she happily fell in with.

Minutes later we were strolling along Bin Yas road in the direction of the Al-Maktoum bridge. She had a gentle and melancholy demeanour and was outpouring her heart on her philosophy of life.

"Here in Dubai people only think about money," she exclaimed. "Life is too hectic and materialistic. In Egypt people are poor but happy. They have their family and friends. People are well-off here, but they're not happy. Most of us are only here because we have to be. We have to earn money to send back to our families."

As we strolled in the warm night air beneath the stars, it seemed as if our thoughts were uniting us towards a shared ideal of life. As we stepped onto the narrow sandy strip of shoreline between the embankment and the Creek, I wanted to embrace her in my arms and shower her face with kisses, but we dared not hold hands even, for fear the police may have been lurking in the shadows.

In two days I should be leaving Dubai forever, and we would never meet again. I felt a pang of pain, but I knew that any attempt at a longer lasting friendship would be more painful still. Our fate, unhappily, lay in circumstances beyond our own volition. Such, surely was the understanding of us both.

As we enjoyed those blissful moments together, and I reflected on the social mores of the Middle East, it struck me that socialising between men and women was psychologically an essential and civilising component of societies aspiring to balance, openness and progress in all its aspects. All-male societies, as indeed, with all-male associations within a specific society, tend towards a rigidity and sterility of thinking, and a harsh conservatism engendering resistance to change.

All-male societies and associations are comfortable, self-satisfying and self-perpetuating in their assurance of exclusivity, unanimity and power, and too often they are havens for prejudice and short sightedness. This was so as they represented the subjective attitudes of only one half of the human race, and there was no way - despite the hardest tried attempts at objectivity - that the total interests of society could be so promoted.

Men and women were different - in fact, no less than opposites - and biological differences led to contrasting visions and attitudes in solving the problems of the world. Those who insisted on equating the concept of Difference with that of Equality were simply confusing the issues of the conflict between the sexes. The question of Equality was irrelevant in determining psycho-scientific fact, for equality was a subsequent consideration, only properly being concerned with the discussion of rights.

The glaring differences between men and women had in the distant past led the patriarchal organisers of society along the easy path of segregation. This may have been an attractive route in allowing each sex to develop certain interests in its own unique way without the interfering bias of the other, but ultimately and inevitably, and by a quiet and unknowing process - devious in its crooked path - it was to lead to the domination of one half of humanity. On awakening to the real truth in the recent past of our history, the realisation was uncovered of the conflict between the sexes. In view of this, surely the happiest and most natural relationship between the two, could only best be achieved finally through their on-going communication in an open environment. Was that not alone the courageous path to true and honest relationships?

I failed to receive the impression that Arab women enjoyed their segregated status - or if they did, it could only have been out of perversity. After all, if the benefits of segregation were "protection" it might then be asked, what kind of woman would be flattered by such condescension? And furthermore, when such "protection" was at the price of subordination, does it not become a euphemism for uninvited domination? From what I had seen of Arab women - usually gleaned from a distance - did not leave me with the impression that they were intrinsically shy, diffident or retiring.

On only one occasion, during my years in Arabia, was I ever introduced to the wife of a Saudi Arab. That was during a Jeddah Spring Fair, when a young Saudi businessman I had met in London - the couple had lived for six months together in England - introduced me to his wife. She was hooded and heavily veiled, but as I took her hand, I saw a demure smile and a pretty face behind the layers of black gauze. Such an introduction was a privilege that would have been denied a Saudi, but as a Westerner it seemingly did not break the inhibitions of convention. Such an introduction was not painful to either husband or wife. Perhaps there were Arab men, even, who would not be averse to greater openness in their own societies.

It may be that women exert a certain unique emphasis on aspects of life desirable for the direction of society. They usually have less aggression in the promotion of abstract notions or ideals. In the sphere of religion they are more interested in the practicality of good works than in the dogmas of belief. As leaders in history they have flourished as peacemakers and defenders of peoples, rather than as warriors and conquerors. As leaders in politics, in the modern era, they have made their mark most notably as reformers for social justice rather than as the promoters of national power measured according to the boosting of the Share Index.

Following the upheavals and bloodshed of the *Völkerwanderungen*

- or the great movements of population in early historical times - it was the women who were finally the peacemakers in absorbing and pacifying conquering peoples through the appeasing power of sexual love. It is women, surely, who are more sensitive to the truth of nature, and are the first, in the face of necessity, to repudiate the idealistic and cultural baggage of oppression, and it is they who initiate the civilising outcome of physical love between the sexes.

The stories and legends from our own European history are enough to demonstrate that it is from such unions that new cultures, new languages, and new civilisations of combined peoples rise from the ashes of destruction. It is love between men and women, and most significantly, the communication and mutuality between them which culminates in those cultural benefits of greatest value. It has often been said that only the saving grace of love can save the world, as it may also save the microcosm of the individual.

Might not the liberation of Arab women some day act as a catalyst to the intellectual modernisation of the Middle East? The Islamic religion, indeed, has great potential for social good. Leading Western thinkers since the close of the 17th century - most notably Bayle, Voltaire and Gibbon - have recognised the superiority of the core theology of Islam, with regard to defining the nature of the deity and in promoting justice and egalitarian values, in contrast to the barbarism, gothic crudities, and superstitious values of Christianity with its church hierarchies and deference to privilege and tyranny.

Because Christianity created a God out of a living being, many peoples throughout the world - irrespective of the truth or non-truth of their conclusions - have come to see the Christian deity as merely a tribal God of the Caucasian peoples. The growing Black Muslim movement in America is the most notable outcome of such a perverse thinking process. The Islamic God, on the other hand, entails an abstraction of the highest good, surpassing the sphere of humanity in the omnipotence of its understanding. It may be argued, that Islam as chronologically the third of the great Semitic faiths, set out and succeeded in refining the core theological beliefs of its two great predecessors. In this sense it may be said to have reached a higher evolutionary status in religious belief.

Might not the liberation of Arab women, in combination with the ideas of the Enlightenment and the more recent conclusions of psychology, facilitate the reform of Islam in creating the most rational, just, and greatest religion on earth? Might not the liberation of Islamic women facilitate a great renaissance of the Arab peoples? Nothing is more hateful today than the fearful prospect of a future conflict between Islam and Christianity, and yet with the passing of the Cold War, this is a threat which is looming between Greater Europe and the Near and Middle East Asia - and especially amongst the mixed and Turkic populations of southern Russia.

Both religions are still dominated by the aggression and intolerance of patriarchal attitudes that are self-destructive. The fundamentalism of Christianity is no less a threat to humanity and progress than is the fundamentalism of any other religion - and even Hinduism, historically amongst the most tolerant of religions, is now developing dangerously its own brand of fundamentalism. Might not the peacemaking influence of Arab women contribute to a reconstruction of Islam, the eventual consequences of which might advance the cause of technology and science with no less energy than that of the West?

In this overview of two cultures competing for moral and political domination there is, of course, another dimension to the future of events. The civilisations of both the West and Islam are loud and arrogant in haranguing the attention of the world, and in this they have perhaps bloated their significance beyond all deserving measure. It should be remembered that combined they form but a small minority of the global population. The values of both Islam and the West may yet be doomed to wither in surrendering to forces more apt in carrying forward the torch of technology and progress.

In the relatively stable and low-crime rate societies of the Far East, might not the secular and far older Confucian values of Harmony and a This-Worldly moral order, bring into fruition a spiritual and intellectual force more suited to the future of the modern world? The complacency and arrogance of the "End of history" theorists of the Anglo-American liberal establishment is blind to both the infinite diversity of human nature and the potential for new forms of political thinking in driving humankind towards yet greater heights of progress. If the civilisations of the West and Islam were to deplete their energies in senseless self-destructive conflict, there may arise in the Far East a greater and more peaceful civilisation, more suited to the values of permanence and progress.

In the New Millennium might not Western liberalism give way before an ethical system as yet un-thought of, yet granting greater justice and opportunity for all? If in the New Millennium a new enlightenment shining from the Far East is to dawn over the peoples of the world in complementing their growing industrial power, then any attempted comparison between the alleged values of the West and Islam, as they are now perceived, would become irrelevant and wasted effort. In that event the cherished values of both Islam and the West would perish, only to be sustained through memory as recorded in the dusty annals of the past. Even a superficial knowledge of the rise and fall of civilisations is sufficient to justify such predicted probabilities.

Those were my thoughts as I walked with the sweet Egyptian.

In the early hours I was awoken by a great banging and crashing in the adjoining room, as if someone was stumbling around, knocking over pieces of furniture. Then I heard a slurred voice in Arabic, using and abusing the phone. A little later there was a noise in the corridor outside. One of the Indian porters was addressing an Arab guest, but it sounded rather as if a naughty child was being chided by its parent.

"Behave yourself! Get back inside your room. I said, get back inside your room. No, you can't have another drink. If you don't stop misbehaving, I'll call for help and you'll be punished."

Curious, I leapt from my bed and peeped outside. An elderly and diminutive Arab, in a brown thobe and red check headscarf, was stumbling around the entrance to his room.

"Now go inside and keep quiet," exclaimed the uniformed porter. "Go to bed and get some sleep - and don't disturb other guests. I don't want to hear from you again."

The Arab was pushed gently into his room, and the porter closed the door and walked down the corridor in my direction.

"Were you disturbed, Sir,?" he asked, as he passed by.

"I was awoken by the crashing of furniture," I answered.

"Was it you who phoned down to complain?"

"No!"

"These Saudis are a menace when they come to Dubai," explained the porter. "He's drunk up all the mini-bottles in his drinks cabinet, and now he's asking for more alcohol. He can't have any! But he should be quiet now. If he wakes you again, just ring down to Reception."

Later that morning I crossed the Creek by abra to visit Ramesh & Sons. A pleasant breeze blew off the waterway as the boat passed by the wharves and dhows on the Deira side, and we approached the landing stage of the old town. I would have unfortunate news for Mr. Chander, but I had warned him in advance that I was unhappy with the annual level of our UAE turnover, and so I did not anticipate encountering difficulties.

As I cut through one of the narrow alleyeways beyond the souk, I was surprised to note that Kamlesh's video shop must have moved to another location, but on entering and crossing Talib road, I was momentarily struck with the sensation of having lost my way. Then I realised that Ramesh & Sons had gone! An Indian bakery had taken its place. I burst into the shop and made my enquiry.

"I can't help you - I've no idea," mumbled the middle-aged proprietor. "The site was empty when we took it over."

I went into the laundry next door.

"Ramesh & Sons? Oh, it was very bad! All the family went back to Bombay," replied the bearded owner. "The business went bankrupt. They left owing money to everyone. Very bad! Their sponsor lost a lot of money. He invested so much in the business. He was very angry. There was no warning. They disappeared in the night. The entire family returned on a single flight to Bombay. That Mr. Chander was a real crook. He was a big talker. Everyone trusted him and lost money."

Again I realised we had severed our links in the nick of time. Anyhow, I had been saved the embarrassment of an explanation.

A day later, two hours before sunset, I was strolling along the wide and magnificent beach in the Gulf of Oman, nearby the Intercontinental. A few people were walking by the shore, and some paddling, and brown jelly fish had been washed up onto the sand. It was a peaceful and idyllic scene. Nearby some vegetation extending down to the sea I met a young Bangladeshi couple, and stopped to speak with them. They were employees of the hotel on their off-duty hours, laying nets to catch fish with which the coastline was enriched. He was the Personnel Manager and she a Secretary in the accounts office, and he told me about the domestic problems of expatriate Asians away from home. He had formerly been employed as a Chargé d'Affaires before working for the hotel group.

Later that night an evening of Indonesian cuisine and music was prepared for the guests in the colourfully illuminated gardens of the hotel. I sat beside an American who was apprehensive and pensive about the immediate future.

"Tomorrow I'm flying home to Denver, and I'm not looking forward to it," he mused, twirling his wine glass between his fingers. "It's always the same when I get back after a long trip: there's the tension and resentment from the other side, and then come the rows."

"I know what you mean," I answered.

"I mean, it's only a job, but the womenfolk don't understand that," continued the American. "They see it only as a pleasure trip. I tell the wife, 'Look here, I work seven days a week when I'm on a trip. I've got a budget to make, and if I don't reach the figures, I'm out of a job.' But they're so stupid, they don't see that. I don't get the support I need at home. Even when I phone the wife, she asks dumb questions and insinuates God knows what. They think you're messing around with women. I ask you, in a place like this, what chance have you got for playing with women?"

"None,!" I answered, feeling a twinge of awkwardness.

"It's impossible - although I did hear a strange story this morning. Did you hear about the Englishman who had a public flogging last week in Ruwi?"

"What happened,?" I asked.

"He was a businessman - passing through - staying at this hotel," began the American. "He was caught screwing an Indian bird on the beach. The idiot! It was so unnecessary. Why didn't he take her to his room?"

"And what became of her,?" I asked.

"She was deported back to her own country," came the reply.

* * *

The morning following the public execution, I awoke early, and lay in bed thinking. It was my final day in the Gulf. I heard a rustle on the carpet beneath the room door. The daily paper had arrived. I jumped up, fetched the paper, and returned to bed, looking for the report on yesterday's event.

Impatiently I turned over the pages, and at first found nothing. Then, on page 3 of the *Saudi Gazette* for the date of 9th Safer 14** (Saturday, 5th December 19**), hidden beneath the following report headed, TWO MEN EXECUTED FOR MURDERS, I read:-

"Muhammed Mussa Hensh Al-Zahrani was beheaded in Jeddah yesterday for stabbing to death Mussa Abdullah Al-Zahrani.

"An Interior Ministry communiqué said that Muhammed Mussa was sentenced to death after he confessed to the crime before the Makkah Court.

"The communiqué said Mohammed Mussa stabbed Mussa Abdullah to death while the victim was asleep. The Security Forces arrested Mussa who later confessed the murder.

"Meanwhile in Riyadh, Tuwairish Bashir Al-Halwi was stoned to death after the Friday prayers for assaulting and killing Master Muhammed Bin Saeed Al-Mabrouk.

"The Interior Ministry said that Tuwairish consumed alcohol with Master Muhammed and then sexually assaulted him before stabbing him to death. He then wrapped the body in a blanket, put it in his car and got rid of it."

This was the full extent of publicity - the first and last mention - of a horrific crime and the punishment that followed. What thoughts - if any - could be passed on such an event? Was there full justification or none for the final act that marked this episode? Is barbarism just a word: meaningless and indefinable in the last resort, when in the mind of one person it may be condemned as the unmentionable, whilst in that of another it is seen as a punitive act of necessary justice? The world may long be divided in its conclusions on this particular episode, given the outrageous crime that evoked such a fearful punishment.

***

Lightning Source UK Ltd.
Milton Keynes UK
UKOW04f0952100817

307052UK00002B/89/P